A SIMPLE GUIDE TO

Mushrooms
of the **Northeast**

by Teresa Marrone and Walt Sturgeon

PUBLICATIONS
Adventure
an imprint of AdventureKEEN

Acknowledgments

Some of this material has appeared in *Mushrooms of the Upper Midwest*, by Teresa Marrone and Kathy Yerich. It may have been edited for the Northeast.

Cover, book design and illustrations by Jonathan Norberg

Page layout by Teresa Marrone

Edited by Brett Ortler

Photo credits by photographer and page number:
Cover photo: *Mycena leaiana* by Walt Sturgeon

All photos by Teresa Marrone, Walt Sturgeon and Kathy Yerich unless noted.

IMAGES USED UNDER LICENSE FROM SHUTTERSTOCK.COM:
7, BGSmith. **10, Bell-shaped:** Martin Fowler; **Egg-shaped:** mikeledray; **Elongated/cylindrical:** Matauw. **11, Veil fragments on edge:** fedsax. **12, Bulbous base:** Maxim Blinkov; **Mycellium:** Martin Fowler. **13, Patterned/reticulated:** CCat82; **Scaly:** Francis Bossé; **Simple ring:** Alba Casals Mitja. **22, Atypical Caps:** Sergiy Palamarchuk. **26, Half-free Morel:** Tony Campbell. **27, Gyromitra esculenta:** Kletr. **29, Wooly Inky Cap:** Martin Fowler. **39, Yellow-foot Chanterelle:** Henrik Larsson. **56, Conifer False Morel:** Kletr. **62, Button stage:** Lumir Jurka Lumis; **Emerging from veil:** Kirsanov Valeriy Vladimirovich. **145, Maturing Blewits:** LFRabanedo; **Young Blewit:** DUSAN ZIDAR. **147, Violet Cort:** Vassiliy Fedorenko. **169, Orange-Capped Leccinum:** Digoarpi. **186,** Jan S. **193, Common Stinkhorn:** Sergiy Palamarchuk. **217,** Jukka Palm. **231, After releasing spores:** Lippert Photography. **241, Veined Cup:** Medwether. **245, Scarlet Cup:** Martin Fowler. **251, White Worm Coral:** N. F. Photography.

Photo credits continued on page 286

20 19 18 17 16 15 14

Mushrooms of the Northeast
Copyright © 2016 by Teresa Marrone and Walt Sturgeon
Published by Adventure Publications
An imprint of AdventureKEEN
310 Garfield Street South
Cambridge, Minnesota 55008
(800) 678-7006
www.adventurepublications.net

Printed in China
ISBN 978-1-59193-591-9 (pbk); ISBN: 978-1-59193-631-2 (ebook)

Table of Contents

About This Book

This book was written with the beginning mushroom enthusiast in mind. It is a pocket-sized field guide featuring hundreds of the most common species in the Northeast, with clear pictures and additional comparisons for each species. Many "beginner" books feature just the top eminently edible and deadly toxic varieties, while leaving out the hundreds—maybe thousands—of other species that grow in the area. Some books are generalized and may present descriptions and photos of mushrooms that don't grow in our area, the Northeast. Given the sheer number of mushroom species in the Northeast alone, one book cannot completely cover every species you are likely to find . . . especially not one you'd care to carry into the field!

This book covers Connecticut, Maine, Massachusetts, New Hampshire, New Jersey, New York, Ohio, Pennsylvania, Rhode Island and Vermont

Our hope is that this book will both spark your interest about mushrooms and provide you with the means to learn more. A list of useful resources is included at the end of this book, as is a list of some mushroom terms you may encounter in those and other resources. First and foremost, we have arranged the entries in this book by what they look like, or their *morphology*. Many of the genus and species names that originally placed a mushroom in a certain family were assigned by experts because of the mushroom's physical appearance, and many other books arrange species based on their names or their scientific classification. But it is hard to look up a mushroom in a book by its name when you don't have a clue what it is yet.

Many misidentifications start with a hopeful guess that guides you to a book entry that, while incorrect, may have numerous features that seem to match the specimen you have found. The temptation is strong to "force" the description to fit what you have in hand. This can be a dangerous path to travel when attempting to identify wild mushrooms; a mistaken identification may prove harmful or, in the worst case, even fatal if a misidentified mushroom is eaten because the reader attempted to make the specimen "fit" the description given in a book. **For this reason, we strongly advise that novice mushroom enthusiasts consult multiple reliable references or, better still, a local authority who can verify the identity of the mushroom in question before it is eaten.**

Remember, too, that when attempting to compare features of mushrooms in various references or when discussing them with other enthusiasts, the scientific name (which is always in Latin) must be used. The colorful, sometimes descriptive and often humorous common names of mushrooms are fun but can vary by region and are not a truly reliable way to label a species. Using the Latin genus and species name, referred to as **taxonomy**, is the standard and most respected way of referring to a specific variety. However, without a microscope it is often impossible to determine the difference between species with similar appearances. Even some scientists have been overheard in the field referring to a drab specimen simply as an LBM ("little brown mushroom").

To make things more complicated, as more species are discovered and scientists have the ability to study them in more depth with microscopic examination, mating studies and DNA sequencing, authorities are finding that many of the mushrooms that were given their Latin name hundreds of years ago may belong to a different genus than that to which they were originally assigned. In fact, some of the names remain in constant flux, creating so much confusion that at any one time a specific mushroom could be referred to by multiple names, depending on your source. Again, we've attempted to list as many species as possible while keeping this pocket-sized book. We've also used single quotes around names (such as *Russula 'densifolia'*) used for species which appear in, say, Europe but not in North America; this means that specimens found in North America are very similar but not exactly the same as their European counterparts, but a new name has not yet been published

There is also a complete index starting on pg. 276 referencing both common and Latin names, and you'll see that we have included both on the ID pages.

We have been greatly aided in our decades-long studies by numerous people who generously shared their expertise with us. In writing this book we have also consulted many excellent books and other sources; a list of the best is included in Helpful Resources and Bibliography, starting on pg. 268.

Walt would like to thank the organizers and participants of the Sam Ristich NEMF Forays. A wealth of information has been obtained on the mushrooms of the Northeast from these events. The late Sam Ristich shared his knowledge with Walt over the years, as did the late Dick Grimm, founder of the Ohio Mushroom Society.

We would also like to thank Kathy Yerich, co-author (with Teresa Marrone) of *Mushrooms of the Upper Midwest*, the first in this series of mushroom identification guides. The basic structure of *Mushrooms of the Northeast* is based on the Upper Midwest book. Some text in the Northeast book is picked up or adapted from the Upper Midwest book, and we gratefully. acknowledge Kathy's contributions.

What Is a Mushroom?

Mycology is the study of mushrooms. In very general terms, mushrooms and macro fungi are the fruiting bodies of organisms from the fungi kingdom. Indeed, many references refer to the aboveground portion of a fungal organism as a *fruitbody*, although the word *mushroom* is far more common in everyday use. Mushrooms are not plants, because unlike plants they do not use sunlight to photosynthesize their food. More like animals, they use enzymes to break down what they consume. In their role as decomposers of organic material, fungi are essential to life on earth, because without them, the world would be buried in its own debris. In the forest, fungi break down dead or dying organic matter and render it into soil, making it usable for new growth.

The *mycelium* or "roots" of the organism may spread for miles underground, or inhabit an entire tree. The part that we see (and harvest, if we so choose) is comparable to the fruit we pick from a tree; the tree—and the mycelium—remains to bear fruit the following season. Like fruits, mushrooms can also assist in reproduction; just as an apple produces seeds that can grow into a new tree, mushrooms produce microscopic *spores* that are dispersed by wind, insects or other vectors, allowing the larger organism to spread into new areas. Of course, that is a very simple description. There are thousands of species of fungi with complicated life cycles and growth patterns. Learning some basic mycological terms and understanding how mushrooms grow and reproduce will help you understand some of what you'll encounter, but because of the staggering amount of diversity you'll run into, it is more important to learn **how** to decipher what you are seeing.

How to Look at Mushrooms

The main goal of an identification book is to teach the reader how to identify, name and understand more about something. With mushrooms, the sheer number of possibilities makes them a challenging but fascinating subject. Besides the large number of different species, there is an amazing variety of characteristics among those species. Additionally, some of the features are tactile or even sensory elements, like smell or taste, which can be described in a book but should really be experienced firsthand. Other features are too small to be seen without a microscope. This book will cover only criteria visible to the naked eye or through a magnifying glass or loupe (called a *hand lens* in this book), or observable by the senses. Removing microscopic features from our view leaves no shortage of traits that can be observed to positively identify a species. These traits provide a wealth of interesting content for a book, but firsthand experience in the field is even more fascinating! So, what we are really sharing in this book is **how to look at a mushroom**. Reading about different traits and studying the images refines our ability to notice them.

Modern digital photography captures details that may not be readily noticed by the naked eye, making it easier to spot subtle ID features. Multiple photos can be taken and reviewed at home, perhaps even shared on blogs and social media sites, creating an almost instant digital field record.

Store-bought white button mushrooms and brown cremini (or crimini) are varieties of the same species. Portabella mushrooms are mature cremini. All three are *Agaricus bisporus*.

Many universities, mycological societies and individuals have created virtual field guides with amazing photos and descriptions (see a list of recommended websites on pg. 268), but as noted, the best learning experience is a trip to the woods with an experienced teacher.

The practice of taking notes and making drawings to highlight features of the specimens you've found is an old exercise but a good way to become aware of important details. Dr. Michael Kuo's wonderful book, *100 Edible Mushrooms* (see Bibliography), recommends trying this with store-bought mushrooms. He suggests studying button mushrooms and portabellas to observe and compare the features of different stages of growth and different varieties of the same species. Some mushrooms have similar features at different stages of growth, beginning as smaller versions of the mature mushroom. Other mushrooms, however, change quite drastically as they grow, going through stages that would be described quite differently. Weather also has a huge effect on the growth, development and size of a mushroom. That is why it is important to look at not only the entire mushroom, but also multiple specimens, if possible. Most proper identification depends on evaluating many distinct features, some of which occur only at certain stages of growth, during specific types of weather or with other various factors. Due to all the factors noted, your mushroom may not look exactly like the ones in the photos.

In this book, we have listed the key identification features for each species in **green**. One of those key elements, which you'll see listed even before the description on the page, is habitat. When you see a mushroom, get used to looking around you. What type of terrain is there? What other plants or trees are nearby? What is your mushroom really growing on? Sometimes, it may look like a mushroom is growing from the soil when in reality it is growing from a buried piece of wood or an underground tree root. Many species are *saprobes*, mushrooms that get their nutrients from decaying or dead organic matter, whether from a specific type of tree or other vegetation. Some species are *parasites*, attacking living plants and insects. Other mushrooms grow from the soil in association with certain trees, in a symbiotic relationship that is called *mycorrhiza*. Getting to know your trees is a good way to look for certain species of mushrooms.

Learning the parts of a mushroom will help you examine them more closely. Many books take a scientific approach to terminology; this book will not. The diagram below gives an overall view of the parts of a mushroom we'll be mentioning in the upcoming descriptions. Rather than list all of the possible variations of those parts, let's start looking at some pictures and save the terminology and definitions for the Glossary at the back of this book. Some of the features you'll need to consider are easier to distinguish in a picture, so we've included close-up photos on the next pages that clearly show these elements.

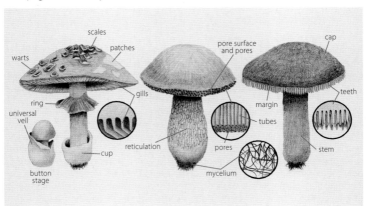

GROWTH STAGES

This discussion focuses on mushrooms—fruiting bodies, actually—that have a distinct cap and stem, resembling familiar store-bought species. Some types of mushrooms take different forms; shelf mushrooms, for example, have no distinct stem, puffballs have neither a traditional stem nor a cap in the common sense of the word, and others, such as coral fungi, are simply structured differently.

Young mushrooms arise from the *mycelium*, microscopic thread-like fungal roots that are underground or growing in another substrate such as rotting wood. Most emerge from the substrate as a *pinhead*, a small rounded bit of tissue that grows rapidly, soon becoming recognizable as what we call a mushroom. The photo sequence below shows a Green-Spored Lepiota (pgs. 60–61) over the course of four days. Some cap-and-stem mushrooms don't develop this quickly, but the stages are similar. (Note that some mushrooms, such as Amanitas and Volvariellas, are encased in a *universal veil*, a thin membrane that encircles the entire developing mushroom; see pg. 62 for photos that show the early growth stages of an Amanita.)

In the photo below at left, the mushroom has emerged from the ground; the cap and stem are distinct and recognizable. At this point, the cap is about 1½ inches wide. The next day, the cap has expanded dramatically to about 4½ inches wide. The photo at right shows the fully expanded cap, which is now about 7½ inches wide. The cap is almost completely flat, with just a slight curve on top, and the darkened gills are visible underneath.

Different species mature at different rates and in different ways. Development is also affected by the weather; mushrooms tend to mature quickly during periods of warm, wet weather and more slowly when it is cool and dry.

CAPS

The cap is generally the first thing that is seen, and its features such as shape, color, size and texture are a good starting point for identification.

As shown on the previous page, the cap's **shape** can change dramatically over the life of a mushroom. The size increases as well; this is particularly dramatic on mushrooms that have the traditional cap-and-stem shape, but caps become larger on other shapes such as shelf mushrooms. Here's a look at some of the common cap shapes.

In the *button stage*—when the specimen has recently emerged from the ground—most caps are *spherical* or *egg-shaped*. As the mushroom grows, the cap expands and begins to open up like an umbrella. Common shapes are shown at right and below.

Spherical

Egg-shaped

Bell-shaped

Conical

Knobbed

Elongated/cylindrical

Rounded/convex

Flat

Bowl-shaped/depressed

Funnel-shaped/vase-shaped

In addition to the shape of the cap, its **texture** must be considered. Some textures are obvious; the egg-shaped cap above is *patchy* (covered with small, slightly raised patches), while the elongated example is *shaggy* (covered with scales that curl or create an irregular, highly textured surface). The rounded example above is *smooth*; however, a smooth cap may feel dry, velvety or slimy, and the best way to know is to touch the cap.

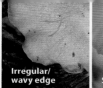
Irregular/wavy edge

Scalloped edge

Upturned edge

Ribbed/striated edge

Cap **edges** also play a part in identification. The edge may be smooth, irregular, scalloped or upturned. It may have faint ribbing; in technical literature, this ribbed texture is referred to as *striated*. Edges also may have fine hairs or *veil fragments* (tissue-like pieces) hanging on them. A hand lens is sometimes needed to observe these characteristics.

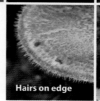
Hairs on edge

Veil fragments on edge

The **color** of the cap may be uniform over the entire surface, but it may also have variations that may be subtle or very obvious. Some are mottled or streaky; others appear to have faint stripes, bands or rings. The center may be a different color than the outer edges; many mushrooms also fade or darken over time. It's not uncommon to have a mushroom change color substantially after it is picked; a digital photo taken before the specimen is picked can be helpful in later identification.

Sometimes, cap colors change on the same specimens depending on the weather. The photo sequence below shows the same group of mushrooms over a three-day period during which the weather changed from rainy to dry and back to rainy (a few of the individuals fell over or were removed from photo to photo). A mushroom whose cap changes color in response to moisture is referred to as *hygrophanous*; if you can observe specimens over the course of a few days, this can be a diagnostic characteristic. Hygrophanous genera include *Agrocybe*, *Galerina*, *Panaeolus*, *Psathyrella* and *Psilocybe*.

Day 1: Wet

Day 2: Dry

Day 3: Wet

11

STEMS

After you've inspected the cap, take a look at the stem underneath it. It's a good idea to study the stem a bit before picking the mushroom, as there are several things you should look for.

Mycelium

Study the base of the stem to look for *mycelium*, thin fungal roots that look like fine threads, cotton or a fuzzy coating. The color, texture and quantity of the mycelium (if present) provide a clue to the mushroom's identity. Mycelium may be found on any substrate that provides a growing medium for mushrooms: soil, decaying wood, live trees—even soggy carpet!

Volva

Next, look for any sign of a *volva*, a fragile, cup-like structure that surrounds the stem base on Amanitas and Volvariellas. You may need to dig around carefully in the dirt at the base of the stem to find the volva, but if you do find one, you're well on your way to identifying the mushroom, since very few types of mushrooms have them. The volva is a remnant of a universal veil; see pgs. 62-63 for more information about this.

Look at the shape, length and thickness of the stem. It may be fairly even in thickness from top to bottom, or it might taper at the top, becoming thicker toward the base. Many can be said to have a *club-shaped* base; this resembles the shape of a baseball bat or may be slightly wider, but gener-

Club-shaped base

Bulbous base

ally the taper is smooth. A *bulbous* base is also broader at the bottom, but the swelling is generally more abrupt and the stem appears to bulge at the base.

Now it is time to pick the mushroom. When you pick it, make sure to get the bottom of the stem, and then turn the whole mushroom over. Note whether the stem is centered on the cap, or if it is off-center (mycologists call this positioning *eccentric*). What do you see under the cap? There may be *gills*, thin blade-like structures that run radially (like spokes of a wheel) between the cap edge and the stem. Instead of gills, some mushrooms have *pores* that look like a very fine sponge. A few, such as Chanterelles (pgs. 38–40), have neither gills nor pores. Gills and pores are discussed in detail on pgs. 14–15.

| Velvety | Scaly | Ridged/grooved | Patterned/reticulated |

Like the cap, the stem may be smooth and fairly featureless, or it may be highly textured. Some of the common textures are illustrated above. Textures can be crucial to identifying your mushroom, so study them carefully; a hand lens may be helpful in some cases. If the stem appears smooth, touch it and note whether it is velvety, slimy or dry.

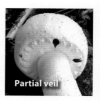

Partial veil

You may notice a ring on the upper part of the stem. This is a remnant of the *partial veil*, a thin tissue that covers the developing gills or pores on some mushroom species (this is not the same thing as the universal veil mentioned at left and discussed in more detail on pgs. 62–63). If you look at a common button mushroom from the grocery store, you'll see a partial veil on small specimens. As the mushroom grows, the cap expands and opens up, tearing the veil away from the cap and allowing the spores to disperse from the gills or pores. The veil remains attached to the stem. It may persist as a *ring* or it may deteriorate, leaving behind a *ring zone*, a sticky band that is often colored by falling spores; sometimes it dis-

| Skirt-like ring | Simple ring | Ring zone |

integrates completely, leaving no trace. The photos above illustrate these features. Note that pieces of the veil may also remain attached to the cap edge, as shown in the photo of veil fragments on pg. 11.

Cortina

Some species have veils that are extremely thin and cobweb-like; this type of veil is called a *cortina*, and it is found on *Cortinarius* species as well as several others. Because the cortina is so insubstantial, it does not leave a classic ring; at most, a faint ring zone remains behind on the stem.

UNDER THE CAP

Some of the most important mushroom features are found under the cap. On cap-and-stem or shelf mushrooms, this area produces *spores*, microscopic particles that function like seeds to help the mushroom reproduce.

Gills

Many mushrooms, including common grocery-store mushrooms (*Agaricus bisporus*), have **gills**, thin blade-like structures (referred to as **lamellae** by mycologists) that grow like the spokes of a wheel between the cap edge and the stem. Spores are produced on the flat faces of the gills and are forcibly ejected when they are mature. The spore color often affects the color of the gills; if you look at a young button mushroom from the grocery store, you'll notice that the gills are pinkish, but on mature specimens the gills have turned chocolate brown from the spores. (Indeed, you may often find a dusting of brownish spores on the tray underneath portabella caps.) When collecting wild mushrooms, it's always a good idea to make a spore print as described on pg. 17; this is the best way to determine the color of the mature spores, which is often key to properly identifying your find.

When you're holding a gilled mushroom you've picked, look closely at the way that the gills are attached to the stem. Mycologists use numerous terms to describe a wide variety of attachment methods; the differences between some of them are so subtle that it's difficult for the layperson to detect them. In this book, we're going to focus on those attachments that are easy to see with the eye, or perhaps with use of a hand lens. Other attachment methods can be included broadly in the three described here.

Attached gills are just what they sound like: the gills are attached to the stem. *Decurrent gills* are attached gills that run down the stem, slightly or a fair distance, rather than ending abruptly. *Free gills* stop short of the stem; when viewed from above, it looks like there is a miniature racetrack around the stem. It's often helpful to cut the mushroom in half from top to bottom to get a clearer view of the attachment, as shown in the first and last photos below.

Attached gills, cross section

Decurrent gills

Free gills

Free gills, cross section

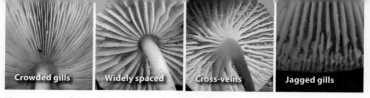

Crowded gills | Widely spaced | Cross-veins | Jagged gills

The spacing of the gills is an important identification point. From tight to loose, spacing is described in this book as crowded, closely spaced, moderately widely spaced, or widely spaced. They may be as straight as a knife blade, or wavy as shown in the photo of decurrent gills on the facing page. Sometimes there are short **cross-veins**, small ridges that connect the gills in a net-like fashion; a hand lens is often needed to see these. Some gills have a jagged texture on the edge; others are forked near the edge of the cap. The color of the gills is an important identifying factor; also note that some species have gills that are a different color along the thin edge. And as previously noted, gills often change color over time as spores collect on them.

Pores

Rather than gills, some mushrooms have **pores**, created by a sponge-like layer of very thin tubes attached to the underside of the cap. The spores develop inside the tubes, then drop down through the open bottom ends of the tubes when they are mature. **Boletes** are the most well-known of the cap-and-stem mushrooms that bear pores.

Bolete tubes, cross section

The pore layer of a bolete can be peeled away from the cap as a fairly cohesive unit; this differentiates it from the pore layer on **polypores**, short-stalked or shelf-like mushrooms that grow on wood.

Like gills, pore surfaces are various colors. The pores may be extremely tiny or fine, appearing almost like a solid, featureless layer unless studied through a hand lens; they may also be large and coarse enough to see easily with the naked eye. Pores may be rounded, angular or hexagonal. Many species have pores that **bruise**, or change color when handled, cut or damaged.

Very fine pores | Larger pores | Angular pores | Bruised pores

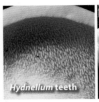
Hydnellum teeth

Hericium teeth

Teeth

Rather than gills or pores, some mushrooms have *teeth*, spine-like structures on which the spores develop. Members of the *Hydnum* genus (pgs. 52–53) and the *Hydnellum* genus (pgs. 254–255) look like standard mushrooms when viewed from above, but they have short teeth on their undersides. *Hericium* species (pgs. 48–49), on the other hand, seem to be composed of nothing but long, dangling teeth.

Folds

These spore-bearing structures look like gills at a quick glance, but further inspection reveals that they are not separate, individual structures like true gills; they are merely thin, raised veins that are part of the mushroom body. Chanterelles (pgs. 38–40) are the best example of this, and the folds are not the only features that differentiate them from look-alikes. They do not have a distinct cap and separate stem; rather, the entire mushroom is a single item that is somewhat trumpet-shaped. Chanterelles are one of

Chanterelle folds

the top edibles and are highly prized, but care must be taken to ensure that the specimen really has folds rather than gills in order to distinguish it from the Jack O'Lantern (pgs. 70–71), a **toxic** look-alike. Black Trumpet (pgs. 50–51) is another mushroom in this book that has spore-bearing folds rather than gills.

Other spore-bearing structures

The mushroom world is complex, and the examples above are only part of the story of how mushrooms spread their spores. Morels (pgs. 24–27) carry their spores on pits between external ridges. Puffballs (pgs. 41–43, 230, 234) are solid sphere-like mushrooms with spores located in the interior flesh; when the spores ripen, the mushroom becomes shrunken and will burst open when lightly touched, scattering its spores. Other mushrooms are shaped like cups, coral or shapes that are too numerous to list here; each shape of mushroom has its own unique way of dispersing its spores.

SPORE PRINTS

As noted on pg. 14, the color of a mushroom's spores is often a major clue to its identity, and we're including information about spore color for every species discussed in this book. Sometimes, a mushroom that is still standing in the woods or field has deposited spores on surrounding vegetation, logs or other mushrooms; in cases like this, you can determine the spore color without any further action. At right is a photo of a Purple-Gilled Laccaria (pg. 142) that has deposited its whitish spores on the green leaf of a nearby plant.

Spore deposit

Most of the time, however, you'll have to make your own spore print at home. It's easy to do and fun to see the results. The spore deposit may be white, black, or nearly any color of the rainbow. White prints won't show up on white paper, and black prints won't show up on black paper, so the best way to make a print is to use a piece of paper that is half-white and half-black; it's easy to run sheets of paper on a laser printer that have a large black field covering half of the paper.

You'll need a completely developed but still-fresh mushroom; specimens that are too young or too old probably won't produce spores. It should not have any trace of a partial veil over the gills. Cut off the stem so it is just a stub that fits inside the cap; a scissors often works better than a knife. Place your black-and-white paper on a table where it can sit undisturbed. Carefully place the mushroom with the spore-producing surface down, positioning it so half of it is over the white paper

and half is over the black area. Cover it with a bowl or glass and let it sit for a half-day, or overnight. Carefully remove the bowl, then the mushroom cap; with any luck, you'll have something that looks like the example at left.

The benefit of the two-colored paper is obvious. The spore print shown here is whitish to pale cream-colored; it shows up well on the black part of the paper, and just a slight trace of it can be seen on the white part of the paper.

Eating Mushrooms

Identifying mushrooms from a book is a good way to begin learning about them, but when edibility is your goal you must be extremely careful. It is recommended to obtain a first-hand, positive ID from an expert before eating any mushroom, as many of the toxic varieties look similar to the edible ones and could make you very ill, or even kill you! Join a local mycological society (see information in the Resources section on pg. 268), or hook up with an experienced forager who is familiar with local species.

Even after you have a positively identified a good edible, always try just a small portion the first time to assess your body's tolerance to it. Never eat more than one new species at a time the first time you try it, because if you combine several and have problems, you won't know which mushroom was the culprit. Don't assume that because others can enjoy a particular species, it will be OK for you, too; a friend who is an amazing outdoorsman recently shared his unfortunate discovery that even though he loves the taste of morels, he found that eating them made him nauseous. Also remember that **wild mushrooms should never be eaten raw**.

It is tempting to look for a simple rule or test that tells you whether an unknown mushroom is edible, but unfortunately no such rule exists. Taking the time to learn how to identify each species by its unique characteristics (even though some may be hard to see) is the only appropriate method. Also read the Top Edibles and Top Toxics section on pg. 21 for additional guidance.

Some common folklore to ignore

- If a mushroom was eaten by animals or insects, it isn't poisonous.
- If you cook a mushroom with a silver utensil or coin in the pot and the metal doesn't turn black, the mushroom isn't poisonous.
- If a mushroom smells and tastes good, it isn't poisonous.
- If a mushroom peels easily, it isn't poisonous.
- Brightly colored mushrooms are the only poisonous ones.
- Pickling or boiling eliminates toxins from poisonous mushrooms.
- Rice will turn red if cooked with poisonous mushrooms.

Digging Deeper into Mycology

Physical features that can be observed with the eye (possibly aided by a hand lens) are enough to identify some mushrooms positively. Many other mushrooms, however, are difficult or impossible to identify unless the spores (the reproductive units) are studied microscopically. Mycologists classify mushrooms into groups (called *phyla*) based on how the spores are dispersed. Two major groups are described briefly below: basidiomycetes and ascomycetes.

Most mushrooms in this book fall into the **basidiomycetes** group, which includes all mushrooms with gills or pores and others such as puffballs. The spores are carried on the surface of club-shaped appendages called *basidia*. The surface of the gills on gilled mushrooms, and the insides of pore tubes on boletes and polypores, are covered with basidia. Each basidium (the singular form of basidia) holds several spores on tiny prongs at the end of the appendage. By the time the tiny spores are on the mycologist's slide, however, they have often been ejected from the basidium, so this appendage is not visible in most microscopic views of the spores.

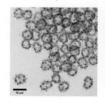

Ascomycetes are also called sac fungi because the spores are contained in a sac-like container called an **ascus**. These sacs are carried on the spore-bearing surface of non-gilled and non-pored mushrooms, including morels, cup fungi and others.

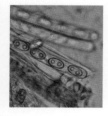

When the spores are ripe, the end of the sac opens to eject the spores. The number and shape of spores in each ascus may vary, although many asci (the plural form of ascus) contain eight spores. As with basidiomycetes, the spores have often been ejected out of the ascus before they are collected for analysis; however, mycologists sometimes shave off a section of the mushroom before the spores are ejected, in order to observe the asci (shown in the detail at left).

This discussion may seem highly technical to the novice; however, it is actually an extremely simplified overview. Mycologists who study mushrooms microscopically use terms that are baffling to the novice when describing the shape and other characteristics of the pores. Should you wish to learn more, check with your local mycological society or a university; some mycological societies offer periodic seminars on studying mushrooms microscopically.

How to Use This Book

As noted in the Introduction, this is an abbreviated field guide designed for ease of use by a layperson—one who is not intimately familiar with mushrooms in the field or on the printed page. It focuses on mushroom features that can be seen without the aid of a microscope, so it is organized a bit differently than other field guides you may have seen.

Many books organize the entries based on an alphabetical listing of the **genus**, which might be thought of as the mushroom's "last name." That is followed by an alphabetical sub-listing of the exact **species**, the mushroom's "first name" that makes it different from other members of its genus. This listing is referred to as the mushroom's **scientific name**, and it is always in Latin. This is a much more reliable system than using "common names" which change depending on the language being spoken; indeed, common names can change from one state to another, making them unreliable.

The King Bolete (pgs. 44–47), for example, is referred to as the Porcini in Italy and the Cep in France. Its scientific name, however, is listed as *Boletus edulis* in all references, regardless of language. *Boletus* is the genus name; *edulis* is the species name. This tells us that this mushroom is closely related to, say, *Boletus subvelutipes*. However, while *Boletus edulis* is a choice, highly prized edible with a brown cap and whitish pores, *Boletus subvelutipes* is toxic, with a reddish cap and bright red pores. Thus, within the same genus, you may have a listing for a brown mushroom followed by a red one; a white one may follow that and another brown one after that. If you know what you're looking for, this type of organization is easy to follow, but if you're not sure what genus your mushroom belongs to, it's difficult to know where to start looking.

Some mushrooms are delicious edibles, while others are dangerously toxic—even deadly. As discussed above, these distinctions do not follow genus classifications. Before you take to the field in search of edibles, it is helpful to know which mushrooms are safe even for beginners, but it is also imperative to become familiar with the deadliest mushrooms so you know what to avoid. This book starts with two sections that offer expanded coverage of the Top Edibles and Top Toxics in our area. The rest of the book is like a catalog of mushrooms, organized by their shape and other visible features.

In this book, mushrooms are grouped by basic categories, and within each of those categories they are grouped by color. Thus, if you find a mushroom that has a distinct cap and stem, and it has gills under the cap, you would go to the section entitled Cap & Stem with Gills, starting on pg. 72 (refer to the listing of Basic

Categories on pgs. 22–23 to locate the proper category). Colors within the section are organized from light to dark, as much as possible. So if your cap-and-stem mushroom is brown, go to pg. 86, where the first of the brown cap-and-stem mushrooms is listed. Compare your specimen to the photos and pay particular attention to the details listed. With luck, you'll find a description that matches your specimen, but if not, use the scientific name of the closest match to search more complete references. Also remember to check the Top Edibles and Top Toxics sections, as well as the abbreviated Others of Note sections found at the end of each category.

TOP EDIBLES AND TOP TOXICS

These special sections highlight two categories of mushrooms you should be very familiar with before collecting anything for the table. First up is a selection of some of the top edibles in our region, chosen not only for edibility but also because these are easy to identify without fear of collecting a toxic species. Following that are the top toxic mushrooms in our area. Some are **deadly**; all will make you very sick if you ingest them. Study them until you can easily recognize them in the field. Remember that it is always best to have an experienced mushroom forager with you when you first learn about edibles—or about toxic species.

The Top Edibles start on pg. 24; the Top Toxics start on pg. 56. Each section includes expanded coverage of highlighted species, along with descriptions of look-alikes to watch out for. Some of the look-alike descriptions include references to other pages in this book; others include photos of species that aren't discussed elsewhere in the book. At the bottom of each of the look-alike photos, you'll find a band that provides information about edibility. A green band indicates that the look-alike is edible. A red band indicates that the look-alike is toxic, while a pinkish band indicates that while it may not be extremely toxic, the look-alike should not be considered edible.

Lilac Bolete
EDIBLE

Angel Wings
NOT RECOMMENDED

Jack O'Lantern (toxic)
TOXIC

Basic Categories

Here are the basic categories used in this book, along with the page range for each section. Notes next to each category give a brief description and also list species that are covered in the Top Edibles or Top Toxics sections. The bands next to the photos indicate the color used for each section.

CAP & STEM WITH GILLS (PGS. 72–163)

Traditional cap-and-stem shape with gills underneath the cap.

In the Edibles section: Inky Caps
In the Toxics section: Deadly Galerina, Green-Spored Lepiota, Amanitas, Jack O'Lantern

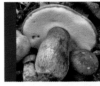

CAP & STEM WITH PORES (PGS. 164–191)

Traditional cap-and-stem shape with pores underneath the cap.

In the Edibles section: King Bolete
In the Toxics section: Toxic Boletes

ATYPICAL CAPS (PGS. 192–195)

Mushrooms that have stems but do not have a traditional cap with gills or pores.

In the Edibles section: Morels, Chanterelles, Hedgehogs
In the Toxics section: False Morels: Gyromitras

SHELF WITH PORES (PGS. 196–219)

Typically growing on trees or wood as a shelf or cluster with pores underneath; lacking a distinct stem.

In the Edibles section: Chicken Mushrooms, Hen of the Woods

SHELF WITH GILLS (PGS. 220–225)

Typically growing on trees or wood as a shelf or cluster with gills underneath; lacking a distinct stem.

In the Edibles section: Oyster Mushrooms

SHELF/OTHER (PGS. 226–229)

Typically growing on trees or wood as a shelf or cluster with neither pores nor gills underneath; lacking a distinct stem.

SPHERICAL MUSHROOMS (PGS. 230–237)

Rounded or ball-like mushrooms that lack a distinct stem.

In the Edibles section: Giant Puffball

CUP-SHAPED MUSHROOMS (PGS. 238–245)

Mushrooms with no distinct stem whose body consists of a cup-like or flattened structure.

CORAL AND CLUB FUNGI (PGS. 246–253)

Irregularly shaped mushrooms that look like branches, soft sticks or sea coral; generally small in stature but often growing in large groups.

MISCELLANEOUS MUSHROOMS (PGS. 254–267)

Mushrooms whose shapes fit no other category.

In the Edibles section: Cauliflower Mushrooms, Lion's Mane, Black Trumpet

FROM THE SOIL NEAR TREES

SPRING

Morels (several)

Morchella spp.

Morels are probably the most sought-after wild mushrooms in our area; they are so popular that they have been named the official state mushroom of Minnesota. Even novices can easily learn to identify Morels with confidence—once they find some to identify. Experienced foragers guard the locations of prized Morel spots like a treasure and have been known to park a mile or more from a favorite spot to throw off anyone who may be following them. The Morel season is very short—typically a few weeks—which adds to their mystique.

Like many other mushrooms, Morels are subject to debate about how many species there are and what they should be called; ongoing DNA studies are redefining traditional concepts and discarding long-standing species names. At the simplest, "classic" Morels can be divided into two categories: Yellow Morels and Black Morels. Half-Free Morels are another "true Morel," but they have some significant differences in appearance (see pg. 26).

Hollow interiors

HABITAT: Typically found **around trees that have recently died**, especially elm but also cottonwood; sometimes found in old fruit orchards. May also grow under live tulip and ash trees. Although it is rare, they may appear under conifers. They are occasionally found in gardens and shrubbery and sometimes appear on wood chips. Areas disturbed by fire the previous year, or cinder banks along old railroads, can produce morel fruitings. Morels typically grow singly or scattered but may also grow gregariously or in small clusters.

DESCRIPTION: Morels have **pitted caps** that appear **honeycombed**. Caps may be conical, egg-shaped, elongated or nearly spherical. Stems have a smooth or granular texture; they are often crumbly or brittle, and there is no ring. Stems are whitish, cream-colored or yellowish. They may have a round profile in cross-section, or may be

green = key identification feature

M. americana

Gray form of
M. americana

M. diminutiva

slightly flattened or irregular; they often appear creased or folded, particularly at the base, which may be slightly wider than the rest of the stem. When sliced lengthwise, both cap and stem are **completely hollow** (photo at left) with **no trace of cottony material** inside. The cap and stem are seamlessly connected so that the hollow space inside is a **single, continuous cavity**. On Black Morels, there is a slight but distinct **rim at the base of the cap** (sometimes called a groove). Half-Free Morels have a **short skirt around the lower half of the cap**, but they *do not have a full, loose skirt that dangles from the top of the stem*.

Yellow Morels have ridges that are typically paler than the pits. • *M. americana* (also known as *M. esculentoides*; previously listed as *M. esculenta* and *M. deliciosa*, which are European species) is the most common in our area, where it is often found under dead or dying elms and living ash. It is typically yellowish but may be gray or whitish when small. The ridges are **irregularly arranged** and are **paler** than the pits. The gray form is often found at the start of the season; in addition to being dark, these early-season Morels are often smaller than the yellow form that follows, making them particularly difficult to find. *M. americana* are typically 2 to 4 inches tall, but size varies quite a bit and they may reach enormous sizes at the end of the season, sometimes growing to a foot in height; older sources list this form as *M. crassipes*, a name which has been invalidated. *M. cryptica* is visually identical to *M. americana* and can be identified only by microscopic examination. • The **Tulip Morel** (*M. diminutiva*) is typically smaller than other Yellow Morels. Caps have **long, vertical pits**, and the stems sometimes seem proportionally longer in relation to the cap than other Morels. Pits are grayish at first, soon becoming the same color as the ridges. They are found near hardwoods and have been reported under tulip trees, ash, oak, cherry, apple and hickory trees.

M. angusticeps

Half-Free Morel

Half-Free
Morel, split

Black Morels have **strongly vertical ridges** bisected by numerous short horizontal ridges; the ridge arrangement may look **ladder-like.** • *M. angusticeps* (previously listed as *M. elata* and *M. conica*, which are European species) is the most common Black Morel in our region. It is found under hardwoods, including ash and cherry trees; it has also been reported under poplars and pine trees. The base of the cap **hangs slightly over the stem**, creating a small rim with a groove underneath. Ridges are tan at first—sometimes nearly the same color as the pits—becoming **much darker than the pits** with maturity, often nearly black. *M. angusticeps* are typically 2 to 5 inches tall, sometimes up to 6 inches; they do not reach the gigantic proportions that Yellow Morels do at the end of the season.

Half-Free Morels (*M. punctipes*; previously listed as *M. semilibera*, which has been determined to be a European species) are true, edible Morels that have a **small cap** perched atop a stem that may be up to 6 inches tall. The **bottom half of the cap is free from the stem**; when the mushroom is halved vertically, the top half of the cap is **part of the same hollow chamber** as the stem, while the bottom half of the cap hangs free like a **short skirt-like extension**. They grow under hardwoods.

SPORE PRINT: Creamy, whitish or yellowish; spore prints are seldom taken.

SEASON: Spring.

OTHER NAMES: Sponge Mushroom, Land Fish, Merkel, Molly Moocher. Yellow Morels that reach enormous sizes at the end of the season are often referred to as Big Foot Morels. The scientific names for Morels are in flux and change periodically; they remain somewhat unsettled at the time of this writing.

V. bohemica

V. bohemica, split

V. conica

COMPARE: Several mushrooms with wrinkled or pitted caps may appear in the woods during spring. • Verpas are found earlier than Morels and continue to grow during the Morel season. *Verpa bohemica* has a cap that is **wrinkled** or pitted; the

Gyromitra esculenta

Gyromitra interior

TOXIC

cap of *V. conica* is **smooth**. With both forms, the cap is attached to the stem **only at the top**; the sides **hang completely free** from the stem, which is at least **partially stuffed** with a cottony material. Verpas can cause gastrointestinal distress and are best considered inedible. • Several *Gyromitra* species (also called False Morels; pgs. 56–57) share the spring woods with Morels; they are often much larger, leading to confusion with large, end-of-season Yellow Morels. Their caps appear **wrinkled, folded or brain-like** rather than pitted, and the interiors are **stuffed with pockmarked flesh**. Colors range from reddish to brownish; stems are whitish or yellowish. Most are regarded as **toxic**; none should be eaten. • Also see **Stinkhorns** (pg. 192) and **Elfin Saddles** (pg. 194) for other mushrooms that have some similarities to Morels.

NOTES: All true Morels are edible when cooked, although Half-Free Morels are considered less desirable. Some people may have a reaction to one variety or another, so small quantities should be eaten at first.

FROM THE SOIL · SPRING THROUGH FALL

Inky Caps (several)

Coprinoid group

This group of related mushrooms is common in both urban and woodland settings. While they're not as highly regarded for the table as some others in this section, they are easy to identify and a good choice for beginners.

HABITAT: Inky Caps are saprobes, mushrooms that get their nutrients from decaying organic matter. They often appear in large clusters but also grow in scattered groupings.

DESCRIPTION: The most obvious feature of Inky Caps is that the gills of mature specimens dissolve, partially or completely, turning into an **inky black fluid** (photo at left). All species discussed here have a partial veil covering the gills of young specimens, and some have a universal veil;

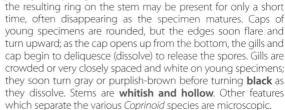

the resulting ring on the stem may be present for only a short time, often disappearing as the specimen matures. Caps of young specimens are rounded, but the edges soon flare and turn upward; as the cap opens up from the bottom, the gills and cap begin to deliquesce (dissolve) to release the spores. Gills are crowded or very closely spaced and white on young specimens; they soon turn gray or purplish-brown before turning **black** as they dissolve. Stems are **whitish and hollow**. Other features which separate the various *Coprinoid* species are microscopic.

Shaggy Manes

- Shaggy Manes (*Coprinus comatus*) are found in grassy areas, on wood chips, on disturbed ground and in areas with compacted soil. Caps of young specimens are shaped like an **elongated oval** and may be nearly **6 inches tall**, although they are usually shorter. They are whitish and covered with **small, elongated, shaggy scales that curl upward**; the very top of the cap is generally smooth and somewhat darker in color. Stems are 3 to 8 inches tall; when cut in half vertically, a **string-like filament** can be seen on the inside, hanging down from the top of the cap into the stem.

green = key identification feature

Alcohol Inky (edible stage)

Alcohol Inky (too old to eat)

• **Alcohol Inky** or **Tippler's Bane** (*Coprinopsis atramentaria*; also listed as *Coprinus atramentarius*) grows on decaying roots and other woody debris that may be buried. They generally grow in **tight, dense clusters** and are often found at the base of stumps and dead trees. Young specimens have **egg-shaped to conical caps** up to 2 inches wide and tall; they are **pewter-gray or grayish-brown**. The surface is **silky** except at the center, which is **finely scaly** and often darker in color; **faint** grooves run upward from the edge of the cap. Stems are 3 to 5½ inches tall.

SPORE PRINT: Blackish to brownish-black.

SEASON: Alcohol Inkies and Shaggy Manes are most common in the fall but also occur in cool weather conditions in spring or early summer.

OTHER NAMES: Inkies; Shaggy Mane is sometimes called Lawyer's Wig.

COMPARE: Several related mushrooms may be confused with the top edible Inky Caps. • **Mica Caps** (pg. 94; edible) have **tawny**, conical caps that are **finely ribbed**, with no hairs, scales or overall patches; young caps are covered with **salt-like granules**. Caps may not dissolve completely. • **Scaly Inky Caps** (pg. 116) have tan to grayish-brown caps that are covered with **large, flaky pale patches**. Some people suffer digestive upset after eating them; like Alcohol Inky, they should not be consumed with alcohol. • **Wooly Inky Cap** (*Coprinopsis lagopus* or *Coprinus lagopus*; inedible) is generally 2 inches tall or less. Young caps are **gray and covered with pale hairs**.

Wooly Inky Cap

NOTES: Collect Inky Caps for the table before the gills darken. They deteriorate very quickly after picking and must be cooked without delay. Alcohol Inky **causes severe illness if consumed within several days of drinking alcohol** (either before or after the mushrooms are eaten). Some compare the reaction to the worst hangover imaginable, or even worse.

NEAR DEAD AND DYING TREES   SUMMER THROUGH FALL

TOP EDIBLES

Cauliflower Mushrooms

Sparassis spathulata, Sparassis americana

Many books show pictures of this mushroom in a basket, on a plate, or being displayed proudly in someone's hands. The first reason is to show the impressive size that this mushroom reaches, but the second may be that hunters who find this delicacy aren't willing to show anyone exactly where in the woods they found it!

HABITAT: Cauliflower Mushrooms are saprobes, getting their nutrients from the buried roots of dying and dead trees. Found alone or in groups in mixed woods next to deciduous and coniferous trees.

DESCRIPTION: This large, brain-like **cluster** mushroom is easy to recognize. It is made up of a mass of **creamy white to tan-colored folds** growing from a **branching base**. Some describe it as looking like a pile of egg noodles. Large examples may be up to 12 inches across, but most specimens are much smaller. This mushroom doesn't have gills or teeth but a **smooth surface** on one side of the folded flesh to release its spores. Two species are found in our area; both look similar and both are highly sought-after edibles.

S. spathulata

green = key identification feature

S. americana

- *S. spathulata* is typically found under **oaks**. It has an underground central base but is not deeply rooted. Individual folds have **distinct color zones or bands**; the folds are spread out and **fairly flat**.

- *S. americana*, sometimes referred to as the Rooting Cauliflower Mushroom, prefers **conifers**. It grows from a **deeply buried root** that is dark brown to black; if the root is not disturbed, it will continue to fruit in the same place from year to year. Individual folds of *S. americana* are **very curly** and **uniformly colored**, with no banding; they are more tightly packed together than the folds of *S. spathulata*. *S. americana* is less common in our area than *S. spathulata*.

SPORE PRINT: Whitish to cream-colored.

SEASON: Summer through fall.

OTHER NAMES: Wood Cauliflower, Noodle Mushroom, Eastern Cauliflower Mushroom. *S. radicata* is sometimes listed as a synonym for *S. americana*, but *S. radicata* is actually a closely related species found in the Pacific Northwest and California. *S. crispa* is listed as another name in some texts but is now thought to be a European species.

COMPARE: Hen of the Woods and its look-alike, the **Umbrella Polypore** (pgs. 54–55), can grow quite large like the Cauliflower Mushroom and are also delicious edibles. They are found at the base of trees (usually oak) but have **fleshy caps** with **porous**, white spore-producing surfaces underneath.

NOTES: Though not easy to find, the Cauliflower Mushroom is quite the treat! A large specimen, however, can require lots of cleaning. Though brittle, they can be pulled apart at the base and soaked in mild saltwater to remove debris and unwanted critters. The flavor and texture of cooked Cauliflower Mushrooms are often compared to buttered noodles. Older, over-mature specimens often have an unpleasant cabbage-like odor.

NEAR OR ON LIVE OR DEAD TREES

LATE SPRING THROUGH FALL

TOP EDIBLES

Chicken Mushrooms (several)
Laetiporus spp.

Unlike other edible mushrooms that seem to use natural camouflage to hide from the eager forager, the Chicken Mushroom announces its presence loudly. Its bright colors, large size and frequently elevated location make it easy to spot from a fair distance.

HABITAT: Found in association with live, dead or dying trees. The appearance of Chicken Mushrooms on a living tree is a signal that the tree has been attacked by the mushroom's parasitic mycelium (thread-like fungal roots), which can sometimes be seen as whitish fibers in cracks in the wood. The fungus causes heart rot of the host tree.

DESCRIPTION: Three *Laetiporus* species are found in our area. All grow as a **grouping of thick, stemless fan-shaped caps**; individual caps may be up to 12 inches wide but are generally smaller. Caps are some shade of **orange to yellow-orange**, with a fair amount of variation among different groupings of the same species. They are smooth to wrinkled and may be leathery but are **not hairy**. Edges may be rounded or scalloped and range from flat to wavy. The underside of each cap is covered with **tiny pores**.

• *L. sulphureus* (also called Sulphur Shelf and *Polyporus sulphureus*) is the most well-known Chicken Mushroom. It grows directly on **deciduous**

L. sulphureus

L. sulphureus, showing yellow pore surface

green = key identification feature

L. cincinnatus, showing white pore surface

wood, favoring oaks; it often grows on standing trees but also is found on stumps and downed wood. The caps are typically arranged in **tight, overlapping shelf-like layers** but may occasionally grow as a rosette. The pore surface is **bright yellow**; cap edges are often yellow.

- White-Pored Chicken Mushroom (*L. cincinnatus;* also listed as *P. cincinnatus*) has a **white to buff** pore surface and usually grows as a **rosette** rather than as a cluster of overlapping shelves. *L. cincinnatus* is most often found **on the ground** or on top of stumps, over buried roots of oak and, occasionally, those of other deciduous trees. It has softer, more muted colors than *L. sulphureus*. Cap edges are often white.

- *L. huroniensis* has an appearance that is identical to *L. sulphureus*, but it grows on **hemlock and pine logs and stumps**. It is usually found in mature conifer forests.

SPORE PRINT: White.

SEASON: Late spring through fall.

OTHER NAMES: Chicken of the Woods, Sulfur Shelf.

COMPARE: Another choice edible, **Hen of the Woods** (pgs. 54–55), also grows as a cluster of caps, but its caps are **tan or gray** and thinner. • **Toxic** Jack O'Lantern (pgs. 70-71) is a bright orange, clustering mushroom that bears some resemblance to Chickens when glimpsed from afar, but closer inspection reveals that Jacks have **distinct stems** and **gills**. • The inedible Orange Mock Oyster (pg. 225) is a fan-shaped orange mushroom that grows on deciduous and coniferous trees. It has **gills** rather than pores, and its caps are **hairy**. It often grows in clusters but may be scattered.

NOTES: Chicken Mushrooms have a meaty, chicken-like texture. Young growth on the cap edge of *L. sulphureus* is tender, but the older center portion becomes tough and requires stewing; many eat only the tender edges. The flesh of *L. cincinnatus* is more tender than that of *L. sulphureus* and the entire fruiting body is generally edible; most foragers consider it a better culinary prize than *L. sulphureus*. Chicken Mushrooms, particularly older specimens, may cause digestive upset in some people.

NEAR OR ON LIVE OR DEAD TREES

LATE SPRING THROUGH EARLY WINTER

TOP EDIBLES

Oyster Mushrooms (several)
Pleurotus spp.

Four *Pleurotus* species in our area are variations of the traditional Oyster Mushroom; they are a choice edible that is easy to identify. All share several common characteristics. They are shelf-like mushrooms that grow in overlapping clusters on living and dead wood; their gills run down the stem, which is often so short as to appear nonexistent. Caps have a smooth upper surface and are often wavy or ruffled around the edges. They hasten decomposition of the wood on which they grow.

HABITAT: Oyster Mushrooms always **grow from wood** and are found on living trees, dying trees, or dead trees, stumps and logs; they also may grow on buried roots, appearing to grow from the soil. They may be found singly, but typically grow in clusters that may be quite large.

DESCRIPTION: The shelf-like cap is the most prominent part of any Oyster Mushroom; it is fan-shaped if growing against a standing tree but may be circular if growing upright from a fallen log or from buried roots. Edges are often wavy, scalloped or irregular. The cap is **smooth** and is **fairly meaty**, especially at the point where the gills come together on the underside. Stems may be short and stubby, or virtually nonexistent; when present and not covered with gills, they are usually

Pleurotus ostreatus

green = key identification feature

Pleurotus pulmonarius

Pleurotus populinus

hairy near the base. Stems have **no ring**. Gills are closely spaced and run down the stem, or may simply taper down to a stem-like stub. The first three Oyster Mushrooms discussed here are similar in so many ways that it may be difficult to determine exactly which species you have found. Below are some traits that may be helpful; however, microscopic examination is necessary for absolute certainty. Happily, all are equally edible, so exact identification is not required.

• "Classic" Oyster Mushrooms (*Pleurotus ostreatus*) are up to **8 inches** across and range from cream-colored to tan to grayish-brown. Gills are white to cream-colored. Most commonly found on deciduous wood, they also grow on conifers and are found from spring through **early winter**. They have a sweet smell that is sometimes described as anise-like. Spores are whitish, lilac-tinged or grayish.

• *Pleurotus pulmonarius*, also called the Pale Oyster or Summer Oyster, is generally **smaller and paler** than Classic Oysters, often with a lung-like shape. They are typically less than 4 inches across. Caps and gills are white to cream-colored to tan. They are found from late spring through early fall on the wood of living and dead deciduous trees. Spores are whitish, lilac-tinged or grayish.

• The **Aspen Oyster** (*Pleurotus populinus*) is similar in size and coloration to *Pleurotus pulmonarius*, but it grows only on the wood of living and dead trees in the *Populus* genus, which includes **poplars, aspens and cottonwoods**. It is found in late spring and, occasionally, into the summer. It has a distinct anise-like scent. Spores are whitish.

• The **Golden Oyster** (*Pleurotus citrinopileatus*) is native to eastern Asia but commonly cultivated in the U.S. New to our woodlands, it is found growing gregariously, likely invasively, on dead or dying deciduous trees, from spring through fall. Large groups of **densely clustered** caps are **bright to egg-yolk yellow**. Caps may be 6 inches across or more and are rounded, with

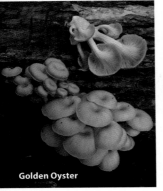
Golden Oyster

a **dimple** in the center. Stems are up to 5 inches long and ½ inch thick; they are **multi-branched**, curving around a central, thicker base. With age, the caps flatten, fading to tan; the central depression may deepen, creating nearly hollow stems. Gills are white; spores are **pale pink**. Golden Oysters are edible and seem relatively bug-resistant. They have thin flesh but dehydrating enhances the texture, which is a good thing since you may find loads. In the past, *Pleurotus citrinopileatus* was considered a variety of *Pleurotus cornucopiae*, a European species. DNA studies to trace origins of the wild strains found in North America are ongoing.

SPORE PRINT: Spores of most Oysters are whitish, but color varies, depending on species; see individual accounts.

SEASON: Late spring through early winter, depending on species.

COMPARE: Numerous mushrooms in our area have some resemblance to traditional Oyster Mushrooms. Some are edible; others are not recommended.

• Veiled Oyster (*Pleurotus dryinus*) is related to other Oyster Mushrooms, but it has a **distinct, stocky stem** up to 4 inches long that is **covered with fuzz**. Caps are up to 6 inches across and **densely fuzzy**. Both caps and gills are white to cream-colored, turning **yellowish** when bruised or old. There is a **partial veil** over the gills of young specimens, which breaks apart as the cap matures, leaving **remnants on the cap edge** and a **thin ring** on the stem; the ring disappears with age. Veiled Oysters grow from midsummer through fall on living and dead oak and other deciduous trees. They are edible but not as choice as other Oysters. • Hairy Lentinus (*Lentinus levis*; also listed as *Pleurotus levis* and *Panus strigosus*) looks similar to Veiled Oyster, but its stem is covered with **coarse white hairs**; there is **no veil or ring**. *L. levis* is edible but tough.

Veiled Oyster
EDIBLE

Angel Wings
(no longer recommended)

Stalkless Paxillus (inedible)

- **Angel Wings** (*Pleurocybella porrigens*) look very similar to white Oyster Mushrooms, but the cap is so thin that it is **partially translucent**; it is smaller than most white Oyster Mushrooms, generally 3½ inches across or less. Angel Wings are found from late summer through fall on dead **conifer wood**. Many sources list Angel Wings as edible, but the North American Mycological Association reports that more than a dozen deaths in 2004 were attributed to ingestion of this mushroom in Japan; it is best to regard it as inedible.

- **Stalkless Paxillus** (*Tapinella panuoides*; also listed as *Paxillus panuoides*) grows on **conifers**. Caps are shell-shaped and up to 4 inches wide, becoming narrower but still fairly broad at the base. The surface is **tan to orangish-brown**; it is downy when young. Gills are yellowish. They have **cross-veins** and are **wavy**, appearing **corrugated**; they may be forked. Its spore print is **yellowish to yellowish-brown**. It is inedible.

- **Creps** (pg. 224) resemble Oyster Mushrooms but are much **smaller**, generally 2 inches across or less; the caps are often very **fragile**. There is no stem. They are found on well-rotted deciduous wood from summer through late fall.

- Gills of *Lentinellus* **species** (pg. 223) have **serrated edges**; caps are **fuzzy or hairy** and up to 4 inches across. Lentinellus are too bitter to be edible.

- **Hairy Panus** (pg. 220) have **hairy caps** that are **tan to purplish** with a **rolled-under edge** and often have a distinct stem. They are bitter and tough, and considered inedible.

- **White Beech Mushrooms** (pg. 84) resemble Oyster Mushrooms but have a **distinct, thick stem** and the gills **do not run down the stem**. The stem has **no ring**. They are edible when young, although they may be bitter and tough.

NOTES: Oyster Mushrooms can be cultivated fairly easily and are available in grow-it-yourself kits.

Chanterelles (several)

Cantharellus spp. and *Craterellus* spp.

At first glance, Chanterelles appear to be gilled mushrooms. Closer inspection reveals that what appears to be gills are actually **blunt-edged folds or ribs**. The folds dent when pressed with a blunt object and can be teased from the cap in small sheets containing numerous folds. True gills have sharp, **knife-like edges**; individual gills break or collapse when pressed with a blunt object and don't peel away easily. The folds are a key characteristic to differentiate between the Chanterelle, a prized edible, and the **toxic** Jack O'Lantern (pgs. 70–71).

The most popular Chanterelle is the Yellow Chanterelle, generally listed as *Cantharellus cibarius*. Many mycologists believe that *Cantharellus cibarius* is a European species that doesn't appear in North America. As reported by Dr. Tom Volk, the Yellow Chanterelles found here should be divided into several new species based on DNA evidence. Research is ongoing and name changes are likely in the future. Regardless of their scientific names, all Chanterelles are edible, although some are considered less delicious than the highly prized Yellow Chanterelle.

Yellow Chanterelle

green = key identification feature

Red Chanterelle

Smooth Chanterelle

Yellow-Foot Chanterelle

HABITAT: Chanterelles grow **from the soil**, singly or in loose groups, under hardwoods (particularly oak and beech) or conifers.

DESCRIPTION: With few exceptions, Chanterelles in our area have distinct, **gill-like folds** under the cap (see further description on pg. 16). The folds are often forked and **continue down the stem** for a short distance below the cap; the folds may feel waxy, and there may be a network of fine veins between the folds. Stems are fairly sturdy and have no rings. Caps are smooth on top; they are rounded with a depressed center and rolled-under edge on young specimens. As the Chanterelle ages, the cap spreads and flattens out, turning upward to form a shallow, funnel-like bowl with edges that are generally **wavy or ruffle-like**. Flesh of the stem and cap is **white**.

- **Yellow Chanterelles** (*Cantharellus 'cibarius'*) are **deep yellow, golden, or golden-orange**. Undersides have numerous forked folds that may be yellowish, whitish or creamy peach. Caps are 1 to 5 inches across. Stems are up to 2¼ inches tall and about one-third as wide; they may be paler than the cap, particularly near the base. Cap edges may bruise darker. They have a fruity or **apricot** odor.

- **Red Chanterelles** (*Cantharellus cinnabarinus*) are **deep orange to reddish-orange**. Caps are less than 2 inches across; stems are up to 1½ inches tall.

- **Smooth Chanterelles** (*Cantharellus lateritius*) **lack the folds under the cap**, or have very faint folds. The color is similar to the Yellow Chanterelle; Smooth Chanterelle may be a bit larger. Look for it under oaks.

- **Yellow-Foot Chanterelles** (*Craterellus tubaeformis*; formerly listed as *Cantharellus tubaeformis*) are similar in size to Red Chanterelles, although often taller. Caps are **brownish to olive-brown**; stems are **yellowish to orangish-tan** and gills are **grayish-lilac**. Folds are very thick, with many forks near the edge

of the cap. *Craterellus lutescens* and *Craterellus ignicolor* are also called Yellow-Foot Chanterelles; caps are **smooth underneath or with a few wide folds near the edge**, and they grow in damp areas. All Yellow-Foots are edible.

• The **Small Chanterelle** (*Cantharellus minor*) is yellowish to orangish, with a cap that is ¼ to 1¼ inches across and a somewhat delicate stem up to 2 inches tall; it grows in mossy or damp areas.

SPORE PRINT: Yellow, Smooth, Yellow-Foot and Small Chanterelles have pale yellow, buff-colored or cream-colored spores. Spores of Red Chanterelles are cream-colored, often with a faint pinkish cast.

SEASON: Chanterelles in our area fruit in summer, sometimes into early fall.

OTHER NAMES: The Yellow Chanterelle is also called Golden Chanterelle. Yellow-Foot Chanterelle is also called the Trumpet Chanterelle.

COMPARE: The **toxic** Jack O'Lantern (pgs. 70–71) is bright orange and resembles the Yellow Chanterelle but has **true, knife-edged gills that can be separated individually from the cap**; gills are **unforked**. Jack O'Lanterns tend to grow in dense clusters and always **on wood** rather than from soil, although the wood may be buried and easy to miss. Its flesh is **orange**. • False Chanterelle (*Hygrophoropsis aurantiaca*) has **true gills**; it is orangish-yellow to brownish with a darker area in the center of the cap and grows from the soil or on woody debris. Its gills are orange; they are **more brightly colored than the cap and fork repeatedly**. Some sources list it as edible, while others say it causes intestinal problems. • Scaly Vase Chanterelle (pg. 266; **toxic**) has **incurved scales** on the top surface; the base is **wrinkled or ribbed overall**.

NOTES: Most Chanterelles have a fruity aroma and a mildly peppery flavor. They often grow in large quantities and are easy to spot due to their color.

Giant Puffball

Calvatia gigantea

You might mistake this round, white mushroom for a softball, a soccer ball or something larger. Fresh, young specimens are a popular edible and the old, brown ones become a giant smoke bomb that kids like to stomp on (be careful not to inhale the spore cloud; it can cause respiratory distress).

HABITAT: Grows from the ground singly, in groups or sometimes in large circles (called fairy rings) in grassy areas or woodlands. A favored habitat is a hillside above a creek or canal.

DESCRIPTION: These generally **spherical, white-skinned** mushrooms are usually 8 to 12 inches across, but can grow up to 3 feet wide! They get more misshapen and dented as they expand but are still attached to the ground with only a **small root-like structure**. The exterior skin encases the spore-producing flesh inside that is **smooth and pure white** when young, much like a loaf of white bread. As it ages,

Giant Puffball

Giant Puffball

Interior of Puffball

the skin develops scaly patches and cracks, becoming more tan in color. The interior becomes yellow, then greenish, until finally the spores are ripe brown. If untouched, it will eventually shed its outer skin to expose the mass of spores, which will be spread by the wind.

SPORE PRINT: Brown.

SEASON: Early summer through fall.

OTHER NAMES: Moon Melon, *Langermannia gigantea*, *Lycoperdon giganteum*.

COMPARE: Two other large puffballs are also found in the Northeast. The **Skull-Shaped Puffball** (*C. craniiformis*) is less spherical overall and doesn't grow as large as the **Giant Puffball**; it is generally less than 10 inches in diameter. The entire mushroom is covered in smooth white to tan skin and has a **narrower, goblet-like base**, making the puffball appear **skull-like**. The base doesn't produce spores and remains attached to the ground even after the ripe, **yellowish-brown** spores have been released and the rest of the puffball disintegrates. • The **Purple-Spored Puffball** (*C. cyathiformis*) is smaller than the Skull-Shaped Puffball. It is generally less than 6 inches in diameter and seems to prefer grassy areas to woodlands. Initially white throughout, it is distinguished from other puffballs when ripe by the **dark brown cracked skin** and by its **purple spore mass**, which may be visible year-round in the remaining nest-like piece that is left attached to the ground after the spores have been released and the rest of the puffball disintegrates. • Many smaller puffball species are common in our area; see pg. 230 for information. • The **Common Earthball** (pg. 234) is spherical like a Puffball, but the surface is **yellowish to tan** and covered with a **dark brown, crackled texture**. Common Earthballs are generally 4 inches across or less. The interior of young specimens is white like a

Skull-Shaped Puffball

Purple-Spored Puffball

EDIBLE

Common Earthball (young)

Split Amanita button

TOXIC

Puffball, but it soon turns darker, becoming **purplish-black to warm black** at maturity. The distinction is important because Common Earthballs are **toxic**.

NOTES: All the puffballs listed here are edible when they are young and the flesh is **pure, featureless white throughout**. If the flesh appears to be anything other than pure, featureless white, the puffball is too mature to eat, or it may be another species. Be particularly cautious with small specimens, as they can be mistaken for a number of cap-and-stem species in the button stage, including **deadly** Amanitas (pgs. 62–66), inedible Agaricus (pg. 80) or the egg stage of Stinkhorns (pg. 192). Note that the button stage of an Amanita is not featureless inside; instead, a faint outline of the developing mushroom can be seen in the interior flesh. The outline is often very subtle, as shown in the photo above right. Small puffballs growing from the ground should always be cut in half to make sure they are not overripe and to eliminate young specimens of Amanita, Agaricus, or Earthballs (pg. 234).

FROM THE SOIL NEAR TREES

LATE SPRING AND LATE SUMMER THROUGH EARLY FALL

TOP EDIBLES

King Bolete
Boletus edulis

As the name King Bolete suggests, *Boletus edulis* is one of the most sought-after edible mushrooms. This is the mushroom that Europeans call the Porcini or Cep. It grows in our area but is more commonly found in large numbers and much larger sizes in the Rocky Mountains. According to experts there are most likely many different species across North America that we simply refer to as *Boletus edulis* due to their similarities and popularity as a good edible. Additionally, there are hundreds of other distinct species of boletes in various colors, shapes and sizes, many of which are inedible or even **toxic** (see pgs. 67–69).

From above, this brown-capped mushroom looks like a typical cap-with-stem shape, but turning it over reveals a **spongy pore surface**. This is really a series of tubes that hold spores. It is the feature that most strongly defines the group of mushrooms called, in general, *boletes*, a term used to refer to many cap-and-stem mushrooms with pores.

King Bolete

green = key identification feature

HABITAT: King Boletes grow from the soil, singly or in loose groups, in association with trees; they are generally found under conifers, especially Norway spruce, hemlock and white pine. It can also be found in mixed woods, where it forms a symbiotic relationship with conifer trees.

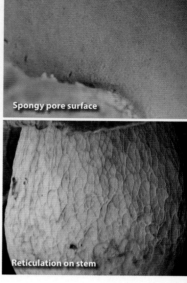

Spongy pore surface

Reticulation on stem

DESCRIPTION: This stout mushroom has a large, somewhat sticky, dull red-dish to pale brown cap, 3 to 10 inches across, that becomes almost polished in old age. When young, the rounded cap may have a flush of white that can remain as a faint edging on the outer rim as it enlarges and flattens out. Immature caps may also seem small in relation to the swollen stem, which tends to be short and bulbous on young specimens. The stem lengthens with age and may be up to 7 inches tall and 1 to 3 inches thick; it is always **white or cream-colored** with surface **reticulation (mesh-like texture)** of the **same color**. The reticulation is most prominent at the top of the stem. The stem has no ring. The interior of the stem is solid, white, and although a little firmer than the cap, is valued just as much for edibility. The interior flesh of the cap is also white. When cut crosswise, it **does not change color** when exposed to air. The flesh and pore surface of many of the other boletes stain or discolor when cut, scraped or bruised; some **toxic** varieties (pgs. 67–69) turn blue. The pore surface of the King is white and very finely textured when young; pores are stuffed, making the surface appear nearly solid. With age the pores turn yellowish and become coarser.

SPORE PRINT: The King Bolete has a **yellow to olive-brown** spore print.

SEASON: Late spring, and again in the late summer and early fall.

OTHER NAMES: Porcini, Cep, Penny Bun, Steinpilz. Other members of the *Boletus edulis* group in our area include *Boletus variipes*, *Boletus separans* (see pg. 46 for both) and *Boletus atkinsonii* and *Boletus subcaerulescens*.

Boletus variipes

Butyriboletus brunneus

COMPARE: Numerous mushrooms in our area look similar to the King Bolete; some are edible, while others are not recommended. Many more bolete species have bright yellow pore surfaces; also see pgs. 67–69.

- *Boletus variipes* is similar to the King but has a more grayish tint to the brown cap, which is often finely cracked when old and dry. Like the cap, the stem is **grayish brown**, but like *Boletus 'edulis,' Boletus variipes* has white reticulation. This edible bolete is found near oaks.

- *Butyriboletus brunneus* (also known as *Boletus speciosus* var. *brunneus*) has a brick-colored cap, **yellow reticulation** on the upper half of the stem and flesh that **quickly bruises blue**. It is edible, with a good taste. It occurs in mixed woods with hemlock.

- The **Lilac Bolete** (*Boletus separans*; also listed as *Xanthoconium separans*) is a choice edible similar in size and stature to the King, but when young the cap and stem have **lilac coloring**. With age, the cap becomes brown, but the stem remains lilac-colored and becomes hollow. The pore surface is white on young specimens, becoming **yellow** with age; it **does not stain or bruise**. **Bicolor Bolete** (pg. 180) may be mistaken for a young Lilac Bolete, but its cap is more intensely red and it has a yellow pore surface that **stains blue**. A drop of common household ammonia on the cap turns deep blue-green if the specimen is a Lilac Bolete, providing a no-fail way to separate the two species. Lilac Bolete grows near hardwoods and occasionally by conifers.

- *Boletus huronensis* has the same stature as the King Bolete. It has a pale tan to light brown cap. Its stem **lacks reticulations**. The flesh may **bruise slightly blue**. It is has caused some serious debilitating vertigo and digestive distress, and is not recommended for eating. More common in the northern areas of the Northeast, it is associated with hemlock.

Lilac Bolete
EDIBLE

Boletus huronensis
NOT RECOMMENDED

Bitter Bolete
NOT RECOMMENDED

- **Bitter Bolete** (*Tylopilus felleus*) is generally larger in our area than the King (mature caps can be up to a foot across!) but appears so similar otherwise that at first glance, you may think you've hit the jackpot. On closer inspection, you'll find that the pore surface has a **pink tinge** and **stains brown** when handled. The reticulation on the stem is **brown** rather than white and is more pronounced, especially at the top of the stem. *T. rubrobrunneus* is another large, bitter bolete, but it has **no reticulation** on the stem and has a darker, more **purplish** cap when young. Bitter Boletes are not toxic, but as the name suggests, they taste extremely bitter and are not collected for the table.

NOTES: Both the cap and stem of the King Bolete are edible and choice. It dries well, and drying intensifies its nutty flavor. Boletes should be cut into evenly thick slices before cooking or drying; this ensures that all pieces cook at the same rate and also allows you to check for insect larvae. The bugs will often beat you to this tasty find.

ON DEAD OR DYING TREES   SUMMER THROUGH FALL

TOP EDIBLES

Lion's Mane (several)

Hericium spp.

This beautiful waterfall-like mushroom is a delight to come upon in the woods. It often grows in large clusters, so if you are lucky enough to find it, you will probably find a lot!

HABITAT: Grows as a parasite and decomposer (called saprobic) of dying and dead deciduous trees; may be found rarely on conifers. Usually found in mixed woods on fallen maple, beech or oak logs.

DESCRIPTION: The sheer number of common names given to this mushroom helps convey its unique look. Rather than a cap or shelf, it is a **large, white mass with dangling teeth** that are actually the spore-producing structures. It can grow up to **one foot** across and is comprised of soft but brittle **white** flesh that becomes yellow or even tinged with brown when old. Three *Hericium* species grow in our region. Due to constant changes in mycology (the study of mushrooms), the scientific names of two Hericium species have been switched with each other, so you may come across conflicting names in older references. Happily, all are edible and delicious.

H. erinaceus

• *H. erinaceus* is easy to identify because it has teeth up to **2 inches long**. The teeth grow from an **unbranching central base**, like a white pom pom. It is commonly cultivated, dried and sold in Asian grocery stores as Monkey Head Mushroom.

green = key identification feature

H. americanum   *H. corralloides*

- *H. americanum* (formerly listed as *H. coralloides*) has **numerous branches** growing from the central base. Its teeth are shorter than those of *H. erinaceus*, generally about 1 inch long or less; they create a tufted appearance.

- *H. coralloides* (formerly listed as *H. ramosum*) resembles coral due to its more **loosely branching** habit and teeth that are **½ inch long or less**.

SPORE PRINT: White.

SEASON: Summer through fall.

OTHER NAMES: Bear's Head Tooth Fungus, Monkey's Head, Icicle Mushroom, Satyr's Beard, Bearded Hedgehog, Goat's Beard, Comb Tooth, Waterfall Hydnum. *H. erinaceus* is sometime referred to as the Pom Pom Mushroom.

COMPARE: Crown-Tipped Coral (pg. 248) grows on fallen logs. It has a more **upright, loose** structure and **does not have teeth**. The branches are white or yellowish and somewhat translucent. Crown-Tipped Coral is edible when young and has a peppery flavor but develops a tough texture with age.
- **Northern Tooth** (pg. 229) is similar in size, habitat and color to Lion's Mane and even has spore-bearing teeth. However, those teeth are found on the underside of **large, rough, overlapping shelves**. It is not edible due to its tough texture and bitter flavor.

NOTES: All Hericium are sought-after edibles, but the Pom Pom version is said to taste the best. They are lovely when sliced and cooked, with a flavor and texture that is sometimes compared to lobster. It is best when young and fresh, because it gets sour or bitter tasting when old. It is popular in Chinese cooking and is also reported to have medicinal properties.

TOP EDIBLES

Black Trumpet

Craterellus fallax

Shaped like a lily blossom, this fragrant mushroom is often found while looking for Chanterelles (pgs. 38–40). However, unlike the brightly colored Chanterelles that seem to want to be found, this lovely edible mushroom could be right under your feet and you might not even notice it!

HABITAT: Occurs on soil, moss or humus; singly, scattered or in small, tight clusters. They are particularly fond of mossy areas. Look for this delicious edible under oak and beech, the two tree species with which it most commonly associates.

DESCRIPTION: These **thin, funnel-shaped** mushrooms are hard to see simply because of their color. Ranging from **gray to brown to black**, they don't stand out against the soil, unless you happen to find a nice clump on a bright green patch of moss. They can also be quite small, ranging from 1 to 3 inches across but may grow prolifically and over large expanses. The edges of these delicate funnels are rolled under when young but become wavy as they grow and may get darker along the edges. Stems are less than 4 inches tall and are **hollow** like a true funnel but may be tightly pinched at the bottom, especially when

Black Trumpets

green = key identification feature

Brownish form

Fragrant Black Trumpet
EDIBLE

growing in a tight cluster. The spore-producing surface on the exterior has **no gills**. It is smooth or slightly wrinkled, ranging in color from **very light gray to brown to charcoal**; it may be salmon-pink when covered with spores. Black Trumpets have a distinctly **fruity scent**, like plums or prunes.

SPORE PRINT: Salmon-pink.

SEASON: Summer through fall.

OTHER NAMES: Horn of Plenty, Black Chanterelle, Trumpet of Death (based on the color only). *Craterellus cornucopioides* is a look-alike European species with whitish spores.

COMPARE: Devil's Urn (pg. 238) could be confused with Black Trumpets, but it grows **on wood** in **early spring**. It is generally regarded as inedible and is not collected for the table. • The **Fragrant Black Trumpet** (*Craterellus foetidus*) is **thicker** and the bottom part of the stem is **solid**. It also has **distinct veins**, much like a **Chanterelle** (pgs. 38–40), and the exterior is light gray with a pink to purple tinge. It is reported to have a much stronger aroma than other Black Trumpets and is equally edible and delicious. • *Craterellus cinereus* (also listed as *Cantharellus cinereus*) is uncommon. Its general appearance is similar to Black Trumpet, but it has a **very pale exterior** with prominent ridges and a strong, sweet smell like the Fragrant Black Trumpet. It is edible but it has a slightly unpleasant, bitter taste.

NOTES: Recent DNA work has shown that the Black Trumpet of the Northeast is *Craterellus fallax* and differs from similar species in the Pacific Northwest and Europe. Black Trumpets are edible and delicious. Drying them further enhances their fruity aroma and flavor.

TOP EDIBLES

Hedgehogs
Hydnum repandum, Hydnum umbilicatum

At first glance, these mushrooms look like Chanterelles or many other cap-and-stem species. When the mushroom is turned over, however, the difference becomes clear: instead of gills or pores, the underside of the cap is covered with **distinct spines or teeth**. Two similar species have long been recognized; both are edible and delicious. In addition, several new *Hydnum* species have recently been identified in the Northeastern United States; the taxonomy is uncertain, and some examples of what are currently called *H. repandum* and *H. umbilicatum* may belong to these newly identified species.

HABITAT: Hedgehogs are mycorrhizal, growing from the ground near living trees; they appear singly and in groups.

DESCRIPTION: Two closely related mushrooms are commonly called Hedgehogs. Both have a **bristly-looking pore surface** under the caps, consisting of spore-bearing spines or teeth.

 • *H. repandum* is the larger of the two, with **cream to tan to apricot** caps that are 2 to **7 inches** wide. The edge of the cap is rolled under

H. repandum

green = key identification feature

when young, becoming flattened and more lobed and wavy as it grows, a bit like Chanterelles (pgs. 38–40). The thick **white** stem is often **off-center** and is less than 4 inches tall; the **cream-colored teeth** may run partway down it. The stem and teeth **bruise**

H. umbilicatum

orangish-brown when handled, and the whitish interior flesh may **discolor yellow** when cut. There is also a white variety which has flesh that shows orange staining when cut. *H. repandum* occurs with both conifers and broadleaf trees, and is often found in mixed woods.

• *H. umbilicatum* is much smaller and prefers a **boggy pine habitat**. It generally has a **darker orangish** cap that is 2 inches wide or less and is **sunken in the center**, lending it the common name of Belly Button Mushroom. The whitish flesh **does not discolor** when cut. The stem is thinner and **more centrally located** and the teeth are darker than those of *H. repandum*.

SPORE PRINT: White to cream.

SEASON: Late summer through fall.

OTHER NAMES: Sweet Tooth, Wood Hedgehog, *Dentinum repandum*.

COMPARE: Several other mushrooms have teeth under the caps. • The inedible **Orange Hydnellum** (pg. 254) is usually found under conifers. Caps are bumpy, **clustered** and often fused; they are orange to brownish with a pale edge. The stocky stems are **orangish to brownish**; spores are **brown**. • The uncommon **Drab Tooth** (*Bankera fuligineo-alba*; inedible) is similar to *H. repandum* in cap color and size; it is found under **conifers**. The teeth and upper part of the stem are white; the bottom part of the stem is **dark brown**. Caps darken to brown with age. It is sometimes called Blushing Fenugreek Tooth because dry specimens may smell like fenugreek (similar to curry).

NOTES: A favorite and easily distinguished edible, Hedgehogs are closely related to Chanterelles and are often found in the same locations and at the same time. Hedgehogs have a lightly fruity aroma and peppery taste and unlike many good edibles, insects seem to leave them alone.

green = key identification feature   53

NEAR LIVE OR DEAD TREES

LATE SUMMER THROUGH LATE FALL

TOP EDIBLES

Hen of the Woods

Grifola frondosa

The discovery of a large Hen of the Woods is a thrill for any mushroom seeker. Not only do the clusters sometimes reach enormous proportions—2 feet across is possible, or even bigger—but the mushrooms have a firm texture and meaty taste that is highly prized. They are also in high demand for medicinal uses in Japan, Korea and China.

HABITAT: Hens grow in clusters **at or near the base of trees**; they are usually found under oak but also reported under beech, wild cherry and yellow birch in the Northeast. Trees may be living or dead. Several clusters may grow around the same tree or on nearby trees.

DESCRIPTION: Hen of the Woods grows as a **tight cluster or rosette** of **many individual fan-shaped caps** arising from a central fleshy base, similar to a cauliflower. The upper surface of the caps may be tan, gray, cream-colored or white; the texture is **smooth to slightly velvety**. Individual caps are **1 to 3 inches across** and may have subtle streaks radiating from the center, or may appear slightly mottled; edges sometimes have a darker band. The undersides are white to cream-colored and covered with **small pores** that descend the base of each cap toward the central base; individual caps have no actual stem. The flesh of both the caps and the base is firm but tender on fresh specimens; older specimens become tough, especially the central base.

Several Hen of the Woods clusters

SPORE PRINT: White.

green = key identification feature

Gray cluster

Pores on underside

SEASON: Late summer through late fall.

OTHER NAMES: Maitake, Sheepshead, Ram's Head, Nusk, *Polyporus frondosus*.

COMPARE: Other clustering shelf-like mushrooms are found in our area near deciduous trees; here is how to distinguish them. • **Black-Staining Polypore** (*Meripilus sumstinei*; also listed in some guides as *M. giganteus*, although that name properly refers to a European species that is not found in North America) has caps that may grow up to **12 inches wide**, although they are often smaller. Caps are grayish to drab yellowish and may appear banded or ringed. They are thicker than the caps of Hens, especially toward the center, and have a **fibrous, tough texture**; when a cap is pulled apart, **thin fibers may be visible**. The pores are **white**; caps slowly **bruise brownish to blackish** when handled. Stems are short and stubby and generally off-center. Young specimens are generally regarded as edible although reports of its flavor range from mild to bitter or sour, and it may cause digestive problems. • Caps of **Umbrella Polypore** (*P. umbellatus*) are **circular**; each has a **central stem** that joins with others in the cluster to form a large, thick, central stalk. Umbrella Polypore is less common than Hen of the Woods and its clusters are smaller, but it is also a delicious edible. It appears from late spring through summer. • **Berkeley's Polypore** (pg. 211) has large, tan to yellowish-brown caps up to **10 inches** across; they are dry in texture and produce milky sap when squeezed. Although edible when found in a young, finger-like growth stage, developed caps are bitter and inedible.

NOTES: Hen of the Woods clusters engulf anything they encounter, and it's not uncommon to find twigs, leaves or other debris embedded in the cluster. Bugs also burrow into the clusters; a soak in a mild saltwater solution should dislodge these unwanted inhabitants. Hen of the Woods typically appears in the same location year after year. It is a favored edible of Italian-Americans, who call it Nusk. Any of these large woodland species are fibrous, and overeating can cause digestive issues.

FROM THE SOIL NEAR TREES

SPRING

TOP TOXICS

False Morels: Gyromitras (several)

Gyromitra spp.

Gyromitras are often found in the spring woods by people seeking Morels (pgs. 24–27). At first glance, the two mushrooms can be confused, but closer inspection reveals some significant differences.

HABITAT: Gyromitras grow singly or scattered from the ground in forests.

DESCRIPTION: Most of the Gyromitras discussed here have caps that look lumpy, with a brain-like, folded or wrinkled texture. Stems are white to pale tan. The interior flesh is **pale and chambered**. Saddle-Shaped False Morel is an exception; see facing page.

- **Conifer False Morel** (*G. esculenta*; found primarily near conifers) is up to 4 inches tall and wide. Its **brownish** cap is covered with **rounded, brain-like wrinkles**. Its medium-width stem may be smooth or creased. The Conifer False Morel is uncommon in the southern portions of our area.

- **Gabled False Morel** (*G. brunnea*; found near deciduous trees) is up to 4 inches tall and wide. Its cap is **tan to reddish-brown with flattened, wavy folds**; it may appear saddle-like. The stem is short and stocky.

- **Bull-Nosed False Morel** (*G. korfii*; found in broadleaf forests and mixed woods) is tan with a **wrinkled or wavy** texture; it is generally less than 3 inches tall and wide. The cap hangs over the stem so much that it

Conifer False Morel

Gabled False Morel

green = key identification feature

may appear **stemless**. It is the most common false morel in our area.

- **Saddle-Shaped False Morel** (*G. infula*; found near conifers and in mixed woodlands) occurs in **late summer and fall**, fruiting on conifer wood or woody humus. Its tan to brownish caps are up to 5 inches tall and have **two or three lobes**. Stems may be colored like the cap but are often paler, sometimes with violet tinges. The interior is generally hollow. See pg. 194 for information on *Helvella* spp. with similar appearance.

Gyromitra **interior**

SPORE PRINT: Spore color is not an identifying factor with Gyromitras.

SEASON: All but the Saddle-Shaped False Morel appear in spring.

OTHER NAMES: Lorchels.

COMPARE: Morels (pgs. 24–27) may appear similar at first glance, but their caps are **pitted and ridged** and the insides are **completely hollow**.

NOTES: All Gyromitras contain compounds in their raw state that are **toxic**. Although some eat Conifer False Morels after boiling them in several changes of water, both it and Saddle-Shaped False Morel can be **fatal**. Well-cooked Gabled and Bull-Nosed False Morels are eaten by some foragers; however, for most people, Gyromitras should be considered inedible and possibly **toxic**.

Bull-Nosed False Morel

Saddle-Shaped False Morel

ON DECAYING WOOD   SPRING THROUGH FALL

Deadly Galerina
Galerina marginata

This pretty little mushroom prefers cool weather; it typically graces the woods in spring, then again in fall. Unfortunately, it is one of the most **toxic** mushrooms around. It contains amatoxins, the same deadly poisons found in Amanitas; for more information on this toxin, see pg. 63.

HABITAT: Deadly Galerina are saprobes, getting their nutrients from dead wood. They grow in **clusters** on decaying deciduous wood; they are often found on rotting logs that are mossy.

DESCRIPTION: Deadly Galerina are small to medium mushrooms, with caps that are generally 1½ inches wide or less; large specimens may be up to 3 inches across. The caps are **rust-colored, tawny or brownish** with a tacky surface, fading and becoming paler with age or upon drying; they may feel slimy in damp weather. They are rounded or bell-shaped when young, opening up and becoming fairly flat with maturity. Stems are slender and generally 2 to 3 inches long; they are fairly equal in width from top to bottom but often curve as they emerge from a rotting log or from a cluster. They are pale gray to brownish; the lower portion of the stem may be darker and somewhat shaggy.

green = key identification feature

Yellowish gills, skirt-like ring

Velvet Foot (pg. 132)
EDIBLE

White mycelium (thread-like fungal roots) can sometimes be seen where the stem grows out of the wood. A **fragile, short skirt-like ring** is present on the upper half of the stem of young specimens. The ring is whitish at first, turning **brown** as it catches falling spores. It often disintegrates, leaving behind a **thin, collar-like ring zone**; the ring may be fairly obvious or may disappear entirely. Gills are **honey-colored** at first, becoming **rust-colored** as the spores develop; they are attached to the stem and closely spaced.

SPORE PRINT: Rust-colored.

SEASON: Deadly Galerina are most common in spring and fall but may appear in summer during periods of cool weather.

OTHER NAMES: Autumn Galerina, Funeral Bell, *G. autumnalis*.

COMPARE: Velvet Foot (pg. 132) is an edible orangish mushroom that thrives in the same habitat and season as Deadly Galerina, but it produces a **white** spore print. Velvet Foot stems have **no ring**, and they turn **dark brown to blackish** with age. Its caps are slimy. Great care must be taken to distinguish between the two species when collecting Velvet Foot for the table, as young Velvet Foot look nearly identical to Deadly Galerina. • Honey Mushrooms (pg. 112) are yellowish to brownish, and are larger and **beefier** than Deadly Galerina; they have a **sturdy ring** on the stem and a **white** spore print. They sometimes fruit on the same log as Deadly Galerina, and at the same time. • Various Little Brown Mushrooms (pg. 114) may resemble Deadly Galerina; the resemblance of LBMs to a species as dangerous as Deadly Galerina should be enough to dissuade anyone from eating most small, brownish mushrooms.

NOTES: Both Deadly Galerina and Velvet Foot are often found by Morel hunters in the spring. Careless collectors of Honey Mushrooms and Velvet Foot have been poisoned by failing to inspect every mushroom.

FROM THE SOIL

EARLY SUMMER THROUGH FALL

Green-Spored Lepiota

Chlorophyllum molybdites

Common in the southern states, the Green-Spored Lepiota is becoming more common in lawns in the Northeast—even in well-manicured yards. It's easy to spot, even from a distance, as young specimens look like elevated white balls on the lawn; small specimens look like golf balls, while larger ones are the size of softballs. Unfortunately, according to a 2005 report from the North American Mycological Association, this **toxic** species is responsible for almost as many poisonings (caused by mushroom species that were positively identified rather than unknown) as the top two *Amanita* species combined. Symptoms include intense vomiting and other severe gastrointestinal problems one to three hours after ingestion.

HABITAT: Found in grassy areas such as lawns and meadows. Grows singly or scattered; may also grow in a ring.

DESCRIPTION: A **sturdy-looking medium to large** mushroom that is whitish overall. Young specimens have a spherical or egg-shaped cap that is white to cream-colored and typically 1½ to 2½ inches wide. The cap expands dramatically as it opens up, becoming softly rounded

green = key identification feature

to flattened, sometimes with upturned edges; it is typically **6 to 9 inches** across when mature but may be larger. Mature caps have **large buff to brownish patches** at the top and smaller scales around the bottom. The stem is whitish to tan, sturdy and typically 4 to 8 inches long; it is typically smooth but may have a few small scales. Once the cap opens, there is a **double ring** near the top of the stem that may disappear on old specimens. The base may be somewhat enlarged but is not bulbous. Gills are closely spaced and **not attached** to the stem; they are white at first, turning **grayish-green** with age.

Young specimens

Mature gills

SPORE PRINT: Greenish to dull olive.

SEASON: Early summer through fall.

OTHER NAMES: Green Gills, *Lepiota morgani*.

COMPARE: Species listed in this section are very similar to Green-Spored Lepiota, but all have **white** spore prints. • Shaggy Parasol (pgs. 76–77) is more **coarsely scaled**; young caps and the patches on mature caps are typically **brown**. It is found in fall. • American Parasol (pgs. 76–77) is **smaller** than Green-Spored Lepiota; its cap is covered with small **rust-colored scales**. • The Parasol

Greenish spore print

Mushroom (pgs. 76–77) has a **narrow, scaly** stem; the cap has a dark, **nipple-like bump** in the center. • Many **toxic** *Amanita* species (pgs. 62–66) have patchy caps and swollen bases; some have a **cup** at the stem base.

NOTES: Other than **toxic** *Amanita* species, the look-alikes listed above are sometimes collected for the table by experts, but this is strongly advised against due to the difficulty of positive identification.

NEAR LIVE TREES (TYP.)

SUMMER THROUGH FALL

Amanitas (numerous)

Amanita spp.

It's probably safe to say that if you asked most people to name just one poisonous mushroom, they would mention the Amanita, although each person might have a different picture in their mind as to what this fungus looks like. Many people would think of the delicate, all-white Destroying Angel, with its skirt-like ring on the stem and its fragile cup at the base. Others might conjure up an image of the Fly Agaric, with its brightly colored cap dotted with numerous small but thick white patches.

The *Amanita* genus is a large, diverse group of mushrooms, encompassing hundreds of species in a wide palette of colors. The species discussed in this book have caps with gills underneath and stems that are centered under the caps; many other key characteristics are microscopic. Common traits shared by many—but not all—are the presence of a ring on the stem and a fragile, cup-like structure called a ***volva*** around the base of the stem. Many also have patches on the caps. All three of these characteristics are remnants of a ***veil***, a thin membrane that covers all or part of the developing mushroom.

All Amanitas start their lives encased in a ***universal veil***, a thin membrane that surrounds the developing mushroom entirely, making it resemble a small, rough-skinned egg; this is often referred to as the ***egg stage***. As the mushroom grows, it breaks through the universal veil. The volva is the

Amanitas, from egg to button stage (different species shown)

Egg stage

Emerging from veil

Button stage

green = key identification feature

part of the universal veil surrounding the base of the stem after the mushroom has emerged from the egg-like sac; it is often necessary to dig around the base to uncover evidence of the volva, which may be covered by dirt and sometimes has disintegrated entirely. The patches on top of the cap, when present, are another remnant of the universal veil; patches may be thick, wart-like and persistent, or thin, insubstantial and easily washed away by rain.

Some Amanitas also have a *partial veil*, a thin membrane attached to both the stem and the lower edge of the young, unopened cap. As the cap expands, the partial veil stretches to cover the gills, finally breaking away from the cap when it becomes too wide. The partial veil remnant often remains attached to the stem under the cap, hanging down and appearing skirt-like or ring-like; fragments may also hang like broken tissue from the edges of the cap.

Skirt-like veil remnant

Some Amanitas are notorious because they contain *amatoxins*, extremely poisonous substances that cause liver and kidney failure and, often, death; the fatality rate for this type of poisoning, according to the North American Mycological Association, is as high as 50 percent unless prompt, sometimes radical treatment is effected. Other Amanitas have no amatoxins but contain other poisonous substances that cause failure of the nervous system, severe gastric problems or hallucinations. A few lack any toxins and are, surprisingly, edible; however, due to the possibility of confusion with toxic species, **no Amanita should be eaten** by any but the most experienced of foragers—and even then, it is risky business that is best avoided.

HABITAT: All Amanitas grow **from the ground**. Most are found near living trees; the mycelium (thread-like fungal roots) has a symbiotic relationship with tree roots (mycorrhizal). They grow singly, scattered or in loose groups.

DESCRIPTION: Although there are many differences in appearance between the numerous *Amanita* species, all share some common aspects. Young Amanitas at the button stage have rounded or egg-shaped caps that are generally 1 to 3 inches across. As the specimen matures, the cap opens up like an umbrella, becoming wider and flatter; mature specimens of the species discussed here are generally 3 to 6 inches wide. The surface texture of the cap varies depending on species. Stems are stocky on young specimens, becoming moderately

Destroying Angel

Fly Agaric, orange

Fly Agaric, yellow

sturdy to slender; all of the toxic species discussed here have a ring or skirt on the stem, although it may deteriorate or fall off with age. All Amanitas have some remnant of the universal veil at the base; it can be cup-like and quite obvious, but it is sometimes buried or broken up. Gills are closely spaced and generally free from the stem or just attached; they are typically white.

• The **Destroying Angel** (*A. bisporigera*) contains amatoxins (pg. 63) and is one of the most **deadly** mushrooms known; *ingestion of a single cap can kill an adult*. This graceful-looking mushroom is common in our area; it grows near deciduous trees, primarily oak. It is typically **pure white** overall but may be pale ivory; the center of the cap may be slightly darker. The cap has a **smooth, silky** texture; very rarely there may be a patch of veil remnant on the cap. Stems may be smooth or slightly shaggy. A **delicate, skirt-like ring** is present near the top of the stem. A cup-like volva surrounds the base, which is often bulbous or swollen; you may need to dig in the dirt to see these important characteristics. Two related species, *A. virosa* and *A. verna*, are also referred to by the same common name; other than slight variations in size, they are inseparable from *A. bisporigera* without aid of a microscope, and some mycologists believe they are European species that do not appear in the United States.

• Fly Agaric (*A. muscaria*) is **toxic** but not generally lethal; among other unpleasant symptoms, including delirium, it causes a coma-like condition that may last for many hours. One of the loveliest of Amanitas, it grows near deciduous and coniferous trees. Its cap, which may be up to **10 inches** wide, is heavily speckled with **buff-colored wart-like patches**; cap edges may be faintly ribbed. Caps of specimens found in the Northeast are typically **orange to yellow**, as shown in the photos above; it can also be white. In the western United States and in Europe, the cap is bright red. Stems are buff-

green = key identification feature

A. velatipes

False Death Cap

colored with a scaly texture that appears **banded**, particularly near the base. A thin, skirt-like ring is generally present near the top of the stem.

- *A. velatipes* has a **collar around the stem base**. Caps are up to 7 inches wide, and **creamy to yellowish** with a brownish center that may fade with age. They are smooth, or slightly sticky when wet, and dotted with **white wart-like patches** that appear in **concentric circles**. Stems are up to 7 inches tall and ¾ inch thick; they often taper slightly toward the top. A sturdy ring is present on the stem; its location is variable and its edge is often flared upward.

- **False Death Cap** (*A. lavendula*; also known as *A. citrina* f. *lavendula* and formerly referred to as *A. citrina*, which is a European species) is generally regarded as **toxic**. It may also be confused with the true Death Cap (*A. phalloides*), a **deadly** mushroom that is occasionally found in our area. Caps of False Death Caps may be whitish-yellow, pale greenish-yellow or lemon-yellow, with more yellowish centers, sometimes with violet tints. They have soft, thick patches that range from whitish to buff to violaceous. Stems are **tall, slender** and whitish, often with scattered hairs on the lower part; the base of the stem is bulbous and **marshmallow-like** in appearance. A thin, skirt-like ring is generally present toward the top of the stem. Crushed flesh smells like raw potatoes. Both the False Death Cap and true Death Cap grow in mixed woods.

- **Yellow Patches** (*A. flavoconia*; also known as Yellow Dust Amanita) is a lovely mushroom that is fairly common in mixed-wood forests. It has a **bright yellow to orangish** cap that is adorned with **yellow patches** when young; the patches typically fall off fairly quickly, leaving a **smooth, slightly sticky** cap surface. Mature caps are up to 3 inches wide and fairly flat. The cap may have slight, faint grooves along the edge, but these grooves may be fairly subtle or lacking entirely. Stems are up to 4 inches high and yellow to whitish;

the base is slightly bulbous and is roughened with small, **scruffy yellow patches**. A delicate, **skirt-like pale yellow ring** is present on the upper part of the stem.

Yellow Patches

- Frost's Amanita (*A. frostiana*) appears similar to Yellow Patches, but is much less common. Caps are **heavily dotted with small, cottony wart-like patches** that are pale yellow, and the edges are **distinctly ribbed**. The top of the bulb-like base has a **collar of yellowish, cottony material**.

SPORE PRINT: White.

SEASON: Summer through fall.

OTHER NAMES: Most Amanitas are called by more than one common name; refer to the scientific names when researching or discussing them.

Frost's Amanita

COMPARE: Grisettes (pg. 100) are a group of mostly non-toxic Amanitas. Their cap edges are **distinctly ribbed** and the stems have **no rings**. • Puffballs (pgs. 41–43, 230) resemble the egg stage of the Amanita; for this reason, all small puffballs collected for the table should be cut in half and inspected as described on pg. 43 to ensure that the specimen is not an Amanita egg. • Volvariella (pg. 154) have a cup at the stem base, but they have **no rings** on the stems and their spore print is **pink to brownish-pink**. They usually grow **on trees or downed wood**. • Agaricus species (pg. 80) have distinct rings on the stems, but they have no cup-like volva at the base of the stem, and their spore prints are some shade of **dark brown**. • Green-Spored Lepiota (pgs. 60–61; toxic) is a white mushroom that has shaggy scales on the cap and a ring on the stem, but it has no volva at the base of the stem; the spore print is **greenish**.

NOTES: Sadly, it is not uncommon to hear of a family or group who has come to America from another country and picked mushrooms that resemble edible species of their homeland—only to discover, too late, that toxic *Amanita* species resemble familiar favorites from home. Making a spore print before consuming mushrooms prevents many tragedies.

green = key identification feature

FROM THE SOIL NEAR TREES   SUMMER THROUGH FALL

TOP TOXICS

Toxic Boletes (numerous)
Boletus spp.

Like the edible King Bolete (pgs. 44–47), the boletes discussed here look like a typical cap-with-stem shape but reveal a **spongy pore surface** when turned over. These pores are the ends of tubes where the spores are produced. Some of the most brightly colored boletes are **toxic** and cause severe gastrointestinal distress if eaten. Others are good edibles but are virtually impossible to distinguish from the toxic ones without a microscope. In general, the easiest way to identify some of the most toxic varieties is by the color of the cap and pore surface and by the tendency of the flesh to **stain or bruise blue**. There are, however, exceptions to this rule, including Frost's Bolete (pg. 69).

HABITAT: Boletes grow **from the soil** and humus, singly or in loose groups, in mixed woods. Most have a symbiotic relationship with trees.

DESCRIPTION: The boletes discussed here have a cap that is reddish, brownish or yellowish and a **bright pore surface** (ranging from yellow to orange to red to brownish); some or all parts **stain blue** when cut or bruised. Some edible and even choice varieties, including Bicolor Bolete (pg. 180), fall into this broad group; because of difficulty in identifying them, however, they should not be collected for the table by any but the most experienced foragers.

Red-Mouthed Boletes

- Boletes with **orangish to red pore surfaces** are often called **Red Mouth Boletes**. They are often referred to as the *Boletus subvelutipes* group, which is poorly defined in North America; names used are often European species that may not occur here. Members of this species group share some characteristics. They are medium-sized, with brownish (or yellowish-brown) caps that typically have **yellow** edges. Stems have no reticulation and are frequently yellow but may be colored like the cap; stem bases are hairy or velvety. All parts **bruise blue**, including the yellow flesh, which **instantly stains blue** when cut. Red Mouth Boletes are found under hardwoods.

- The **Brick-Cap Bolete** (*Boletus sensibilis*) grows in mixed deciduous woods. It has a **brick-red** cap up to **6 inches** across on a **smooth** stem that is 5 inches tall or less; the cap color may fade to brown with age. The stem is **yellowish**, often tinged with red on the lower part. The pore surface and interior flesh are **bright yellow** and **instantly stain blue** when bruised or cut, as does the stem. It may smell like curry, but this is not always noticeable. The stem of the similar *Lanmaoa pseudosensibilis* (formerly *Boletus pseudosensibilis*) bruises blue more faintly, and its cap is more brownish; other differences are microscopic.

Brick-Cap Bolete

green = key identification feature

SPORE PRINT: Olive-brown.

SEASON: Summer through fall.

OTHER NAMES: Two-Color Boletes.

COMPARE: Frost's Bolete (*Exsudoporus frostii*; formerly *Butyriboletus frostii* or *Boletus frostii*, also called Apple Bolete) has a **deep red cap, red pore surface** and **deeply textured stem** that may be reddish overall or a mix of red, pinkish, orangish or yellowish.

Frost's Bolete

Caps are up to 6 inches wide. The pore surface and yellow flesh **quickly bruise blue** when damaged. Most sources say it is edible when well cooked, with a slightly sour or lemony flavor that pairs well with seafood. • Smaller species with features similar to Brick-Cap include the **Sulfur Bolete** (*Hortiboletus campestris*; formerly *Boletus campestris*) and **Ruby Bolete** (*H. rubellus*; formerly *Boletus rubellus* or *Xerocomellus rubellus*); see photo on pg. 181. Caps of both are less than 2 inches across and typically **deep rose to pinkish red**; with age, they fade and often develop surface cracks. Until recently, both were included with *Boletus fraternus* as a species group, but DNA studies determined that *Boletus fraternus* is identical to *Boletus rubellus*; all were moved to the *Hortiboletus* genus. The *Hortiboletus* listed here are difficult to tell apart; while generally regarded as edible, they can be so similar to small, **toxic** Brick-Caps that even some experts do not collect them for the table. • **Peppery Boletes** (pg. 189) are **rust-red overall** when young. Caps are **1 to 3 inches** across and fade to tan with age. The pore surface bruises **dark brown**. The stem base is yellow; cap flesh is yellowish to pinkish. • Red-capped **Bicolor Boletes** (pg. 180; edible) have stems that are **red overall** except at the top, which is yellow. Its bright yellow pore surface stains blue; interior flesh is yellow and stains blue very slowly and faintly, if at all.

NOTES: Adding to the uncertainty when attempting to identify toxic boletes, there is a good deal of variety among specimens depending on geography, age, and growing conditions. Though the many names and descriptions discussed here get confusing, **the key point is simple**: *boletes with red, orange or yellow pore surfaces that bruise blue should be not be eaten*. That may cause you to skip a potentially edible variety, but you will also avoid getting sick. There are no known deadly bolete species, but the gastrointestinal distress can be quite severe. Boletes are abundant, beautiful to photograph and excellent subjects to hone your species identification skills.

ON DECAYING WOOD

SUMMER THROUGH LATE FALL

TOP TOXICS

Jack O'Lantern
Omphalotus illudens

These stunning mushrooms appear similar to the highly edible Chanterelle (pgs. 38–40). Unfortunately, Jacks are not simply inedible; according to the North American Mycological Association they contain muscarine and other toxins that cause severe gastrointestinal distress, breathing difficulties, visual disturbances and lowered blood pressure.

Luckily it's fairly easy to distinguish Jack O'Lanterns from Chanterelles. A key difference is that Jacks have **true, knife-edged gills that can be separated individually from the cap**. Chanterelles, in contrast, have folds or ribs rather than gills; the folds are actually just a textural feature of the cap and stem and can be separated **in a sheet** but not individually. The flesh of Chanterelles is **whitish** throughout.

HABITAT: Always grows from decaying wood, although they may appear to be growing directly from the ground if the wood is buried (as seen on pg. 71, bottom right). Often found at the base of trees.

DESCRIPTION: Bright orange mushrooms with **sharp, thin gills that run partway down the stems**; gills are **unforked** and closely spaced. Jacks almost always grow in **dense clusters** rather than individually. Caps of mature specimens are 3 to 7½ inches wide; stems are up to 8 inches tall and are generally curved at the base. Flesh is evenly **orange** throughout. The cap is smooth above, turning upward as the specimens age.

SPORE PRINT: Cream-colored to pale yellow.

SEASON: Summer through late fall.

OTHER NAMES: Also called *O. olearius*, a similar species not in our area.

COMPARE: As noted above, Jacks resemble edible Chanterelles. They also could be confused with the **False Chanterelle** (pg. 40), but False Chanterelles have **forked gills**; the cap surface and stems are more brownish than orange. • **Chicken Mushrooms** (pgs. 32–33) grow on wood and may be bright orange, but they have **pores** rather than gills.

NOTES: Jack O'Lanterns get their name not only from the bright orange color but also because the gills of fresh specimens can produce a slight greenish glow in complete darkness.

green = key identification feature

Young specimens
growing on hidden roots

SPRING THROUGH FALL

Tiny Fragile Mushrooms (numerous)
Various species

HABITAT: Tiny fragile mushrooms of various types grow in an array of habitats, including woodlands and fields, on dead wood and on debris. They typically grow in scattered groups but may be found singly or in clusters.

DESCRIPTION: Tiny mushrooms are very common but are so small that they are often overlooked unless they are brightly colored and/or growing in a large cluster. The mushrooms included here have **long, thin stems**. Caps are **fragile** and rounded or conical; they are generally less than 1 inch wide at maturity, and many are less than ½ inch wide. Microscopic examination is required to identify many species; indeed, a hand lens is needed to properly examine them in the field. • *Marasmius* species have **tough** stems that may be wiry. They are found during or after periods of **wet weather**, growing from decaying organic matter on the ground. Marasmius can withstand periods of dry weather, shriveling and going dormant for weeks. They are revived by rain, returning to fresh condition and resuming spore production; they are sometimes referred to as Resurrection Fungi. • Many *Mycena* species are also tiny and fragile, but their stems are **brittle** rather than tough or wiry. They may be brightly or subtly colored, or have brownish hues like those on pgs. 92 and 136. • *Parasola*, *Conocybe*, and some *Coprinellus* and *Entoloma* also fall into the tiny, fragile category (some *Entoloma* are larger and easier to identify; these appear elsewhere in this book).

SPORE PRINT: If you want to try to place your tiny fragile mushrooms into a genus, the first step is making a spore print. Here are some generalizations to get you started. *Marasmius* and *Mycena* have white spores. *Conocybe* have rust-brown spores. *Coprinellus* and *Parasola* have dark brown to blackish spores. *Entoloma* have salmon-pink or brownish spores.

SEASON: Spring through fall, depending on species.

COMPARE: See also **Little Brown Mushrooms** (pg. 114), **Orange to Red Wax Caps** (pg. 122) and **Fuzzy Foot** (pg. 124) for other small mushrooms; most of these have somewhat larger caps, shorter stems and are a bit less fragile.

NOTES: These tiny mushrooms are too small to eat, and it's unknown if they are edible.

Marasmius siccus

Mycena crocea

Parasola spp.

Entoloma quadratum

Sweetbread Mushroom

Clitopilus prunulus

HABITAT: These saprobes are found growing from the ground, **scattered** or in **small groups**, in open deciduous and coniferous woodlands and grassy areas.

DESCRIPTION: Although young Sweetbread Mushrooms resemble any number of whitish cap-and-stem mushrooms, developed specimens have caps that characteristically appear **wavy or lobed**; the edge is turned under and is often frilly. Caps are 2 to 4 inches across and may be depressed in the center; the texture is **suede-like or felt-like**. The cap and stem are both cream-colored to dirty white. Stems are up to 3¼ inches tall and may have a slightly swollen base; the cap is often attached to the stem slightly **off-center**. The stem has no ring. Several specimens may grow together from a common base. The gills are very closely spaced and **run down the stem for a short distance**; they are creamy white at first, turning **pale pink** with age. Sweetbread Mushrooms have a fragrance that has been compared to the **scent of grain, flour and unbaked yeast bread**.

SPORE PRINT: Pinkish-buff to salmon-colored.

SEASON: Spring through fall.

OTHER NAMES: The Miller, due to its yeasty or grain-like fragrance. Some guides list *Clitopilus orcella* as a distinct species, separated from *Clitopilus prunulus* by its sticky cap, but it is now considered a synonym.

COMPARE: Several other species are whitish, with gills that run down the stem and other characteristics similar to the Sweetbread. • *Lepista subconnexa* (also known as *Clitocybe subconnexa*) grows in **tight clusters**; its spores are **pinkish to whitish**. The **smooth white** stems may have a bit of a **sheen**. The gills may run down the stem slightly, or may be simply attached to the cap. • **The Sweater** (pg. 152) is a **toxic** Clitocybe that is much smaller than the Sweetbread; its spore print is **white**. • **Aborting Entoloma** (pg. 110) resembles the Sweetbread; it has **cucumber-like** odor. Other *Entoloma* species may also resemble the Sweetbread; some, such as *E. sinuatum* (see pg. 110), are **toxic** and none should be eaten.

NOTES: Sweetbread Mushrooms are edible but not recommended for amateurs due to the possibility of confusing them with **toxic** species.

Sweetbread Mushroom

Lepista subconnexa

American Parasol

Leucoagaricus americanus

ON DECAYING WOOD AND WOODY DEBRIS

MIDSUMMER THROUGH EARLY FALL

HABITAT: These handsome mushrooms are saprobes, found growing singly or in small groups on rotting wood and woody debris such as wood chips, stumps, mulch piles, sawdust heaps and fallen logs from which they get nutrients.

DESCRIPTION: Caps of young specimens are softly conical; with age the cap flattens out and may be 5 inches across when mature. It is white to buff with **numerous small scales** that form a ring-like pattern around the softly pointed center. Scales are pale at first, turning **rust-colored**. The cap turns brownish with age and often has tattered edges which may be upturned. The stem is up to 5 inches tall and smooth or a bit fibrous; it is pale at first, turning reddish-brown. The base is **swollen**, sometimes appearing pear-shaped. There is **no cup** around the base. Young specimens have a thin veil over the gills; the veil disintegrates as the cap expands, leaving a **thin ring** which may deteriorate with age. Gills are closely spaced and are not attached to the stem; they are white when young, turning **reddish** with age. The cap and stem bruise yellowish-orange to reddish when handled.

SPORE PRINT: White.

SEASON: Midsummer through early fall.

OTHER NAMES: Reddening Lepiota, *Lepiota* (or *Leucocoprinus*) *americana*.

COMPARE: Green-Spored Lepiota (pgs. 60–61; **toxic**) has tan patches on its cap, **greenish** spores and gills that turn **grayish-green** with age. • Shaggy Parasol (*Chlorophyllum rachodes*; also called *Macrolepiota rachodes* or *Lepiota rachodes*) appears similar to Green-Spored Lepiota, but its patches are **darker brown**. Its spores are white; gills turn **brownish** with age. • The species in our area that is called **Parasol Mushroom** (generally listed as *M. procera*) has a **narrow, straight, scaly** stem up to **8 inches tall**; the cap has a dark , **nipple-like bump** in the center. Experts say the true Parasol Mushroom is found only in Europe; the species found in our area has yet to be named. • Many *Amanita* **species** (pgs. 62–66; **toxic**) have patchy caps and swollen bases; some have a **cup** at the stem base. • *Lepiota cristata* has a **red-scaled** cap less than 2 inches wide and a **very thin stem**; it has a foul odor. Edibility is uncertain; some sources list it as toxic.

NOTES: American Parasol and Shaggy Parasol are edible, but for experts only as there are several **toxic** look-alikes.

American Parasol

Green-Spored Lepiota

Shaggy Parasol

Parasol Mushroom

Deceptive Milky
Lactifluus deceptivus

FROM THE SOIL NEAR LIVE TREES

SUMMER THROUGH LATE FALL

HABITAT: Mycorrhizal, growing from the soil in association with oak, hemlock and other deciduous trees and conifers. Found scattered or in large groups.

DESCRIPTION: All Milk Caps (*Lactarius* and *Lactifluus* spp.) produce **milky latex when cut**. Deceptive Milky has **white** latex that **remains white**, but it stains the flesh and gills **brownish**; it is very bitter. Caps of young specimens are white, with rolled-under edges that are **cottony** and may **partially cover the gills**. With age, the cap enlarges and flattens out, becoming **scaly** and funnel-shaped; it develops **brownish splotches** and may become yellowish-brown overall. The cap of a mature specimen may be as wide as **10 inches**, although most specimens are smaller. The stem is white, developing brown splotches; it is 1½ to 4 inches tall and about one-third as wide. It is dry and may be scaly but is not pock-marked; there is no ring. The gills are **moderately closely spaced** and attached to the stem or run slightly down it; they are white, becoming tan with age.

SPORE PRINT: White to pale yellowish.

SEASON: Summer through late fall.

OTHER NAMES: Cottonroll Milkcap, *Lactarius deceptivus*. Species listed below as *Lactifluus* were formerly included in the *Lactarius* genus; some references may still list them that way.

COMPARE: Several other Milk Caps in our area are whitish. **Peppery Milky** (*Lactifluus piperatus*) and *Lactarius glaucescens* have **very crowded gills** and **smooth** caps and produce **abundant** latex; Peppery Milky is up to 6 inches across and has white latex that remains white or turns slightly yellowish, while *Lactarius glaucescens* is less than 4 inches across and has white latex that slowly turns **greenish**. · *Lactifluus luteolus* is up to 3 inches wide; it has a **fishy** smell and mild-tasting **sticky, abundant** latex that stains the cap, stem and gills (and fingers) brown. · *Lactarius subvernalis* is less than 2½ inches across; its flesh and gills turn **salmon-pink** when bruised. · Caps and stems of *Lactifluus subvellereus* are **velvety or chalky**. The latex is white, turning yellowish slowly if at all. The gills are **more widely spaced** than those of Deceptive Milky, and it lacks the cottony margin at the edge of the cap. · *Russula brevipes* resembles the Deceptive Milky but **does not produce latex** when cut.

NOTES: *Lactifluus luteolus* has a mild taste, but the other Milk Caps above are bitter or hot and are usually not eaten; some sources list *Lactarius glaucescens* as toxic.

Deceptive Milky

Peppery Milky

FROM THE SOIL IN GRASSY AREAS

LATE SUMMER THROUGH EARLY FALL

Meadow Mushroom
Agaricus campestris

HABITAT: Growing singly, in groups or rings in **grassy areas such as meadows, fields and lawns.** They are saprobes, feeding on decaying organic matter.

DESCRIPTION: Looks like its relative, the grocery-store Button Mushroom (*A. bisporus*). When young, the Meadow Mushroom has a **veil over the gills** and a smooth, rounded cap that is whitish to grayish-brown. With age, the cap expands and pulls the veil apart, leaving a **thin ring** on the stem; the cap is up to 4½ inches wide when fully opened, and the ring may disappear with age. The stem is stubby and generally 1 to 2½ inches tall; it may taper slightly at the base. Gills are closely spaced and **pink** at first, maturing to brownish-black; they are not attached to the stem.

SPORE PRINT: Blackish-brown or dark purplish-brown.

SEASON: Late summer through early fall.

OTHER NAMES: Field Mushroom, Pink Bottom.

COMPARE: Caps of **Wood Mushroom** (*A. sylvicola*) and **Horse Mushroom** (*A. fissuratus* or *A. arvensis*) **turn yellowish when rubbed**. Gills are **white** at first, soon turning pink, then brown. Both have a **large, skirt-like ring** and a **sweet, anise-like odor**. Wood Mushroom inhabits **forested areas**; caps are up to 4½ inches wide. Horse Mushroom is found in grassy areas; caps are up to **8 inches wide** and the veil has a **cog-wheeled** appearance. • The cap of **Eastern Flat-Topped Agaricus** (*A. placomyces*) is covered with brownish fibers that are **concentrated at the center**, giving it a bull's-eye appearance. The stem base **turns bright yellow when cut** and is often slightly swollen. The veil may have **yellowish or brownish droplets** on it when still attached to the cap edge. • **Spring Agaricus** (*A. bitorquis* or *A. rodmani*) is stubby and has a **double ring**; it grows in **hard soil**, often near sidewalks. It may start fruiting in **late spring**.

NOTES: Spring Agaricus is a choice edible. Meadow, Wood and Horse Mushrooms are edible, but Wood and Horse Mushrooms may cause intestinal problems. Eastern Flat-Topped Agaricus is inedible. Be cautious when collecting *Agaricus* to eat; **toxic** Amanitas (pgs. 62-66) may look similar but have **white spores**. Also watch out for **toxic** Yellow-Foot Agaricus (*A. xanthodermus*); its cap bruises yellow and its **stem base turns yellow when cut**. It smells like **tar**.

Meadow Mushroom

Eastern Flat-Topped Agaricus

Wood Mushroom

Horse Mushroom

ON DECAYING WOOD AND WOODY DEBRIS

LATE SUMMER THROUGH EARLY FALL

Decorated Pholiota
Leucopholiota decorosa

HABITAT: Decorated Pholiota is a saprobe, feeding on decaying wood. It grows most commonly in beech-maple forests, often on rotting logs and stumps, **especially those of sugar maple**. It occurs singly, scattered or in small clusters.

DESCRIPTION: This attractive mushroom has a cap that is tan to brown due to a **dense covering of pointed tan-to-rusty-brown scales**. The cap edge is hairy and rolled inward. Caps are 1 to 3 inches wide and convex to nearly flat at maturity. The cap flesh is white and does not change color when bruised. Stems are 1 to 3 inches tall and ½ inch wide. They are usually slightly enlarged at the base but may be nearly equal from top to bottom. The tops of the stems are smooth and white. There is a dense covering of rusty brown scales and hairs that spans from the bottom up to the **flaring, shaggy ring zone**. Gills are closely spaced and white. They are slightly notched at the stem and their edges are uneven. Decorated Pholiota do not have a distinctive odor.

SPORE PRINT: White.

SEASON: Late summer through early fall.

OTHER NAMES: *Armillaria decorosa*.

COMPARE: *Pholiota* species also have scaly caps, but produce **brown** spore prints. (Note that *Pholiota* species can be difficult to identify based on physical characteristics alone; microscopic analysis is generally used for accurate identification.) • Both *P. squarrosa* and *P. squarrosoides* are called Scaly Pholiota. They grow in **dense clusters** with caps up to **4 inches** across. Cap color is **pale yellow to tan** with spiky brown scales that are **more densely arranged towards the center**. *P. squarrosa* has **dry** caps. Its white gills turn **greenish** before turning brownish from the spores; it often has an odor of **garlic or radishes**. Nearly identical *P. squarrosoides* has **sticky** caps in damp weather and gills do not have a greenish stage before turning brown. • Golden Pholiota (pg. 156) caps tend to be **more yellowish overall**, with a **slimy or tacky** texture.

NOTES: The contrast of the tan scales on the cap and lower stem with the pure white gills highlight this attractive mushroom. It is not considered edible. Once considered rare, Decorated Pholiota can now be found most years on logs in mature forests in our area.

Decorated Pholiota

P. squarrosoides

ON LIVE OR DEAD TREES

LATE SUMMER THROUGH LATE FALL

White Beech Mushroom

Hypsizygus marmoreus

HABITAT: Occurs on logs and stumps of broadleaf trees, often in **clusters**. It is common in northern hardwood forests. Like many mushrooms growing on stumps and logs, it is an important recycler of woody debris.

DESCRIPTION: At first glance, the White Beech Mushroom is often mistaken for an Oyster Mushroom (pgs. 34–37), but closer inspection reveals that the White Beech Mushroom has a **distinct stem that is well delineated from the cap**, whereas Oyster Mushrooms have only a very short stem or none at all. White Beech Mushrooms are **white, cream-colored or tan** overall. Caps of young specimens are smooth and rounded. As the specimen matures, the cap expands and flattens and may be **up to 6 inches across**; edges may be slightly cracked, and the surface often has a **water-spotted appearance**. Stems are 2 to 4 inches long and up to ¾ inch thick and may be attached to the caps slightly off-center; they are often curved and may appear to have faint ridges running from the cap to the base. Gills are moderately spaced and are **attached to the stem but do not run down it**; the stem has no ring.

SPORE PRINT: White to buff.

SEASON: Late summer through late fall.

OTHER NAMES: Elm Oyster, Beech Mushroom. Some texts refer to White Beech Mushroom as *H. tessulatus*, but that is a smaller pinkish-buff species that may not occur in the Northeast, except in markets where it has been imported.

COMPARE: Elm Cap (*H. ulmarius*) is an edible white mushroom that often grows on deciduous tree wounds. It is **not usually clustered,** and **its cap is not water-spotted**. • The Train Wrecker (*Neolentinus lepideus* or *Lentinus lepideus*; cap edible when young) appears similar to the White Beech Mushroom and grows in clusters on decaying wood including logs, stumps and railroad ties; its cap and stem have numerous **brown scales** and its gills have **jagged edges**.

NOTES: White Beech Mushrooms are edible but may be bitter and are tougher than Oyster Mushrooms. Some prefer to parboil them before frying. White Beech Mushrooms and *H. tessulatus* (also referred to as Brown Beech Mushroom and sometimes spelled *H. tessellatus*) are available in grow-it-yourself kits; the cultivated mushrooms are sold as Shimeji.

green = key identification feature

White Beech Mushroom

Elm Cap

Spring Agrocybe
Agrocybe praecox

FROM DECAYING GROUND DEBRIS

SPRING TO EARLY SUMMER

HABITAT: Spring Agrocybe are saprobes, getting nutrients from woody debris and other decaying organic matter that may be underground. Often seen in great profusion in wood-mulched flowerbeds, it also occurs in woodlands.

DESCRIPTION: Young specimens have a rounded cap up to 1¾ inches wide, with a white partial veil over the gills. As the cap expands, the veil is pulled apart; fragments **hang from the cap rim** or may appear as **small, cottony projections** around the edge of the cap. Caps are **cream- to buff-colored**, often with a slightly raised center. Fresh caps have a **silky-smooth** texture and may feel greasy. Mature caps are up to **4 inches** across and may crack in dry weather. Stems are colored like the cap or slightly paler, becoming darker with age. They are up to **4 inches tall** and fairly sturdy-looking. Stems are smooth or faintly grooved; there may be a **faint, irregular flattened ring** that is darkened by falling spores, but the ring may be incomplete or missing entirely. Whitish mycelium (thread-like fungal roots) cling to the base of the stem. Gills are closely spaced and attached to the stem or very slightly separated from it; they are cream-colored at first, turning grayish, then brown, as spores develop.

SPORE PRINT: Dark chocolate brown.

SEASON: Spring to early summer.

OTHER NAMES: Spring Fieldcap, Spring Agaric.

COMPARE: Several *Agrocybe* species are very similar and require a microscope for positive identification. *A. molesta* (also called *A. dura*) is one of these; it grows exclusively in **grass** and is white when young, turning yellowish-brown as it ages.
• **Common Agrocybe** (*A. pediades*; photo on pg. 115) is smaller, with a **yellowish** cap less than **1½ inches** wide and a **thin** stem less than 2 inches tall; the ring is visible only on very young specimens. It appears in summer on lawns after rain.
• *A. firma* has a **dark brown** cap; edges are paler. The cap becomes tawny with age. Gills of fresh specimens are **brownish**, becoming yellowish-brown with age. The stem is solid and relatively hard. The spore print is **cinnamon-brown**.

NOTES: *Agrocybe* are hard to identify with certainty; some, such as Common Agrocybe, may be confused with toxic species. Although all species listed above but *A. firma* are considered edible, they are for experts only. Grow-it-yourself mushrooms called Velvet Pioppino are sometimes listed as *A. aegerita*, but also are sold as *Cyclocybe aegerita*.

Spring Agrocybe

Cracked caps of
Spring Agrocybe

A. firma

FROM THE SOIL NEAR LIVE TREES

SPRING THROUGH FALL

Common Laccaria
Laccaria laccata

HABITAT: Growing from the ground, scattered or in groups, near deciduous trees and conifers with which they have a mycorrhizal relationship. Often found in leaf litter.

DESCRIPTION: Common Laccaria can be difficult to identify without resorting to microscopic analysis, as the color changes throughout the life of the mushroom and is also affected by the weather. They appear in various brownish colors, ranging from reddish- or orangish-brown to tan to nearly white. Caps are smooth to finely scaly and may have a slightly translucent skin; the center is sometimes slightly depressed but may also be raised. Caps of young specimens are small and rounded, sometimes appearing softly folded around the edge. As the mushroom matures, the cap enlarges and flattens out, often flaring upwards to form a shallow bowl; it is up to 2 inches wide at maturity and may have wavy or frilly edges that are often split. Gills are **pinkish to tan, thick and widely spaced**. They are attached to the stem and may run down the stem for a short distance; additional short gills are attached around the edge of the cap. Stems are somewhat **slender**, up to 4 inches long and often somewhat twisted or curved; they are dry and fibrous with fine hairs or scales on the surface and are typically a **darker shade of the cap color**. The stem has no ring.

SPORE PRINT: White.

SEASON: Spring through fall.

OTHER NAMES: Deceiver, *L. laccata* var. *pallidifolia*.

COMPARE: Sandy Laccaria (*L. trullisata*; also spelled *trullissata*) is similar but slightly larger, with a cap up to 2¾ across and a **thick stem** that may be enlarged at the base. Its gills are **purplish** and it fruits in **very sandy areas**, typically near conifers. • Purple-Gilled Laccaria (pg. 142) is up to **6 inches across** and has **purple** gills. • Many **toxic** *Cortinarius* are brownish (pg. 118) or orangish (pg. 126), but young specimens have a **cobwebby veil** over the gills; the spore print of mature specimens is **rust-brown**.

NOTES: Common Laccaria are edible but not recommended for amateurs due to the difficulty in identifying them and the possibility of confusing them with **toxic** Cortinarius.

Common Laccaria

Sandy Laccaria

ON DECAYING WOOD   SPRING THROUGH FALL

Deer Mushroom
Pluteus cervinus

HABITAT: Growing singly or scattered in deciduous, coniferous and mixed wood-lands from rotten logs, sawdust piles, wood chips, decaying roots and other woody debris that may be underground. They are saprobes, getting nutrients from decaying organic matter.

DESCRIPTION: A very common, medium-sized mushroom. The cap is **brownish**, ranging from pale tan to brownish-gray to dark brown; it is smooth and often streaked with fibers that radiate from the center of the cap, which is tacky in damp weather and may appear glossy. Bell-shaped when young, the cap expands to become broadly convex or flat; it may grow to 4¾ inches wide. The slender stem, which is up to 4 inches tall, is **white** to grayish and may be streaked with dark fibers. There is no ring on the stem and **no cup** around the base. Gills are closely spaced and are **not attached to the stem**; they are white at first, turning **pale salmon-pink** as the spores develop.

SPORE PRINT: Salmon-pink.

SEASON: Spring through fall.

OTHER NAMES: Fawn Mushroom, *P. atricapillus*.

COMPARE: Other Pluteus with pink spores and similar growth habits are found in our area. *P. petasatus* often grows in **clusters** from buried wood; its cap may be slightly larger than the Deer Mushroom and is **white** with a **brownish center**. • Pleated Pluteus (*P. longistriatus*) has **ribbing** around the bottom half to two-thirds of the cap, which is about 2 inches wide. The top half is brownish, becoming **paler gray** around the edges; the stem is whitish with gray fibers. • Black-Edged Pluteus (*P. atromarginatus*) has a dark brown to **black** cap up to 4 inches wide that is streaked with small black fibers and may feel velvety. The gills are white with **black or dark gray edges**; the stem is covered with dark fibers. • Members of the *Volvariella* genus (pg. 154) are similar to *Pluteus* species, but they have a **cup** around the base of the stem.

NOTES: This is a complex group of species that requires microscopic study to positively identify. None are known to be deadly poisonous, but their soft texture and unremarkable taste make them mediocre edibles at best.

Deer Mushroom

P. petasatus

Tan Mycena (several)
Mycena spp.

HABITAT: Most *Mycena* species grow from decaying organic material, either on ground litter or on dead trees and stumps; a few grow from the bark of live trees. They often grow in large numbers.

DESCRIPTION: Mycena are small to tiny mushrooms in the *Mycenoid* group; most have caps less than 1½ inches wide at maturity. Caps are typically conical or softly rounded. Some species have caps that appear pleated; others are smooth. Stems of most are thin and have a **soft or fragile** texture; there is no ring. Gills of many Mycena are darker on the edge than on the inner sides. Microscopic examination is required to identify most species; a hand lens is helpful to examine them in the field. • **Common Mycena** (*M. galericulata*) is one of the larger Mycena, with a **tan to grayish** cap up to **2 inches** wide, a brownish stem up to 3½ inches tall and pink-tinged gills. • **Clustered Bonnet** (*M. inclinata*) has tan caps up to 1 inch wide with a **darker brown center** and a **scalloped outer edge**. The stem is **white at the top** with a **reddish-brown base**; it is up to 3 inches tall. Clustered Bonnet has a **rancid odor**. • **Bleeding Mycena** (pg. 136) has a powdery **reddish to pinkish** cap up to 1 inch wide that fades to **pinkish-tan to pale buff** with age; gills are white. The stem is brownish and up to 3 inches tall; it **oozes deep purplish-red liquid** when cut. • **Lilac Bonnet** (pgs. 144–145) grows **from the ground**, usually under **conifers**. Its 2-inch caps are **purplish** to pink when young, fading to tan with age. It has a **radish-like odor**.

SPORE PRINT: White.

SEASON: Spring through fall, depending on species.

OTHER NAMES: The *Mycenoid* group also includes *Hydropus*, *Rickenella* and others; as noted, a microscope is often needed for exact identification.

COMPARE: See also **Tiny Fragile Mushrooms** (pg. 72) and **Little Brown Mushrooms** (pg. 114) for more small to tiny mushrooms you may encounter.

NOTES: Most of these dainty mushrooms are not considered edible and are too small to be of culinary value; most enthusiasts simply photograph them.

Common Mycena

Clustered Bonnet

FROM DECAYING GROUND DEBRIS

SPRING THROUGH FALL

Mica Cap
Coprinellus micaceus

HABITAT: Mica Caps are saprobes, getting nutrients from decaying roots and other woody debris that may be underground. They are found in woodlands and urban parks. They generally grow in **tight, dense clusters** and are frequently found at the base of stumps and dead or dying trees.

DESCRIPTION: Young Mica Caps have **hollow egg-shaped to conical caps**, generally ¾ to 1½ inches wide, that are covered with **small but prominent glistening salt-like granules** which may be washed away by rain. Thin grooves run from near the top of the cap to the edges. Caps are **honey-colored to tawny**; they may be patchy at the top depending on the weather. As the specimen matures, the cap turns brown and opens up, splitting around the edges; old specimens have flared, upturned edges. Stems are 1 to 3 inches tall; they are hollow and white with a fine, silky texture. There may be a faint ring remnant near the base. Gills are closely spaced and whitish on young specimens; they become brownish and turn **black or sooty gray**, finally **partially dissolving** into an inky fluid.

SPORE PRINT: Black.

SEASON: Most common in spring but may be present through fall.

OTHER NAMES: Glistening Inky Cap, *Coprinus micaceus*. There are numerous *Coprinellus* species that are so similar to *Coprinellus micaceus* that microscopic examination is required to separate individual members of this species complex.

COMPARE: Domestic Inky Cap (*Coprinellus domesticus*) and **Orange-Mat Coprinus** (*Coprinellus radians*, a related species distinguished from *C. domesticus* by microscopic features) are a bit larger overall; the granules are larger and more scale-like and may be concentrated toward the top of the cap. More significantly, these two mushrooms produce a **shaggy orange carpet-like mat** of mycelium (thread-like fungal roots) over the substrate on which they grow; the mat may appear before the mushroom develops. These two mushrooms may grow indoors on damp flooring. • Alcohol Inky (pg. 29) is larger, **lacks the granules** and is **grayish**.

NOTES: Mica Caps are edible when young but should be cooked soon after harvesting to prevent them from deteriorating. They are soft with a mild flavor. Like Alcohol Inky, Mica Caps must never be consumed with alcohol; see pg. 29 for more information. Most sources list *C. domesticus* and *C. radians* as inedible.

Granules on caps

Old Mica Caps

Rooting Collybia
Hymenopellis megalospora

HABITAT: Rooting Collybia are saprobes, getting their nutrients from decaying woody deciduous debris that is usually buried; they are often found in lawns near buried stump remnants. They grow singly, scattered or in small groups.

DESCRIPTION: These tall, slender-stemmed mushrooms have a **distinct root** that is often 3 to 5 inches long, or even longer. The root is thick near the soil but becomes quite thin; it is necessary to dig around the base of the stem to extract the root, so it is often missed and the thinner portion usually breaks off. Caps of mature specimens are up to 3 inches wide; they feel chamois-like when dry, becoming slimy when wet. Colors range from whitish to tan to buff. The center has a slightly darker **knob** that is frequently surrounded by a **puckered** area that may appear sunken; the cap may become fairly flat with age but the knob will still be present. The slender stems are up to 5 inches tall and may be slightly twisted. They are whitish and silky, often with fine band-like patterning; there is no ring. Gills are attached to the stem; they are white and **moderately widely spaced**. Gill edges may be ruffled near the cap edge.

SPORE PRINT: White.

SEASON: Spring through fall.

OTHER NAMES: Formerly known as *Xerula megalospora*. *Collybia radicata* is sometimes used as a synonym, while other sources list this as a separate species.

COMPARE: There are several other *Hymenopellis* species; a microscope is needed for positive identification. The most common is *H. furfuracea*, which has a **smoky brownish** cap up to **4¾ inches** wide and a hairy stem that is brownish on the lower half. • **Melanoleuca** have a knobbed cap and slender stem but **no root**; gills are **crowded**. Yellow-White Melanoleuca (*M. alboflavida*) has a whitish to buff cap up to 4 inches wide and a stem up to 6 inches tall. **Changeable Melanoleuca** (*M. melaleuca*) has a **brownish** cap up to 3 inches wide and a stem up to 3 inches tall. • Twisted-Stalked Entoloma (*Entoloma strictius*; **toxic**) has a tall, slender stem and a knobbed **grayish-brown** cap; its spore print is **salmon-pink** and it has **no root**.

NOTES: The *Hymenopellis* and *Melanoleuca* species discussed here are edible but for experts only, due to possible confusion with **toxic** *Entoloma* species.

Rooting Collybia

Root (partial)

Ruffled gills

Yellow-White
Melanoleuca

FROM DECAYING GROUND DEBRIS

LATE SPRING THROUGH EARLY FALL

Oak Collybia

Gymnopus dryophilus

HABITAT: Found in deciduous, coniferous or mixed forests; they are saprobes, getting nutrients from decaying roots and other woody debris that may be underground. They grow singly, scattered, in small groups or in tight clusters; several individual specimens may grow from a fused base.

DESCRIPTION: This common mushroom has a smooth **tawny to reddish-brown** cap that turns **tan, orangish-tan or buff** as the specimen matures. The cap is generally ½ to 1½ inches wide, although it may be up to 2½ inches wide on mature specimens. It is rounded at first, opening up and becoming flat or developing a wavy top as it matures. The edge of the cap is often wavy and sometimes lighter in color. The stem, which may be whitish, buff-colored or the same color as the cap, is up to 3½ inches tall; it is smooth, brittle and hollow, and there may be **white mycelium** (thread-like fungal roots) at the base. The stem has no ring. Gills are **white** and closely spaced; they may be attached to the stem or free from it.

SPORE PRINT: White to pale yellowish-white.

SEASON: Late spring through early fall.

OTHER NAMES: Oak-Loving Collybia, *Collybia dryophila*.

COMPARE: Buttery Collybia (*Rhodocollybia butyracea*; also called *Collybia butyracea*) has a reddish-brown to orangish-brown cap that feels **buttery** when moist; the cap becomes tawny with age. Its stems are up to **4 inches tall** and often wider at the base, looking rather like an inverted baseball bat. Its spore print is whitish to pinkish and its gills may have **jagged edges**. Buttery Collybia grows near conifers from late summer through fall. • Clustered Collybia (*Connopus acervatus*; also called *G. acervatus* and *Collybia acervata*) is similar but has more reddish tones; its stem is reddish-brown and may be up to **4½ inches tall**. It grows in **tight, dense clusters** on conifer logs and decaying wood.

NOTES: Some sources list Oak Collybia as edible but suggest discarding the stalk due to its tough texture; others recommend against eating it altogether. Oak Collybia is sometimes attacked by Collybia Jelly (pgs. 260–261), a fungus that causes white growths on the cap.

Oak Collybia

Buttery Collybia

Clustered Collybia

FROM THE SOIL NEAR LIVE TREES

SPRING THROUGH FALL

Grisettes (several)
Amanita vaginata group

HABITAT: Grisettes are mycorrhizal, growing in mixed woods from the soil and humus in a symbiotic relationship with living trees. They are often found in grass and are common in urban areas; they grow singly or scattered.

DESCRIPTION: The name Grisette is used for a related group of Amanita mushrooms referred to collectively as the *A. vaginata* complex. Key features in this group are distinct **ribbing on the cap margin**, the presence of a **volva** (sac-like cup at the base of the stem), **scattered or no patches** on the cap and the **lack of a ring** on the stem. Over 200 members of this group have been described; each is genetically distinct. Caps are typically 2 to 4 inches wide but may be wider; cap color may be white, gray, brown or tan. Stems are 4 to 8 inches tall and whitish; they may be smooth or somewhat scaly. The volva may be obvious, or may be fragile and easy to miss (dig carefully in the dirt around the stem base to search for it). Gills are **closely spaced** and **white** when fresh; they are free from the stem or barely attached. Flesh is white. *Grisette* refers to gray, which is the color of *A. vaginata* caps. • **White Grisette** (*A. vaginata*) is **white overall**. • **Tawny Grisette** (*A. fulva*) has a **fawn-brown to tan** cap.

SPORE PRINT: White.

SEASON: Spring through fall. Most common in summer.

OTHER NAMES: *Amanitopsis*.

COMPARE: Please read about other Amanitas on pgs. 62–66.

NOTES: All these names are from mushrooms described in Europe. North American mushrooms look similar but are different microscopically; the names are in flux but will undoubtedly be changed upon further study. Many Grisettes are edible, but even most experts shy away from them due to possible confusion with **toxic** Amanitas. Definitely not for novices.

A. vaginata

Button stage with volva fragment

White Grisette

Tawny Grisette

FROM DECAYING GROUND DEBRIS

SUMMER THROUGH FALL

Big Laughing Gym
Gymnopilus junonius

HABITAT: These saprobes are found in mixed woodlands, where they feed on nutrients from rotting trees, decaying roots and woody debris that may be buried. They often grow in dense clusters; also found in small groups or singly.

DESCRIPTION: With its large stature and clustered growth habit, this mushroom is hard to miss in the woods. Caps of mature specimens are up to **8 inches across** but may be smaller. The stem is thick and up to **8 inches tall**. Caps and stems are yellowish-brown, golden or brownish-orange; gills are similarly colored or slightly paler, turning darker with age. The cap is dry and may be finely scaly; the center is often slightly humped. Stems, which are often curved or twisted, have a **distinct, dark-capped ring** near the top; below the ring, the stems are **streaked with coarse fibers**. Gills are closely spaced and attached to the stem or running down it slightly. The mushroom has a pleasant odor similar to almond extract but a very bitter taste.

SPORE PRINT: Bright orangish-brown or rust-orange.

SEASON: Summer through fall.

OTHER NAMES: Laughing Mushroom, Waraitake, *G. spectabilis*.

COMPARE: Several related Gymnopilus with somewhat different attributes may be found in parts of our area. *G. luteus* has a **saffron-yellow** cap that is less than 4 inches wide and yellow gills; its stem is 3 inches tall or less and its ring is often **very faint**. • *G. luteofolius* has a **scaly, reddish-brown** cap up to 3 inches wide and yellow gills; its stem is up to 4 inches tall and brownish with pale streaks, and it generally has a ring. • *G. sapineus* and *G. penetrans* (sometimes considered to be variations of a single species) are found with conifers; caps are orangish-yellow and less than 3 inches wide and stems are 3 inches or shorter. Caps are often scaly and the stems have **no ring**; they are sometimes called Rustgills because the gills develop **brown splotches** before turning completely rust-brown.

NOTES: Big Laughing Gym is a hallucinogenic mushroom that may induce experiences similar to those caused by LSD. Like that drug, Big Laughing Gym contains a controlled substance that is illegal. Other *Gymnopilus* may have similar effects; none should be eaten or used as a drug.

Big Laughing Gym

Dark-capped ring

G. luteus

ON DECAYING WOOD   SUMMER THROUGH FALL

Velvet-Footed Pax

Tapinella atrotomentosa

HABITAT: Velvet-Footed Pax is a saprobe, getting nutrients from decaying woody debris. It grows in woodlands and urban parks, usually **on rotting conifer stumps**, especially pine and hemlock. It also appears on the ground, emerging from decaying roots or stumps that may be buried. It can be common at times in older conifer woodlands.

DESCRIPTION: Caps are dry, dull to velvety, and yellow-brown to brown. This medium to large mushroom is 2 to 6 inches across. The cap margin is curved under at first; the cap becomes flat in age, often with a depressed center. The cap edge is often paler that the rest of the cap. Flesh inside the cap is thick and pale buff colored. When young, the stems are proportionally large in relation to the caps. The 2 to 5 inch stem is robust and **covered with a dark brown to black wooly coating**. It may be centrally attached, but is usually off-center. The stem has no ring. At times, several stems may be fused at the base, forming pairs or small clusters. The cream to yellowish gills are attached to the stem or running down the upper stem. They are closely spaced; near the stem, the gills are forked or may have cross veins. The gills are easily separated from the cap. Velvet-Footed Pax has a mild to slightly sour odor.

SPORE PRINT: Yellowish to tan.

SEASON: Summer through fall.

OTHER NAMES: *Paxillus atrotomentosus*, Velvet Rollrim, Velvet Paxillus.

COMPARE: The Velvet-Footed Pax is a distinctive species. It slightly resembles the **Common Rollrim** (*Paxillus involutus*), which **lacks the fuzzy, dark hairs on the stem**.

NOTES: Velvet-Footed Pax is considered inedible due to its poor taste; many sources list it as **toxic**. It is used to make dye to color yarns.

Funnel Caps

Infundibulicybe gibba, Clitocybe squamulosa

HABITAT: Funnel Caps are saprobes, getting their nutrients from decaying organic matter. They grow from the ground near trees and may grow singly but are more often found in groups or fairy rings (large circles).

DESCRIPTION: These light tan to pinkish mushrooms have distinctly funnel-shaped caps that are **smooth** and may be 3 to 4 inches across but are often smaller. They may be flat when young or have a wavy edge at maturity but always have a distinct **dimple** in the center. Caps may get paler with age but are always darker than the **crowded** gills, which are white or cream-colored and run down the stem. White mycelium (thread-like fungal roots) are often attached to the bottom. Stems have no ring. • The **Common Funnel Cap** (*I. gibba*) is usually found near **oaks**. It has a smooth, light-colored stem that grows to 3 inches tall and may be slightly swollen at the base. • *C. squamulosa* is found under **conifers** and has a slightly darker cap and stem that are cinnamon to golden brown. The cap may be faintly scaly (called squamulose), and the cream-colored gills are **less crowded** than those of *C. gibba*.

SPORE PRINT: White.

SEASON: Summer through late fall.

OTHER NAMES: Funnel Clitocybe. *I. gibba* was formerly listed as *C. gibba*.

COMPARE: Club-Footed Clitocybe (pg. 162) generally has a more distinctively **swollen base**. Mature caps may become wavy and turned up on the edges; they often have a **knob** rather than a dimple in the center. • The Sweater (pg. 152; also known as Ivory Funnel Cap) is smaller than the Funnel Caps listed above, with a pale, wavy cap less than 1⅝ inches wide; the top is often irregular and **mottled**. It grows in grassy areas and open woods. It is **toxic**.

NOTES: The Common Funnel Cap may have a sweet odor and is considered edible, but it is for experts only because there are too many inedible look-alikes. The Sweater is **toxic**; the other mushrooms discussed above are inedible.

Common Funnel Cap

C. squamulosa

ON DECAYING WOOD

SUMMER THROUGH LATE FALL

Decorated Mop

Tricholomopsis decora

HABITAT: Grows on dead or dying coniferous trees, logs and stumps; found singly or in scattered groupings. They are saprobes, mushrooms that get their nutrients from decaying organic matter.

DESCRIPTION: A medium-sized wood-loving species that is typically **deep golden yellow overall**; it may also be tan or yellowish-brown. Caps are generally 2 to 3 inches wide at maturity, occasionally larger; they are **covered with tiny brown scales** that are concentrated in the center. The surface is **moist**, particularly on young specimens, but it is not sticky or slimy. Stems are generally 2 to 3 inches tall but will be longer on larger specimens. They may be smooth or dotted with fine scales or hairs; there is no ring. Gills are **bright yellow or orangish**; they are closely spaced and attached to the stem.

SPORE PRINT: White.

SEASON: Summer through late fall.

OTHER NAMES: Formerly called *Clitocybe decora*. According to Michael Kuo (mushroomexpert.com), other members of the *Tricholomopsis* genus share many similarities and may form a "species cluster" with *Tricholomopsis decora*; these include *Tricholomopsis sulphureoides* (see below), *Tricholomopsis thompsoniana* and *Tricholomopsis bella*.

COMPARE: The cap of *Tricholomopsis sulphureoides* is **pale yellow** and often has a **mottled appearance**. It is finely hairy; the center often has a slight knob. Gills are **pale yellow** like the cap. The stem, which is frequently off-center, is slightly paler than the gills and often curved at the base. • **Man on Horseback** (*Tricholoma equestre* or *Tricholoma flavovirens*) is broadly related and about the same size, but it grows **from the ground** near conifers rather than from dead wood; it may be found into early winter. It has a yellow cap with dark fibers in the center, yellow gills and a **stocky, whitish** stem.

NOTES: Decorated Mop is inedible and may be **toxic** to some people. *Tricholomopsis sulphureoides* is considered inedible. Man on Horseback has been a popular edible in Europe for centuries, but recent reports of serious poisonings suggest it should not be eaten.

Decorated Mop

Tricholomopsis sulphureoides

Aborting Entoloma
Entoloma abortivum

HABITAT: Parasitic on species of *Armillaria* (pg. 112) and possibly saprobic as well on deciduous wood and woody debris. It may grow singly, scattered or in small clusters. Entoloma often appear in the same area for many years.

DESCRIPTION: Caps are **pale grayish-brown to dove-gray**; they are small and rounded when young, expanding and flattening out until they are up to 4 inches across, often with **wavy edges**. Stems are 2 to 4 inches tall and slightly paler than the cap; they are **moderately stout** and typically **wider at the base**, which is often covered with **whitish mycelium** (thread-like fungal roots). The stem has no ring. Gills are closely spaced and are **gray** at first, turning **pinkish** with age; they are attached to the stem or run down it slightly. The mushroom has a cucumber-like odor.

SPORE PRINT: Salmon-pink.

SEASON: Late summer through fall.

OTHER NAMES: Hunter's Heart, *Clitopilus abortivus*; the lumpy form (described below and shown at right) is sometimes called Earth Prune or Pig Snout.

COMPARE: Lead Poisoner (*E. sinuatum*; also called *E. lividum*) could be confused with Aborting Entoloma, but its cap may be up to **6 inches** across and is slippery when moist. • Twisted-Stalk Entoloma (*E. strictius* var. *isabellinus*) has a brownish cap that is **slightly pointed** in the center; its stem is **slender and gray** with a subtle **twisting pattern**. Both of these Entoloma are **toxic**.

NOTES: The cauliflower-like fungi in the photo at right are the result of the *Entoloma* parasitizing a species of *Armillaria* (pg. 112). This misshapen "aborted" form is edible but some find the taste a bit metallic and the texture off-putting. The gilled *Entoloma* is edible but not recommended for beginners due to the possibility of confusing it with similar **toxic** species. The aborted mushrooms are often more common than the gilled parasite.

Caps of the lower mushrooms here are colored by spores dropped from the mushrooms above

Lumpy, aborted form

NEAR OR BENEATH LIVE OR DYING TREES

SUMMER THROUGH FALL

Honey Mushrooms (several)

Armillaria mellea and others

HABITAT: Growing in **clusters** at the base of living, dead or dying deciduous trees; also grows from hidden roots in open areas near trees. They are parasitic mushrooms, with black root-like strands (rhizomorphs) that cause rot; the strands look like dark shoestrings and may be visible on tree trunks.

DESCRIPTION: Honey Mushrooms are a group of related species with variable characteristics. The classic example has **honey-colored** caps with **tiny dark scales or hairs** at the center, which is **darker** and often knob-like. The cap edge may be lighter in color. Young caps are small and rounded; they expand and flatten with age, growing to 4 inches wide or more. A **thin veil** covers the gills of young specimens. Stems are whitish at first, becoming darker and wooly near the base; they are 3 to 6 inches tall. Once the cap expands, a **prominent ring** is visible near the top of the stem; the ring may have a yellow edge. Stem bases may be fused together. Gills are white and fairly close, attached to the stem or running down it slightly; they may darken or turn spotty with age.

SPORE PRINT: White.

SEASON: Summer through fall; found during moist periods.

OTHER NAMES: Honey Cap, Bootlace Fungus, Podpinki, *Armillariella mellea*.

COMPARE: Caps of *Armillaria gallica* are more **brownish** and its stems often have a wider base; it fruits alone or in small clusters. Its veil is **cobwebby** and the ring is filmy or nearly absent. • *Armillaria solidipes* (also called *Armillaria ostoyae*) is common in the fall on both conifer and hardwood stumps and logs. Its caps are **tan to brown** and usually **prominently scaly**. The stem has a persistent ring. • *Desarmillaria tabescens* (previously listed as *Armillaria tabescens*) is **cinnamon-colored**; its stem has **no ring** and its entire cap has a scattering of fine scales. • Several unrelated yellowish or brownish mushrooms may appear similar to Honey Mushrooms. **Deadly Galerina** (pgs. 58–59; **toxic**) has a **rust-brown** spore print; its ring is **thin** or absent. • **Big Laughing Gym** (pg. 102; **toxic**) has an **orangish-brown** spore print. • **Sulfur Tuft** (pgs. 140–141; **toxic**) has a **purplish-brown** spore print; its ring is **thin** or absent.

NOTES: Honey Mushroom caps are edible but mildly bitter; stems are too tough to eat but may be used in broth. Be sure to cook *very* thoroughly, to break down heat-sensitive toxins. Always check spore prints to eliminate **toxic** lookalikes.

Armillaria mellea

Hairs on cap
(*Armillaria mellea*)

Armillaria gallica

Armillaria solidipes

Thin veil
(*Armillaria gallica*)

EARLY SPRING THROUGH LATE FALL

LBMs: Little Brown Mushrooms

Various species

HABITAT: Little Brown Mushrooms (LBMs for short) grow in all habitat types and may be found in woodlands and fields, on dead wood, or on debris.

DESCRIPTION: This catch-all term is used even by professional mycologists to refer to any of a number of common, **small to medium-sized brownish mushrooms** that are difficult to identify precisely—and are usually considered not worth the bother. *Naucoria, Panaeolina, Panaeolus, Pluteus, Psathyrella, Psilocybe* and *Tubaria* are a few of the genera included in this group. Some *Agaricus, Agrocybe, Collybia, Entoloma, Galerina, Gymnopus, Inocybe, Marasmiellus, Mycena* and *Pholiota* also fall into this category, although some species in these genera can be more readily identified and appear elsewhere in this book. Some LBMs are **toxic**; none should be eaten due to the difficulty in identification.

SPORE PRINT: If you want to try to place your LBMs into a genus, the first step is making a spore print. Here are some generalizations to get you started; colors here apply to most species within the genera listed, although there may be exceptions. *Agrocybe, Galerina, Inocybe, Naucoria, Pholiota*, many *Agaricus* and some *Pluteus* have brownish spores (ranging from ochre to pinkish-tan to chocolate brown). *Collybia* have whitish, buff or pinkish spores. *Gymnopus, Marasmiellus* and *Mycena* have white spores. *Entoloma* and some *Pluteus* have pinkish spores. *Panaeolus, Panaeolina*, many *Psathyrella* and some *Agaricus* have dark brown to blackish spores. *Psilocybe* and some *Agaricus* have purplish-brown spores. *Tubaria* have orangish-brown spores.

SEASON: Early spring through late fall.

OTHER NAMES: Little Boring Mushrooms.

COMPARE: Some tiny fragile species on pg. 72 are brownish. Also see **Common Agrocybe** in "Compare" section on pg. 86, and **"Fairy Ring Fungus"** on pg. 155.

NOTES: It's frustrating to find a large crop of mushrooms that you can't identify—but it's also very common, since field guides can't cover everything you're likely to find. You may enjoy studying them to hone your observation skills and to see how far you get in attempting to identify them. Since you should never eat any mushroom that you can't identify with **absolute certainty**, you should never eat unidentified or poorly identified LBMs.

Panaeolina foenisecii

Inocybe unicolor

Tubaria confragosa

Common Agrocybe
(*Agrocybe pediades*)

ON DECAYING WOOD   SPRING THROUGH FALL

Scaly Inky Cap
Coprinopsis variegata

HABITAT: Scaly Inky Caps are saprobes, getting nutrients from decaying woody debris. They grow in woodlands and urban parks, often on rotting deciduous logs; they also appear on wood chips, at the base of dead trees and on decaying roots or stumps that may be buried. In urban areas they often grow in a circular clump where trees have been removed.

DESCRIPTION: Appearances of Scaly Inky Caps may vary depending on habitat, but all share similar traits. Caps are tan, grayish-brown or grayish and covered with **large, flaky white to tan patches** that vary in size from group to group. The centers are often darker, providing additional contrast to the pale patches. Caps are 1 to 3 inches wide and up to 3 inches tall; they are hollow and egg-shaped when young, becoming bell-shaped. As the specimens mature, the edges flare out, rolling upward at the edges; the caps become **darker, broad and fairly flat**. Stems are whitish and 2 to 4 inches tall, with a felt-like surface; they are hollow inside. Ring remnants may be present on the stem but are often absent. Gills are crowded; they are whitish on young specimens, becoming grayish before turning black and **beginning to dissolve** into a gooey substance. Unlike some other Inky Caps (pgs. 28–29), the gills **may not dissolve completely**.

SPORE PRINT: Blackish.

SEASON: Spring through fall.

OTHER NAMES: *Coprinus quadrifidus.*

COMPARE: Mica Caps (pg. 94) are similar, but caps of young, fresh specimens are covered with **small glistening granules** rather than patches; the surface is **finely ribbed.** • Shaggy Mane (pg. 28) is similar, but it is **whitish**; its cap is elongated and covered with **shaggy scales**.

NOTES: Generally regarded as edible, although the flavor is disagreeable in some collections; they deteriorate quickly after picking and must be cooked promptly. They cause digestive upset in some people; like Alcohol Inky (pg. 29), Scaly Inky Caps cause illness if consumed within several days of drinking alcohol (either before or after the mushrooms are eaten).

Brownish Cortinarius (several)

Cortinarius spp.

HABITAT: *Cortinarius* species are mycorrhizal, growing from the soil in a symbiotic relationship with living trees. The species discussed on this page are found near deciduous trees.

DESCRIPTION: Cortinarius have a **cobwebby veil** (called a cortina; pg. 13) covering the gills of young specimens. The veil disintegrates with age, sometimes leaving a ring remnant on the stem. Spores are brownish; they typically darken the mature gills and may also coat the ring remnant, turning it brown. Caps are conical at first, becoming wider and fairly flat, often with a central hump. Stems often have a swollen, club-shaped base. Our area has numerous Cortinarius with brownish attributes; those listed here are medium to large, with mature caps that are typically 4 to 5 inches wide. • Banded Cort (*C. armillatus*) favors birch trees; it has a yellow-brown to brick-colored cap and tan gills. Its pale stem is up to 6 inches tall, with several **orangish-red bands** that may be solid or broken. • *C. trivialis* is similar to Banded Cort, but its cap is **covered with slime**; the lower half of the stem is partially covered with **shaggy brownish scales**. Gills of young specimens are gray to lilac-colored, turning brownish with age. It is sometimes considered a variation of *C. collinitus*, but the stalk of *C. collinitus* is **violet** and lacks the brownish bands. • *C. corrugatus* has a **wrinkled**, brownish-orange cap. Gills are lilac-colored, whitish or pale gray on young specimens, turning brownish with age; the stem is yellowish and up to 4¼ inches tall.

SPORE PRINT: Rust-brown.

SEASON: Summer through fall.

OTHER NAMES: Some sources refer to *Cortinarius* species as Webcaps.

COMPARE: Also see **Orange to Reddish Cortinarius** on pg. 126.

NOTES: None of the species above should be eaten; some Cortinarius are **toxic**.

Banded Cort

C. corrugatus

C. trivialis

FROM THE SOIL NEAR LIVE TREES

SUMMER THROUGH LATE FALL

Brownish to Blackish Milk Caps (several)

Lactarius spp.

HABITAT: Milk Caps are mycorrhizal, growing from the soil in a symbiotic relationship with living trees.

DESCRIPTION: Milk Caps (*Lactarius* spp.) are a large family of brittle-fleshed, gilled mushrooms that produce **milky latex when cut**. Caps of young specimens are rounded with a sunken center; most become vase-like with age. Caps of the species discussed here are typically 1 to 4½ inches across; stems are typically 2 to 4 inches tall, and the stem bases are **powdery**. The stems have no rings. Gills are attached to the stem or running slightly down it. • Red-Hot Milky (*L. rufus*) has a **rough**, dry **reddish-brown** cap; the stem is paler than the cap, turning darker. Gills are closely spaced and **tan**, turning darker or blotchy. Its latex is white, with a **very bitter, hot taste**, giving it the common name. It is found near conifers, in mossy bogs and also in sandy areas. • Sometimes called the **Coconut Milk Cap** because of its **coconut-like odor**, *L. hibbardiae* is a fall mushroom of conifer and mixed woods. The cap is **plush and gray with a brownish coloration** under the gray coating. Gills are closely spaced and white, becoming yellowish in age. The latex is white and peppery-tasting. • *L. lignyotus* is sometimes called Chocolate Milky because its cap and stem are typically **dark brown** and **velvety**, although they range from smoky tan to nearly black and the stem may be paler than the cap. The cap often has a small pointed knob in the center. Gills are whitish and **moderately close**. Its latex is white and mildly bitter; it turns pinkish as it dries and may stain the gills. This species is found near conifers; it also grows on well-decayed wood and in mossy areas.

SPORE PRINT: Creamy white to pale yellow; *L. lignyotus* spores may also be orangish, while those of *L. rufus* may have a salmon-pink hue.

SEASON: Summer through late fall; Red-Hot Milky may also appear in late spring.

OTHER NAMES: Although usually referred to as Chocolate Milky, *L. lignyotus* is sometimes called Smoky Milky; however, most sources reserve that common name for *L. fumosus*.

COMPARE: Also see Orangish Milk Caps on pg. 128.

NOTES: The Milk Caps discussed here are inedible; Red-Hot Milky is **toxic**.

Red-Hot Milky

Coconut Milk Cap

L. lignyotus

FROM DECAYING GROUND DEBRIS

SPRING THROUGH FALL

Orange to Red Wax Caps (several)

Hygrocybe spp.

HABITAT: Most Wax Caps are saprobes, but some may be parasitic. Commonly found in moss, they also occur in grassy areas and mixed woodlands.

DESCRIPTION: Several *Hygrocybe* with orangish to red attributes are found in our area; exact identification is often a matter for experts. All are small to medium in size. Caps of young specimens are conical or rounded, flattening with maturity; cap colors also fade with age. Caps are generally **waxy or slimy** when wet. Stems have no rings. • *H. cantharellus* has a rounded cap **less than 1 inch wide** and a thin, long orange stem. The yellow gills are fairly widely spaced and **run noticeably down the stem**. • Fresh, young specimens of *H. conica* have caps up to 2¾ inches wide that are often **sharply conical**; edges are slightly ribbed. Stems are yellowish or orangish and **twisted at the base**; all parts turn **blackish** when handled or with age. • *H. miniata* has rounded caps up to 1½ inches wide; they are bright reddish-orange to scarlet at first, fading to orange or yellowish. Gills are yellow and **attached to the stem** or run slightly down it. • *H. punicea* has a shiny, **dark red** cap up to **4 inches** wide and paler gills; its stem is up to **5 inches** tall and yellowish with a reddish base and **ribbed texture**. • *H. coccinea* is **scarlet-red overall** and typically less than 2¼ inches wide and tall. • **Candy Apple Wax Cap** (*H. cuspidata*) has a conical cap that is **bright red** and **slimy**. The stem is colored like the cap or paler, and is whitish at the base. Candy Apple Wax Cap is often found in groups along roads and in other very **disturbed areas**.

SPORE PRINT: White.

SEASON: Spring through fall.

OTHER NAMES: Both *H. punicea* and *H. coccinea* may be listed as Scarlet Waxy Cap; *H. coccinea* and *H. conica* are often called Witches' Hat.

COMPARE: Orange Mycena (*Mycena leaiana*) is orangish overall. Its cap is up to 1½ inches wide and the stem is up to 3 inches tall. Gills are orange with **reddish edges**. It grows in **clusters** on decaying wood. When handled, the mushrooms often **stain hands orange**.

NOTES: Some *Hygrocybe* are edible, while others are toxic; none should be eaten due to difficulties with identification. Orange Mycena are considered inedible.

H. cantharellus

H. conica

H. miniata

ON DECAYING WOOD

SPRING THROUGH LATE FALL

Fuzzy Foot

Xeromphalina campanella, Xeromphalina kauffmanii

HABITAT: Fuzzy Foot mushrooms typically grow gregariously in dense clusters on dead wood, but may be more scattered at times; they may also fruit occasionally on living wood. *X. campanella* grows on coniferous wood, and *X. kauffmanii* grows on deciduous wood such as wild cherries; other than the habitat differences they are impossible to tell apart with the naked eye.

DESCRIPTION: Although small, Fuzzy Foot are easy to spot. Caps are orange, yellowish or yellowish-brown and ¼ to 1 inch wide; they are **broadly convex** to nearly flat. The center is **darker and sunken**; edges have subtle ribbing and are thin enough to be somewhat translucent. Stems are slender and up to 2 inches long; they are yellow at the top, turning reddish-brown and **velvety** below. **Orange tufts** of stiff hairs called *hyphae* grow around the base. Stems have no ring. Gills are pale yellow to orangish and widely spaced; they run down the stem a fair amount. There are numerous **cross-veins** between the gills (visible with a hand lens).

SPORE PRINT: White to light buff.

SEASON: Spring through late fall; may appear into winter in warmer areas.

OTHER NAMES: Cross-Veined Troop Mushroom, *Omphalia campanella*.

COMPARE: *X. tenuipes* has an **orangish-brown** cap up to 1¾ **inches** wide; its stem is **brownish and velvety overall**. It grows from early spring through midsummer on dead deciduous wood. • Orange Mycena (*Mycena leaiana*) is orangish overall and slightly larger. When handled, the mushrooms often **stain hands orange**. • Two small *Entoloma* species appear similar, but they have **conical caps** with a **sharp, pointed center** that looks like a small horn; spores are **salmon-pink**. **Yellow Unicorn Entoloma** (*E. murraii*) is bright yellow to yellowish-orange overall; it grows in swampy areas and damp woods. **Salmon Unicorn Entoloma** (*E. quadratum*, also listed as *E. salmoneum*; photo on pg. 73) is **salmon-colored** overall; it grows from ground debris in deciduous forests and is also found in damp conifer forests, frequently growing from rotting logs. • Also see **Orange to Red Wax Caps** on pg. 122.

NOTES: All mushrooms discussed above are regarded as inedible.

Cross-veins

Hyphae

Orange to Reddish Cortinarius (several)

Cortinarius spp.

FROM THE SOIL NEAR LIVE TREES

SUMMER THROUGH FALL

HABITAT: *Cortinarius* species are mycorrhizal, growing from the soil in a symbiotic relationship with living trees. The species discussed on this page are found in mixed-wood forests.

DESCRIPTION: Cortinarius have a **cobwebby veil** (called a cortina; pg. 13) covering the gills of young specimens. The veil disintegrates with age, sometimes leaving a ring remnant on the stem. Spores are brownish; they typically darken the mature gills and may also coat the ring remnant, turning it brown. Caps are conical at first, becoming wider and fairly flat, often with a central hump. Our area has several *Cortinarius* species with orange to reddish attributes; scientific names differ depending on the source (see Notes, below). Stems of the species listed here lack the bulbous base found on many Cortinarius. • **Red-Gilled Cort** (*C. semisanguineus*) has a **yellowish-brown cap** up to 2½ inches wide, **yellowish-brown stem** and **red gills**; it prefers conifers. • Fresh, young specimens of **Orange Webcap** (*C. mucosus*) have **slimy**, brownish-orange caps that fade to yellowish with age; they are up to **4 inches** wide. The stem is **white and silky**, and may have a darker ring zone. Gills of young specimens are **whitish to cream-colored** and covered with a **slimy veil**; gills of mature specimens become cinnamon-colored as the spores mature. Orange Webcaps are found in association with **conifers and broadleaf trees**. • **Dappled Cort** (*C. bolaris*) has **yellowish gills** and a cap up to 3 inches wide; both cap and stem are pale and **mottled with numerous brick-red scales**.

SPORE PRINT: Rust-brown or cinnamon-colored.

SEASON: Summer through fall.

OTHER NAMES: Cortinarius are sometimes called Webcaps. Some sources list these reddish species as *Dermocybe* rather than *Cortinarius*.

COMPARE: Also see **Brownish Cortinarius** on pg. 118.

NOTES: Many scientific names used for these Cortinarius refer to European species; some experts say these names should not be used for North American specimens, which have subtle differences. As experts attempt to categorize Cortinarius, new names are used, but not all experts agree on them. None of the species above should be eaten; some Cortinarius are **toxic**.

Red-Gilled Cort

Orange Webcap

Dappled Cort

Orangish Milk Caps (several)
Lactarius and *Lactifluus* spp.

HABITAT: Milk Caps (*Lactarius* and *Lactifluus* spp.) are mycorrhizal, growing from soil, humus, and moss in a symbiotic relationship with living trees.

DESCRIPTION: Milk Caps produce **milky latex when cut**. Caps of young specimens are rounded with a sunken center; some become vase-like with age. Stems have no rings. Gills are attached to the stem or run slightly down it. • *Lactarius thyinos* is orangish **overall**, and less than 3½ inches wide and tall. The cap has **concentric bands** that alternate from bright to pale orange. Its stocky stem may be smooth or have shallow pockmarks; it is sticky on young specimens. Latex is **orange**. Gills are **moderately closely spaced** and **bruise brownish**, as does the stem. Found near **conifers**, often in swampy areas. • **Orange Milkcap** (*Lactarius croceus*) has a **fruity odor**. Smooth **yellowish-orange** caps are 2 to 4 inches wide, often with faint rings; caps may be **slimy** when wet. Pale stems are 1 to 3 inches tall. Gills are **cream-colored** and **closely spaced**. The bitter latex is **sparse** and whitish, drying to **yellowish-orange**. Found in deciduous and mixed woods, often near oaks. • **Tawny Milkcap** (*Lactifluus volemus*) has a **fishy odor**. Caps are orangish-brown and up to **5½ inches** wide. Pale stems are up to 4 inches tall and may be **faintly ribbed**. Gills are **whitish** and **closely spaced**. It produces **copious** white latex that stains all parts of the mushroom **brown**. Found near deciduous and coniferous trees. • *Lactifluus hygrophoroides* has orangish-brown caps 2 to 3 inches wide and pale stems are up to 2 inches tall; both are dry and may be velvety. Gills are **whitish** and **widely spaced**; its white latex is abundant. Found near conifers and deciduous trees, especially oaks.

SPORE PRINT: Whitish, creamy or pale yellowish.

SEASON: Summer through fall.

OTHER NAMES: Tawny Milkcap is also called Voluminous-Latex Milky or Bradley. The species listed as *Lactifluus* above were formerly included in the *Lactarius* genus; some references still list them that way.

COMPARE: Corrugated Milky Caps (*Lactifluus corrugis*) have **reddish-brown** caps that are **wrinkled**, especially near the margins. Gills are usually darker. • Also see **Brownish to Blackish Milk Caps** (pg. 120) and **Deceptive Milky** (pg. 78).

NOTES: *Lactifluus hygrophoroides,* and Tawny and Corrugated Milky Caps, are edible. *Lactarius thyinos* is edible but less favored. Orange Milkcap is inedible.

Lactarius thyinos

Orange Milkcap

Tawny Milkcap

Pumpkin Cap
Leratiomyces squamosus

HABITAT: The Pumpkin Cap is a saprobe, getting nutrients from decaying woody debris. It grows in woodlands, often along streams where sand or dirt has partially covered fallen limbs. It is often seen emerging from the soil at the base of a fallen log. This growth habit makes it appear terrestrial but **its food source is wood**. It usually fruits gregariously in broadleaf forests or in mixed woods with hemlock.

DESCRIPTION: This striking mushroom stands out due to its color and its tall stature. Caps are pumpkin to brownish-orange or reddish-orange. They are 1 to 3 inches across and are convex to bell-shaped when young, often with hanging veil remnants around the edge. At maturity they may become flat with an uplifted margin. **Whitish scales are scattered over the cap** and may be very abundant near the margin. The cap flesh is white. Gills are moderately close and attached to the stem. They are pale grayish to purplish; edges become whitish at maturity. Stems are thin and 2 to 5 inches in length. They are colored like a paler version of the cap, sometimes appearing almost white. A **prominent, flaring ring** is generally present near the top of the stem; it is white at first, becoming purplish-brown on top as the spores are released from the gills. The surface of the ring may be striated. Above the ring the stem is whitish and smooth to fuzzy. Below the ring the color is obscured by a **dense covering of whitish scales**.

SPORE PRINT: Dark purplish.

SEASON: Late summer through early fall.

OTHER NAMES: *Psilocybe thrausta, Stropharia thrausta, Stropharia squamosa* var. *thrausta*.

COMPARE: Brick Tops (pg. 140) fruit in a **clustered** manner and are usually found **directly on wood**. The caps are pale on the margins and the ring, if present, is not prominent. Stems are only **slightly scaly**.

NOTES: Although its odor and taste are not distinctive, Pumpkin Cap is **toxic**. Considered to be rare in many areas, it is not uncommon in western New York, western Pennsylvania and eastern Ohio.

Velvet Foot
Flammulina velutipes

ON OR NEAR LIVE OR DEAD TREES

FALL THROUGH SPRING

HABITAT: This saprobe grows from the decaying wood of broadleaf trees, especially elm. It is frequently found on the side of a standing dead tree, often quite high up and out of reach, but it also fruits on stumps and other woody debris that may be buried. It typically grows in clusters but may be found singly.

DESCRIPTION: These medium-sized mushrooms are a fairly common sight in late fall and again in early spring, when other edible mushrooms are scarce. The cap is typically orangish-brown to yellowish-brown but may be honey-colored or tan, particularly on older specimens; the edges are lighter in color. Caps are rounded on young specimens, becoming flatter and wider with age; mature caps are up to 2¾ inches across and may be wavy or distorted, particularly when crowded by neighboring specimens. The surface is **moist and slimy** during wet weather; when the caps dry, they are often glossy. Stems are up to 3 inches tall and have a **velvety texture**; they are pale on young specimens, darkening from the base up until they are **dark brown or blackish** overall except at the very top. The stem has **no ring**. Gills are white to creamy yellow, eventually developing subtle brownish bruises; they are fairly closely spaced and attached to the stem.

SPORE PRINT: White.

SEASON: Fall through spring; may occasionally appear during summer cold spells.

OTHER NAMES: Winter Mushroom, Velvet Shank, *Collybia velutipes*.

COMPARE: Deadly Galerina (pgs. 58–59) can appear very similar and may grow in the same locations, but it has **rust-brown** spores and a **thin ring** on the stem; as its name suggests, it is **deadly**. • Orange Mycena (*Mycena leaiana*; inedible) appears somewhat similar to Velvet Foot and has white spores, but Orange Mycena is smaller; it is **orange overall** with **reddish gill edges**, and its stems are **sticky rather than velvety**.

NOTES: Velvet Foot caps are edible, although they are sticky and trap dirt; stems are tough and are generally not eaten. Make a spore print of every specimen assumed to be a Velvet Foot, and check the stem for a ring, to eliminate **toxic** Deadly Galerina. Velvet Foot is the same species as cultivated Enoki mushrooms; however, Enoki are grown in conditions that cause them to look completely different than wild Velvet Foot.

Dark stems

FROM DECAYING GROUND DEBRIS

SPRING THROUGH FALL

Wine Caps

Stropharia rugosoannulata

HABITAT: Wine Caps grow scattered or in small groups on wood chips, mulch, straw and sawdust; also found in gardens, lawns and cultivated areas. They are saprobes, getting nutrients from decaying organic matter that is often underground.

DESCRIPTION: Although the cap of this mushroom may be as wide as 8 inches, it is generally smaller. Young specimens have pillowy caps with a **thick white partial veil** underneath; the bottom of the veil has an **irregular edge**, somewhat resembling a gear or cogwheel. The cap expands with age, becoming broadly convex. It is generally 2 to 5½ inches wide and is **burgundy to reddish-brown**, with a dry, smooth surface; older specimens may fade to tan and can develop cracks, especially in dry conditions. The veil remnants form a persistent ring on the upper stem; the ring retains the cogwheel-shaped edges and the upper side of the ring is **finely ribbed**. Stems are typically 4 to 6 inches tall and white or cream-colored; they are moderately stout and typically wider at the base, which often is surrounded by whitish mycelium (thread-like fungal roots) that may be visible in the growing substrate. Gills are closely spaced and attached to the stem; they are white at first, turning **grayish-lilac to purplish-black**.

SPORE PRINT: Purplish-brown to blackish.

SEASON: Spring through fall; less common during summer but still present.

OTHER NAMES: Wine-Cap Stropharia, Garden Giant, King Stropharia.

COMPARE: Some *Russula* species (pg. 138; inedible or **toxic**) have reddish caps; stems have **no ring** and the spores are **creamy yellowish to pale orangish-yellow**. Russulas grow near trees. • Brick Tops (pg. 140; edible) have brick-red caps; stems have a **filmy ring remnant or no ring**. • Some **toxic** *Amanita* species (pgs. 62–66) have reddish caps and rings on the stem, but they have **white spores** and a **cup** around the stem base; the cup may be obvious but is sometimes partially or completely buried.

NOTES: Wine Caps are delicious; make a spore print of each specimen to avoid **toxic** look-alikes. Wine Caps are available in grow-it-yourself kits; they are easy to grow in outdoor gardens on wood chips.

Gills and ring

ON DECAYING WOOD

LATE SPRING THROUGH FALL

Bleeding Mycena
Mycena haematopus

HABITAT: The Bleeding Mycena is a wood rotter. It fruits from **well-decayed, bark free logs and stumps** of broadleaf trees. Often the wood is covered in moss. Bleeding Mycena fruits in small clusters or scattered individual specimens. It is common throughout the Northeast.

DESCRIPTION: This is a rather fragile species with thin, pale flesh. Caps are convex to conical or broadly bell-shaped. They are ½ to 2 inches across; the cap edge is scalloped or ragged, particularly on young specimens, and usually paler than the rest of the cap. Striations or slight grooves are often visible on the cap margin. Caps are red-wine–colored to dark brownish-red, fading to pale buff; the center is often darker than the cap edges. The cap surface is bald and dry, appearing slightly dusty-whitish on young specimens. In age the cap becomes moist and slightly tacky. The **thin**, hollow stems are up to 3 inches tall and equal in width from top to bottom. They are brownish-red to reddish-purple, and are bald or lightly adorned with pale reddish hairs. Like the caps, the stems fade with age, especially upon drying. There is no ring. Gills are closely spaced and attached to the stem; they are whitish, darkening with age. Caps and stems typically **ooze purplish-red liquid** when cut; this is particularly evident at the base of the stem. The odor is mild and the taste mild or slightly bitter.

SPORE PRINT: White.

SEASON: Late spring through fall; most common in June and September.

OTHER NAMES: Blood Foot Mushroom, Bleeding Fairy Helmet.

COMPARE: Bleeding Bonnet (*M. sanguinolenta*) is very similar. It occurs **on humus and litter** and has **dark red gill edges**.

NOTES: No species of *Mycena* is considered edible. The common and scientific names of this attractive little mushroom refer to the blood-like liquid it oozes when damaged or cut. This species is often attacked by *Spinellus fusiger*, a thread-like parasitic mold.

"Bleeding"

Reddish Russulas (several)
Russula spp.

HABITAT: Growing from the ground, singly or in small groups, in woods or lawns near living broadleaf or conifer trees; they grow in a mycorrhizal association with trees.

DESCRIPTION: All Russulas, and especially red ones, are notoriously difficult to identify. Like other Russula species, most reddish Russulas have **brittle gills, caps flesh and stems**. The stems have **no rings** and will break like chalk. Caps on young specimens are rounded, spreading and flattening out with age then turning upward to form a shallow, wide-rimmed bowl; some or much of **the skin can be peeled off the cap**. Gills of species discussed here are closely spaced and white to cream-colored; they are attached to the stem or running slightly down it. • Usually found with oaks, **Mary's Russula** (*R. mariae*) has a **velvety purplish** cap, often with a **whitish bloom**; it is up to 3½ inches wide. The cap can be greenish-buff when covered by leaves. Its stem is up to 3¼ inches tall and whitish, with a purplish blush in areas. • The **Sickener** (*R. emetica*) has a **slimy reddish** cap up to 3 inches across. The stem is up to 4 inches tall and white to pale yellow. The Sickener typically grows in **mossy areas** such as bogs (particularly sphagnum) in coniferous or mixed-wood forests. • **Peck's Russula** (*R. peckii*) has a rosy to deep red cap that may be nearly **4 inches** across but is usually smaller. The stem is up to 4 inches tall and is white, often with a pinkish blush. The most distinctive characteristic is its gills, which have **saw-tooth edges** (referred to as serrate).

SPORE PRINT: Spores of the Russulas discussed here are white, cream-colored or pale yellow.

SEASON: Midsummer through mid-fall.

OTHER NAMES: Russulas are often referred to as Brittle Gills. *R. emetica* is also called the Vomiting Russula.

COMPARE: In the Northeast, any mushroom with a ring is something other than a Russula. The closely related milk mushrooms in the genus *Lactarius* can resemble Russulas but few of them are red and they **exude latex** when cut.

NOTES: Many Russulas have an acrid taste. The Sickener, as might be guessed from its name, is **toxic**, causing intestinal problems. Mary's Russula is edible. Peck's Russula is reported as inedible. The authors have not tried eating it.

Mary's Russula

The Sickener

Peck's Russula

Peck's Russula
serrate gills

ON DECAYING WOOD

LATE SUMMER THROUGH LATE FALL

Brick Tops
Hypholoma lateritium

HABITAT: Grows in clusters **on decaying deciduous logs and stumps**. They often appear on the same log or stump in successive years. They are saprobes, getting nutrients from decaying organic matter.

DESCRIPTION: These medium-sized mushrooms are fairly easy to spot in the fall because they are colorful and grow in tight clusters. Caps are chubby and rounded when young, with a rolled-under margin and a **thin, webby partial veil** over the gills. The caps flatten with age, becoming convex; they are up to 4 inches wide and **brick-red with pale edges**. The surface is smooth but may develop cracks with age. The veil often leaves a thin, filmy remnant near the top of the stem, but this remnant may not be present or noticeable; there is no other ring. The stem is up to 4 inches tall and up to ⅝ inch thick; it is often curved or bent as it twists its way out of the cluster. The top half of the stem is whitish or pale yellow, and there may be an irregular brownish stain near the cap where falling spores have been caught by the veil remnant. The base of the stem is **reddish-brown** and often mottled. Gills are dull **whitish** on young specimens, becoming **purplish-brown**; they are closely spaced and attached to the stem.

SPORE PRINT: Purplish-brown.

SEASON: Late summer through late fall.

OTHER NAMES: Brick Caps, *H. sublateritium*, *Naematoloma sublateritium*.

COMPARE: Several wood-inhabiting species with some similarities in appearance are found in our area. **Sulfur Tuft** (*H. fasciculare*) has **yellowish** caps; its stem is tawny and up to 4¾ inches tall, and its gills are **yellowish**, becoming **greenish** to olive-brown. Sulfur Tuft is extremely bitter and considered **toxic**. • The edible *H. capnoides* has an **orangish-brown** to tan cap and **gray** gills that turn reddish-brown; it grows on conifer wood. • Wine Caps (pg. 134; edible) prefer wood chips. They have burgundy caps and a **cogwheel-edged ring**. • The Pumpkin Cap (pg. 130) has a longer stem with a **prominent ring**. It is **toxic**.

NOTES: Young Brick Tops are edible and eagerly collected by some foragers, who note a nutty taste; others find them bitter. Be certain that the gills are whitish rather than yellow or greenish, to avoid the **toxic** Sulfur Tuft.

Brick Tops

Sulfur Tuft

H. capnoides

FROM THE SOIL NEAR LIVE TREES

MIDSUMMER THROUGH FALL

Purple-Gilled Laccaria

Laccaria ochropurpurea

HABITAT: Growing from the ground, scattered or in groups, in mixed forests, particularly under oak, beech and white pine. They are mycorrhizal, growing in a symbiotic relationship with living trees.

DESCRIPTION: When fresh, young and moist, this mushroom has a lilac to light brownish-purple cap; as it matures, its color fades to gray or white. Caps may be smooth or finely scaly. On very young specimens, caps are small and rounded, often perched atop a grossly **swollen, bulbous** stem. The cap enlarges and flattens out with age; it may be up to **6 inches** wide at maturity, often with wavy edges and a depressed center. Gills are **purple, thick and moderately spaced**, with a waxy texture. They are attached to the stem and may run down the stem for a short distance. Stems are **stocky**, up to **7 inches** tall and often somewhat twisted or curved. They are colored like the cap or slightly darker; they typically have a dry, fibrous texture and coarse hairs or scales on the surface. There is no ring. The base is often slightly swollen and covered with soft lilac-colored mycelium (thread-like fungal roots; it may be necessary to dig around the base to see the swelling and mycelium).

SPORE PRINT: White or pale lilac.

SEASON: Midsummer through fall.

OTHER NAMES: None.

COMPARE: Amethyst Laccaria (*L. amethystina*; also called Purple Laccaria and Amethyst Deceiver) is much smaller than Purple-Gilled Laccaria and is **violet overall** when young; with age the cap and stem fade to buff, gray or brownish. Caps are less than **1½ inches** wide; stems are **slender** and 1 to 4 inches tall. • Blewits (pg. 144) are purplish when young but have **closely spaced gills** and a **pinkish** spore print. • Purplish Cortinarius (pg. 146; **toxic**) have a **cobwebby veil** over the gills of young specimens and **rust-brown** spores. • Sandy Laccaria (pg. 88) has purple gills, but its cap is less than 3 inches wide; it grows in **sandy areas**. • Common Laccaria (pg. 88) is typically tan to orangish; its gills are **pinkish to tan** and its stems are **slender**.

NOTES: Caps of Purple-Gilled Laccaria and Amethyst Laccaria are edible, with a mild flavor; the stems are tough and fibrous and are generally not eaten.

Purple-Gilled Laccaria

Amethyst Laccaria

Blewit

Lepista nuda

HABITAT: Blewits are saprobes, getting nutrients from decaying organic matter including leaf litter, compost, grass clippings and wood mulch. Found under brambles and hedgerows and in deciduous and coniferous forests. They grow singly or in small groups and may grow in a ring.

DESCRIPTION: Young Blewits are **lavender, violet-blue or purplish** overall; stems are paler. Mature specimens are **tan to brownish**, often with slight mottling; gills may retain some purplish coloration, particularly around the cap edge. Gills are closely spaced and attached to the stem; they may be slightly notched at the stem, appearing to curve upwards. Caps are 1½ to 6 inches wide with a smooth surface. Caps of young Blewits are softly rounded with slightly rolled-under edges, but as the mushrooms age the caps flare out and may develop wavy edges and irregular tops; some have a rounded point in the center. Stems are generally 1 to 3 inches tall and **stocky** with a rough texture; there is no ring. The base is often swollen or bulbous and may have a network of **fine purplish mycelium** (thread-like fungal roots). Blewits have a **sweet**, floral fragrance.

SPORE PRINT: Pale pink to pinkish-buff.

SEASON: Late summer through late fall.

OTHER NAMES: Wood Blewit, *Clitocybe nuda, Tricholoma nudum*.

COMPARE: Other purplish mushrooms may be encountered; some, such as *Cortinarius* spp. (pg. 146), are **toxic**. Young Cortinarius have a **cobwebby veil** over the gills, and mature Cortinarius have **rust-brown spores**. • Some *Laccaria* (pg. 142; edible) are purplish but the gills are **moderately to widely spaced** and spores are **white to lilac**. • Lilac Bonnet (*Mycena pura*; edible) is smaller, with a cap less than 2 inches wide and a **thin, hollow stem**; it has a **radish-like** odor and **white** spore print. It may turn tan with age.

NOTES: Blewits are edible but not recommended for amateurs due to similarities to **toxic** Cortinarius species. Always look for any trace of a cobwebby veil (present on Cortinarius but not Blewits) and make a spore print of every mushroom assumed to be a Blewit before eating it. Blewits should never be eaten raw.

Maturing Blewits

Young Blewit

Lilac Bonnet

FROM THE SOIL NEAR LIVE TREES

LATE SUMMER THROUGH LATE FALL

Purplish Cortinarius (several)

Cortinarius spp.

HABITAT: Species in the genus *Cortinarius* are mycorrhizal with a variety of trees. They can be found in soil, moss and humus but always near trees.

DESCRIPTION: Cortinarius have a **cobwebby veil** (called a cortina; see photo on facing page) covering the gills of young specimens. The veil disintegrates with age, sometimes leaving strands or a ring remnant on the stem. Gills of the species listed here are closely spaced except for Violet Cort, whose gills are somewhat widely spaced. Spores are brownish; they typically darken the mature gills and may also coat the ring remnant on the stem, turning it brown. Caps are conical at first, becoming wider and fairly flat. Stems of some species have a swollen base. Our area has numerous *Cortinarius* species with purplish attributes. • *C. iodes* has a purplish cap less than 2 inches wide that often develops **yellowish spots** with age; the cylindrical stem is pale, and both cap and stem are **slimy**. It grows near deciduous trees, favoring oak. • **Violet Cort** (*C. violaceus*) is **dark violet overall** when young, turning brownish with age; the cap is dry, covered with **fine whitish tufts** and is up to 5 inches across. The stem is slightly club-like. It is found near conifers and deciduous trees. • Found around conifers, *C. traganus* has a lavender to violet cap up to 5 inches wide that may be **cracked or patchy in the center**; the stem color matches the cap. The flesh has orange tinges. It has a pungent odor that is sometimes described as **goat-like**. • *C. camphoratus* is similar to *C. traganus* and is found in similar habitat. Its odor is often compared to that of **mothballs**. • *C. azureus* is **pale purple overall** with a cap less than 3 inches wide; it grows in association with **beech trees**.

SPORE PRINT: Rust-brown or cinnamon-colored.

SEASON: Most common from late summer through late fall.

OTHER NAMES: *C. camphoratus* is listed in some references as Goatcheese Webcap. *Cortinarius* species in general are called Webcaps or Corts.

COMPARE: Blewits (pg. 144) are purplish but **lack the cobwebby veil**; their spore print is **pale pink to pinkish-buff**. Blewits are the species most commonly confused with purplish *Cortinarius*. Blewits are edible but not recommended for amateurs due to the possibility of misidentification. • Some *Laccaria* (pg. 142; edible) are purplish but the gills are **widely spaced** and spores are **white**.

NOTES: Many *Cortinarius* are **toxic**; all should be considered inedible.

C. iodes

Cortina

Violet Cort

FROM THE SOIL NEAR LIVE TREES

LATE SPRING THROUGH FALL

Green-Capped Russulas (several)

Russula spp.

HABITAT: Growing from the ground, singly or in small groups, under deciduous trees or conifers. Russulas are mycorrhizal, growing from the soil in a symbiotic relationship with living trees.

DESCRIPTION: Russulas have **sturdy stems that lack rings**. Caps on young specimens are pillowy, spreading and flattening out with age, then turning upward to form a shallow, wide-rimmed bowl; some or much of **the skin can be peeled off the cap**. Gills are white to cream-colored and attached to the stem; gills of the species discussed here are closely spaced. The flesh is white and **brittle**. • Two species are referred to as **Quilted Green Russula**. *R. 'virescens'* is a name in common usage, although this is a European species that does not grow in North America. The species found here has a greenish-yellow cap up to **6 inches across** that is dotted with **small patches**; the stem is up to 3½ inches tall. The cap of *R. parvovirescens* is less than 3 inches across; it is **bluish-green** and the patches are up to ¼ inch wide. • **Tacky Russula** (*R. aeruginea*) has a yellowish-green cap that is less than 3 inches across; the cap is **smooth and uniformly** colored, lacking the patches.

SPORE PRINT: *R. parvovirescens* have whitish spores; those of *R. aeruginea* are creamy, **pale yellow or yellowish-orange**.

SEASON: Primarily summer through fall; may also be found in late spring.

OTHER NAMES: Mossy Green Russula, Green-Cracking Russula.

COMPARE: *R. crustosa* is similar to *R. parvovirescens* in stature and cap surface, but its cap color is variable; it is often **buff-colored** but may be pinkish, purplish, yellowish-brown, reddish-brown or even blue-green. • *R. cyanoxantha* and *R. variata* have caps that are typically **purplish or brownish mottled with green** and gills that feel somewhat **greasy**; *R. cyanoxantha* has a stem that is **up to 5 inches tall** and gills that are mostly unforked, while gills of *R. variata* have **numerous, conspicuous forks**. • **Green-Capped Russulas** may also be confused with several greenish Milk Caps (pg. 150).

NOTES: Quilted Green Russulas are considered a delicious edible. The other Russulas discussed here are edible but not as favored; *R. variata* is often somewhat acrid.

R. parvovirescens

R. variata

R. crustosa

Bluish to Greenish Milk Caps (several)

Lactarius spp.

HABITAT: Milk Caps are mycorrhizal, growing from the soil in a symbiotic relationship with living trees. The Celandine Milk Cap is found with pine trees; the others discussed here associate with both coniferous and deciduous trees.

DESCRIPTION: Milk Caps (*Lactarius* spp.) are a large family of brittle-fleshed, gilled mushrooms that produce **milky latex when cut**. Caps of young and middle-age specimens are rounded with a sunken center and rolled-under edges; many become vase-like with age. The species on this page have **stocky** stems up to 3 inches tall; their gills are closely spaced and attached to the stem or running down it slightly. Stems have no rings. • **Indigo Milky** (*L. indigo*) is the most stunning. Its cap and stem are **deep blue to grayish-blue**, sometimes with greenish bruises; caps are up to 5 inches wide or larger, often with darker rings or scattered dots. Gills are **deep, rich blue**, turning yellowish as spores develop. When cut, all parts **immediately turn dark blue**, then greenish; the **gills ooze** a bit of **dark blue** latex. • Caps of the **Celandine Milk Cap** (*L. chelidonium*) are up to 4 inches wide; they are generally **buff-colored and mottled with pale blue or green** when young, turning yellowish-brown and finally **mottled greenish-bronze**. Gills are **tan** to brownish-orange, sometimes with greenish areas. When cut, caps and stems turn bluish, then greenish; gills bruise greenish. Fresh specimens ooze a small amount of **yellowish-brown** latex when cut. • Caps of **Dingy Milk Cap** (*L. sordidus*) are up to 4 inches wide. They are **dirty-looking yellowish-brown** with dull **olive tinges concentrated around the center**, and have a tacky texture, especially when wet. Gills are cream-colored to yellowish, becoming brownish-spotted and darker with age; the stem is pockmarked.

SPORE PRINT: Cream, buff, white or yellowish.

SEASON: Summer through fall.

OTHER NAMES: Milky Caps, Milkcaps, Milky.

COMPARE: Some **Russula** in our area have greenish attributes (pg. 148), but their gills are **whitish** and **do not produce the milky latex** when cut.

NOTES: Indigo Milky and the Celandine Milk Cap are edible; Dingy Milk Cap is not considered edible.

Indigo Milky

Celandine Milk Cap

The Sweater

Clitocybe rivulosa (also known as Ivory Funnel Cap and *C. dealbata*)

This small, **toxic** mushroom appears in pastures, grassy areas and open woods; it often grows in a ring. It is white, pale grayish-white or buff-colored overall; the cap may appear pinkish when it is moist and often becomes **mottled with darker, wet-looking splotches**. Mature caps are generally ½ to 1⅝ inches wide; the edge is turned under. The cap surface is irregular but smooth; it may be slippery on young specimens but becomes dry with maturity. Stems are 1 to 1½ inches tall and may be a slightly darker shade than the cap; the cap is often attached to the stem slightly **off-center**. The stem has no ring. Several specimens may grow together from a common base. Gills are **closely spaced** and **run down the stem for a short distance**; they are creamy white at first, turning **tan to pinkish-tan** with age. Its spore print is **white**; it is found from mid to late summer.

COMPARE: The Sweetbread Mushroom (pg. 74) is similar in overall appearance but is generally larger and its spore print is **pinkish**. • Funnel Caps (pg. 106) are up to 4 inches across and pinkish-tan with a **deep funnel shape**. • Snowy Waxy Cap (pg. 153) and other whitish waxy caps appear similar to the Sweater, but their caps are **waxy or covered with sticky slime** and their gills are **widely spaced**.

NOTES: The Sweater contains the **toxic** compound muscarine, which causes intense sweating, salivation, tear formation and intestinal distress.

Snowy Waxy Cap

Cuphophyllus virgineus (also known as *Hygrocybe virginea*)

This small mushroom is found in grassy areas, pastures, parks and mossy patches, sometimes near forest edges; it grows from dead and decaying matter which is often underground. It is white overall and may appear slightly translucent. The cap is up to 2 inches wide and feels **waxy or slippery** but not slimy; it may be slightly humped or wavy, and older specimens may appear to be turned inside-out. Stems are smooth and up to 3¼ inches tall; there is no ring. The gills are **widely spaced** and **run down the stem** for a short distance; they are **thick and waxy or greasy-feeling**. Snowy Waxy Cap has a white spore print and is found from summer through fall.

COMPARE: Ivory Waxy Cap (*Hygrophorus eburneus*) is slightly larger and its cap and stem are **very slimy**, especially when wet; it may turn slightly yellowish with age. • Golden-Spotted Waxy Cap (*Hygrophorus chrysodon*) has a white cap with a slightly sticky surface and fine **yellowish-gold flakes** that may wash away or fade with age; it is often found near conifers. • The **toxic** Sweater (pg. 152) is similar in size to Snowy Waxy Cap, but its caps are **mottled** and its gills are **closely spaced**.

NOTES: Snowy Waxy Caps are edible but not tasty; not recommended for amateurs due to the possibility of confusing them with toxic species. This may also be listed as *Hygrophorus borealis* or *Hygrophorus virgineus*.

Silky Volvariella
Volvariella bombycina

This large, pale-colored mushroom is most often seen **growing singly on a living tree emerging from a wound where the heartwood has been exposed**. It can also be found on logs and stumps of various broadleaf trees, especially maple. Caps are white to yellowish-white. The surface is **silky-fibrous** to hairy and not ribbed. Ranging from 3 to 7 inches in diameter, this is a striking mushroom. The 4- to 7-inch stem is whitish, equal and often curved. At the stem base is a **prominent yellowish to brownish sac-like volva** (cup). There is **no ring**. Gills are white, becoming pinkish, and not attached to the stem. The spore print is **salmon-colored**. It is found from summer through fall. The Silky Volvariella is not usually abundant, but once seen it is an unforgettable mushroom.

COMPARE: *Amanita* species (pgs. 62–66) have **white spores** and **rings** on the stem; they **grow on the ground**. • *Pluteus* species (pg. 90) **lack the cup** at the bottom of the stem. • Other *Volvariella* species are smaller and **lack the silky cap surface**.

NOTES: This edible species is not recommended due to its resemblance to **deadly** poisonous *Amanita* species. It has a soft texture and reports on its taste vary from mediocre to excellent. When in pristine condition, it is a prime subject for photographers. It is also known as the Silky Sheath and Silky Tree Mushroom.

"Fairy Ring Fungus"
Marasmius oreades (also known as Scotch Bonnet)

Although this mushroom is referred to as the Fairy Ring, that name is also used for other species so it is best to use the scientific name, *Marasmius oreades*. It is found in grassy areas and is common in urban settings; it grows in small clusters, often in a ring where a tree has been removed. The cap is **buff or tan** and is often slightly darker in the center. Caps are rounded at first but flatten out quickly; they are typically somewhat **wavy with a central hump**. Mature specimens are up to 2 inches wide. The stem is up to 3 inches tall and fairly slender; it is generally colored like the cap. It feels somewhat felt-like and has a rubbery, tough consistency. There is no ring. Gills are cream-colored and **fairly widely spaced**. They are typically attached to the stem but **never run down it**; sometimes the gills appear slightly notched where they are attached to the stem. The spore print is white. These mushrooms are present from spring through fall.

COMPARE: Numerous small to medium-sized mushrooms can be confused with *M. oreades*. The **toxic Sweater** (pg. 152) grows in similar habitat and is about the same size and overall shape. Its gills are **closely spaced** and **run down the stem** slightly, and its cap is often mottled with wet-looking splotches. Also see **Spring Agrocybe** (pg. 86), **Common Laccaria** (pg. 88) and **Little Brown Mushrooms** (pg. 114) for other mushrooms that may appear somewhat similar to Fairy Ring Fungus.

NOTES: Although its flesh is somewhat tough, *M. oreades* is edible, but beginners must seek expert help to avoid **toxic** look-alikes.

Golden Pholiota

Pholiota aurivella, P. limonella, P. squarrosoadiposa

Golden Pholiota is a name used for several *Pholiota* species that can't be positively separated from one another without a microscope; the three listed above are often grouped together. The **yellow** to yellowish-orange caps are up to 6 inches wide and **very slimy**, with **irregularly placed reddish-brown to purplish scales** that may eventually fall off. Young caps have a webby partial veil over the gills that often leaves a thin band-like remnant near the top of the stem; there is no other ring. The stem is up to 4 inches tall; it is cottony and white at the top, becoming **scaly** and yellowish to brownish-yellow below the veil remnant. Gills are cream-colored, turning tan to **reddish-brown** with age; they are closely spaced and attached to the stem. Spores are **rusty brown**, and may darken the veil remnant. Golden Pholiota appear from midsummer through late fall in clusters or singly on living or dead deciduous and coniferous trees, logs and stumps.

COMPARE: Decorated Pholiota (pg. 82) have tan caps that are covered with **pointed tan to rusty brown scales**. The spore print is **white**. · Yellow Pholiota (*P. flammans;* inedible) is **bright yellow** and **hairy-shaggy overall**. · Scaly Pholiota (*P. squarrosa;* **toxic**) has a **dry, pale yellow to tan** cap with prominent, **spiky brown** scales. Its gills turn **greenish** before turning brownish from the spores.

NOTES: Golden Pholiota is often listed as an acceptable edible once the cap is peeled; other sources state that it is bitter and may cause intestinal problems.

R. ochroleucoides

Yellow Russulas (several)

Russula spp.

Several yellow-capped *Russula* species grow in our area; they are identified by habitat, slight variations in appearance and microscopic analysis. The listed species have a yellowish cap that is 3 to 4 inches wide at maturity; the center is depressed and the surface is often tacky when moist. Stems are sturdy and smooth; there is no ring. Gills are white, cream-colored or yellowish. They are attached to the stem and fairly closely spaced. Spore prints are white, cream-colored or yellowish. Species listed here are found in summer and fall. • Caps of young *R. ochroleucoides* are rich yellow with a pinkish-orange center, eventually turning yellow overall; older caps may fade to buff. Stems are white, and **bruise brownish**. *R. ochroleucoides* is found near oak and beech trees. • *R. claroflava* (also listed as *R. flava*) is called Yellow Swamp Russula because it grows in **boggy conifer-birch** forests. Stems are white, turning **gray** when bruised. • *R. flavida* has a **yellow stem**; its cap may be slightly orangish. The stem **does not change color** when bruised. *R. flavida* grows near oaks and other deciduous trees.

COMPARE: Almond-Scented Russula (*R. grata*; also listed as *R. laurocerasi*) and Fragrant Brittle Gill (*R. fragrantissima*) are larger, with dull yellow caps up to 5 inches wide; they **smell like almonds**.

NOTES: The Russulas listed above are edible but may be slightly bitter or hot; *R. flavida* is generally mild-tasting.

The Gypsy

Cortinarius caperatus (also known as *Rozites caperata*)

The Gypsy is mycorrhizal, growing **from the soil** in a symbiotic relationship with deciduous trees and conifers. It seems to prefer acidic soil near **conifers** and blueberry bushes and can be found singly or in large groups. The cap is up to 5 inches wide and **yellowish** to light brown; it is covered with fine, **silky white fibers**, mainly in the center, making it appear slightly **frosted**. Caps are conical to slightly knobbed and are often wrinkled (*caperata* means "wrinkled" in Latin). The **attached gills** are closely spaced and putty-colored when young. They are initially covered by a partial veil that breaks to form a **white ring** on the stem, which is white to light tan and may be swollen at the base. Gills darken with age to a **rusty brown** color that matches the spore print. It fruits from late summer through fall.

COMPARE: Other *Cortinarius* species (pgs. 118, 126) may look similar in some regards, but buttons typically have a **cobwebby cortina** (partial veil) and mature specimens lack the ring on the stem. • *Agaricus* species (pg. 80) may be tan with a prominent ring, but the gills are **not attached** to the stem and spores are **dark brown**. • Big Laughing Gym (pg. 102; **toxic**) grows in clusters on **wood** and has a **dark-capped** ring.

NOTES: The Gypsy is being studied for antiviral properties. It is a good edible when properly identified; some of the other species listed above are **toxic**.

Platterful Mushroom

Megacollybia rodmani (also known as *Tricholomopsis platyphylla*)

From spring through fall, this mushroom can be found **singly** or in **small groups**, growing from **dead and decaying wood**, stumps and buried woody debris. Its cap is up to 5 inches wide and is brownish-gray, streaked with **fine, dark fibers** running from the center to the edges; it may look **silky** depending on the light. On mature specimens, the top of the cap may be uneven; edges are often wavy and/or cracked. Stems are up to 5 inches tall and fairly stout; they are white and have **fine, white vertical fibers**. There is no ring on the stem. White mycelium (thread-like fungal roots) are often visible at the base. The white to cream-colored gills are very broad and moderately widely spaced. They are attached to the stem, and the edges near the cap may appear **ruffled or wavy**. Its spore print is **white**.

COMPARE: The Deer Mushroom and Black-Edged Pluteus (pg. 90) may appear somewhat similar, but both have **salmon-pink** spores. • Fried Chicken Mushroom (*Lyophyllum decastes*; edible) is the same stature as Platterful. Its cap may be grayish, brownish or yellowish-brown, but it lacks the dark fibers. It has a white stem, white gills and white spores. It grows in **dense clusters** in **grassy areas** and along roads from summer through fall. • *M. platyphylla* looks similar and is often listed in field guides, but it is a European species that does not grow in the United States.

NOTES: Platterful Mushrooms are edible when young; some people may experience gastrointestinal problems, so try only a small portion at first. Some people refer to this species as Broadgill.

Reddening Russula

Russula 'densifolia'

This mycorrhizal species grows from the ground, scattered or in small groups, under deciduous trees or conifers. Reddening Russula **bruises red, then blackish**, when cut or bruised. Young specimens have pillowy or convex caps that spread and flatten out with age, turning upward to form a shallow bowl up to 6 inches wide. Caps and stems are whitish at first, turning brownish or brownish-gray, often with a mottled appearance; both eventually turn black. The cap is **sticky** when wet. Skin on the cap can be easily peeled to about the middle. Stems are smooth and stocky, up to 3½ inches tall; they have no ring. Gills are **closely spaced** and attached to the stem or running very slightly down it. They are white at first, turning red, then black, when damaged. Flesh is white and brittle. The spore print is white. Reddening Russula grows from summer through early fall.

COMPARE: Black-Staining Russula (*R. dissimulans*) also bruises red, then slowly turns black when cut or bruised. Its gills are **moderately closely spaced**. The cap is **dry** and smooth. The cap skin can't be peeled easily. • *R. pectinatoides* has a buff-colored cap that is **slightly ribbed** around the edge; much of the **skin can be peeled off** the cap starting at the edge. It smells sweet and waxy, and it **does not change color** when cut. • Deceptive Milky (pg. 78) looks similar to young Reddening Russula, but it produces a **milky white latex** when cut.

NOTES: Although Black-Staining Russula is considered edible, it is difficult to identify and should be eaten by experts only. The others listed above are inedible.

Sooty Wax Cap
Hygrophorus fuligineus

When fresh, this is an attractive mushroom despite its drab cap color. The Sooty Wax Cap is mycorrhizal with white pine. It is a cool-weather species, most common in late September and October. The cap is nearly black at first, looking much like a **shiny black marble**. Eventually it becomes **blackish-brown**, at times with olive tones. The shiny appearance is due to a rather thick coating of slime. When the slime dries, there will be needles and leaves sticking to the cap surface. The cap is 1½ to 4 inches in diameter. The gills are attached to the stem and are white, sometimes with a pinkish tinge. The 1- to 4-inch stem is solid and white. It has a slime coating which ends on the upper portion. The white flesh is thick. Odor and taste are not distinctive. It has a white spore print.

COMPARE: The Sooty Wax Cap often fruits with the **Yellow-Centered Waxcap** (*H. flavodiscus*; also called Butterscotch Wax Cap). This edible species is also slimy but its cap is **yellowish-tan to orangish-tan** with a darker center; the cap becomes paler with age. • The **Herald of Winter** (*H. hypothejus*) is another autumn mushroom which has a dark, slimy cap but it develops **yellowish-orange stains** in age. It is also an edible species.

NOTES: Also called Sooty Hygrophorus, this is an edible species with no similar poisonous look-alikes. Some may be put off by the slime but this can be removed by peeling the cap. Some choose not to peel this mushroom and add it to soups or stews where the slime may help thicken the liquid.

Club-Footed Clitocybe

Ampulloclitocybe clavipes (also known as *Clitocybe clavipes*)

Growing in woodlands, primarily coniferous; may also be found in mixed-wood forests. They grow singly, scattered or in loose groups and may grow in a ring. This mushroom's distinguishing feature is its **broad, club-like base**, although it may not be notable in every specimen. Young specimens often have a disproportionately tiny cap, ½ to 1 inch wide, sitting atop a stem with a narrow neck and a bulbous base. The cap expands with age, becoming flat with a rolled-under edge and, often, a knob in the center. On mature specimens the cap flares up to form a **shallow, wavy-edged bowl** up to 3¼ inches wide. Caps are smooth or felty and tan, reddish-brown or dark brown, typically with a light margin and darker center. The stem is cream-colored to brownish, **stout** and up to 2½ inches tall; the base is typically **swollen** and may be up to 1¼ inches wide. The stem has no ring. Gills are white or cream-colored and moderately close; they **run down the stem** for some distance. It has a white spore print and grows from late summer through fall.

COMPARE: Numerous *Clitocybe* (pgs. 74–75, 106, 144 and 152) species may appear similar, and many of them can't be easily separated from one another without the use of a microscope. Some, such as **The Sweater** (pg. 152), are **toxic**.

NOTES: Club-Footed Clitocybe should be considered inedible.

Plums and Custard

Tricholomopsis rutilans (also known as *Tricholoma rutilans*)

This attractive mushroom, also known as Variegated Mop, grows scattered or in small clusters from **decaying conifer stumps and logs** that may be underground. Both cap and stem are **yellow** and have a coating of **reddish to purplish-red fibers and scales** that are sometimes so dense on the cap that it may appear entirely red. Caps of mature specimens are up to **4¾ inches** wide, often with a wavy or scalloped edge. Stems are stocky and up to 4 inches tall; the base may be somewhat flattened. The stem has no ring. Gills are **deep yellow** and closely spaced; they are attached to the stem or slightly notched. The flesh is yellow. The spores are **white**. It grows from late spring through fall, particularly during cool periods.

COMPARE: Decorated Mop (pg. 108) is smaller, with a cap that is generally less than 3 inches across and a stem that is less than 3 inches tall. It is typically **golden yellow overall** and **lacks the reddish fibers**; it has **tiny brown scales** that are concentrated on the center of the cap. • Brick Tops (pg. 140) grow in **tight clusters** from decaying deciduous logs and stumps. They have caps that are brick-red with pale edges; gills are **white** and the spore print is **purplish-brown**.

NOTES: In spite of its delicious-sounding name, Plums and Custard is considered a poor edible.

ON DECAYING OR DOWNED WOOD

SPRING (GROWING SEASON)

Fringed Polypore

Lentinus arcularius

HABITAT: Fringed Polypores are saprobes, and are often found on fallen trees, branches and sticks of hardwoods, especially birch and poplar. They may also grow on buried wood, giving them the appearance of growing from the ground.

DESCRIPTION: This small funnel-shaped mushroom, which is generally less than 2 inches across and tall, has a beautiful pore surface under the cap. The **large, angular pores** are arranged around and run slightly down the stem, creating a **honeycomb-like pattern** that is white to pale yellow, turning tan with age. The cap is brown, with fine, lighter-colored cracks that expand as it grows. It is covered with **fine hairs** that extend beyond the edges. This **hairy cap edge** is the easiest way to separate this from other similar mushrooms. It grows early in the spring and can be found singly or in groups. The tough, thin stems are also tan to brown like the cap. There is no ring on the stem.

SPORE PRINT: White.

SEASON: Grows in spring; present year-round.

OTHER NAMES: Spring Polypore, Early Brown Funnel Polypore, *Polyporus arcularius*.

COMPARE: Winter Polypore (*L. brumalis*; formerly *P. brumalis*) is a similar size and is found in the same habitat, but its cap is **darker**. The pores are **finer**, and rounded to slightly angular. When young, the cap is hairy like Fringed Polypore, but it becomes **smooth and velvety** as it grows; the **cap edge is hairless**. It grows later in the summer through fall. • Big Black Foot and Little Black Foot (pg. 166) could be mistaken for Fringed Polypore and are found in the same habitat, but as the common names suggest, both have stems that are **partially black**. Both also have a fine **white pore surface** under the caps. Big Black Foot is much larger than any of the other species listed above, with caps up to **8 inches** across. • Hexagonal-Pored Polypore (pg. 214) is common in the spring and has pores that are similar to those of the Fringed Polypore. Its cap is **orange** and its stem is **off-center**.

NOTES: All of the mushrooms listed above cause white rot of dead trees, and old specimens can be found year-round. They are not edible due to their tough texture and lack of flavor, though Fringed Polypore is being studied for medicinal properties.

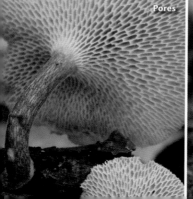

Pores

Hairs on cap edge

ON DOWNED WOOD   EARLY SUMMER THROUGH FALL (GROWING SEASON)

Black Foot Mushrooms

Cerioporus varius, Pipices badius

HABITAT: These mushrooms are saprobes that get their nutrients from decaying wood. They grow singly or in groups from fallen trees, branches and sticks of deciduous trees.

DESCRIPTION: Two Black Foot species are common in our area. Both have thin, smooth, funnel-shaped caps that grow flatter as they expand, often developing a **wavy edge**. Under the cap they have a **fine white pore surface** that runs partway down the stem. The stem may be whitish, tan or brown at the top but is always **black at the bottom**; there is no ring. The stem location varies from centered to completely off to one side and everywhere in between. It may be so short that these mushrooms often look like a shelf fungus at first glance. • **Little Black Foot** (*C. varius*) has a uniformly colored cap that is light cream, tan or brown (*varius* means "variable" in Latin); it is up to 4 inches across. • **Big Black Foot** (*Pipices badius*; also listed as *Polyporus badius, Polyporus picipes* and *Royoporus badius*) is much larger, with caps up to **8 inches** across. It is typically much **darker or reddish brown**, but may be pale tan with a darker center, particularly when young. The center is often nearly black, becoming lighter toward the wavy outer edge.

SPORE PRINT: White.

SEASON: Grows from early summer through fall; present year-round.

OTHER NAMES: *C. varius* is also called the Elegant Polypore, and listed as *Polyporus varius* or *Polyporus elegans*. Some describe *Polyporus elegans* as a distinct species that is larger than *C. varius* and has faint ridges radiating outward on the cap; it may also be called Light Cap Black Foot (*C. leptocephalus* or *Polyporus leptocephalus*), although some references describe that as a separate species.

COMPARE: Winter Polypore (pg. 164) has the same habitat and growth pattern and is small like Little Black Foot, but it has a **darker, more velvety** cap surface and a light tan to brown stem that is **not black** at the bottom.

NOTES: Black Foot Mushrooms cause white rot of dead wood. They fruit annually but can be found year-round due to their tough, leathery flesh. They are not edible but are often used in dried floral arrangements.

Little Black Foot

Big Black Foot

FROM THE SOIL NEAR LIVE TREES

SUMMER THROUGH FALL

Scaber Stalks (several)

Leccinum spp.

HABITAT: These mycorrhizal species grow under or near birch, aspen, oak and conifers. They are also found in open grassy areas near stands of trees.

DESCRIPTION: The hallmark of *Leccinum* species are **scabers**, minute raised scales covering the stems. The scabers of the species discussed here are generally somewhat darker than the stems and often darken further with age, becoming more prominent. Caps of the species listed here are dull and smooth when dry but slippery when wet; stems are **whitish** with no rings. The pore surface is white to brownish and deeply sunken next to the stem; pores **bruise brown**. • Members of the *L. insigne* group are sometimes called Orange-Capped Leccinum because of their cap color, which may be **apricot, orange or reddish-orange**; they often become brownish with age. Caps are typically 2 to 4 inches across at maturity; stems are sturdy and 3 to 5 inches tall. They are also called Aspen Boletes, due to their frequent association with that species • Caps of **Brown Birch Bolete** or Common Scaber Stalk (*L. scabrum*; also called *Boletus scaber*) are **brownish** and less than 4 inches across; stems may be bluish-green at the base and are usually slender. The flesh **remains white or turns pale pinkish** when cut. It is found near birch trees. • **White Birch Bolete** (*L. holopus*) is very similar to Brown Birch Bolete but its cap is **dingy white**, developing a greenish tinge; the stem base often stains bluish. Its scabers are pale and coarse on young specimens, darkening with age. It is found in **damp areas** such as bogs and soggy birch woods.

SPORE PRINT: Yellowish-brown to olive-brown.

SEASON: Summer through fall.

OTHER NAMES: See text above.

COMPARE: Also see *Hemileccinum subglabripes* (pg. 170) for other *Leccinum* species.

NOTES: The *L. insigne* group previously included *L. aurantiacum*, but it has been determined that this is a European species that does not appear in North America. The *Leccinum* listed above were considered good edibles, but they are no longer recommended due to reports of gastrointestinal problems.

Orange-Capped Leccinum

Brown Birch Bolete

White Birch Bolete

Hemileccinum subglabripes
(no common name)

HABITAT: This mycorrhizal species grows singly or scattered under birch and aspen. In the southern part of our region, it is also found occasionally under oak.

DESCRIPTION: Although it doesn't appear in many guidebooks, this mushroom is not uncommon in our area. Its cap is generally 3 to 4 inches wide and is brownish-orange to tan with a smooth surface that may be tacky in damp weather. The stem is more slender than many other boletes; it is up to 4 inches tall and yellow with **subtle scabers** (minute raised scales; see Scaber Stalks, pg. 168) that are the same color as the stem, making them fairly inconspicuous. The top of the stem may be smooth and bright yellow; the lower part of the stem is often streaked with dusky red, although it may be faint. The stem has no ring. Pores are bright yellow and **do not bruise**; the pore surface is deeply sunken next to the stem. Flesh is **yellow** and does not bruise when cut; the stem may turn faint blue or reddish when cut.

SPORE PRINT: Olive-brown.

SEASON: Midsummer through early fall.

OTHER NAMES: *Boletus subglabripes, Leccinum subglabripes.*

COMPARE: The **Wrinkled Leccinum** (*Leccinellum rugosiceps;* previously *Leccinum rugosiceps*) has a **wrinkled cap** that can become **cracked in age**. The Wrinkled Leccinum occurs under oaks and is most commonly reported from the more southerly portions of the Northeast. • **Butter Foot Bolete** (*Boletus auripes*) has a tan to brownish cap; it may grow to **8 inches** wide and it has a finely **velvety** surface that is never tacky. Its pore surface is bright yellow and does not bruise when cut. The stem is stocky and **bright yellow overall**, with a **fine, net-like pattern** on the top half or overall. It is found under hardwoods, favoring oaks.

NOTES: All species listed above are edible; *Hemileccinum subglabripes* may cause digestive upset if eaten fresh, but is reportedly safe to eat after drying.

Stem detail

Leccinum subglabripes

Wrinkled Leccinum

Butter Foot Bolete

Both's Bolete
Bothia castanella

HABITAT: Both's Bolete is **symbiotic with oaks** and possibly other deciduous trees. In the corresponding nutrient exchange, the tree provides carbohydrates and the mushroom provides minerals and water. It grows in woodlands, cemeteries and urban parks, often along trails, wood edges and in lawns. It is widely distributed in the Northeast, wherever oaks are found.

DESCRIPTION: This rather distinctive bolete has been placed in its own genus after years of questions regarding its relationship to other boletes. The caps are 2 to 4 inches across. Brown is the predominant color, ranging from reddish to yellowish brown. The cap flesh is white and unchanging in color when exposed. Caps are convex at first, becoming nearly flat, sometimes depressed in the center. The surface is dry, somewhat soft, and velvety to slightly fuzzy at first, becoming bald in mature caps. Stems are 2 to 3 inches tall and ½ to 1 inch wide; they may be roughly equal in diameter or may taper slightly toward the base or toward the top. They are brownish, with a **net-like pattern on the upper portion**. The stem is usually central but may be off-center at times. The stem has no ring. White mycelium (thread-like fungal roots) are sometimes visible at the base of the stem. The pore surface **extends a bit onto the upper stem**. The pores are **angular and radially arranged**. Pores are buff to golden tan or yellowish-brown in color. The pores stain brownish when bruised. Both's Bolete does not have a distinctive odor.

SPORE PRINT: Dull yellow to yellowish brown.

SEASON: Summer through early fall.

OTHER NAMES: *Suillus castanellus, Boletinus castanellus, Boletinus squarrosoides.*

COMPARE: Ash Bolete (pg. 174) is **associated with ash trees**. Its stem is generally **short** and stubby and grows **off-center**, sometimes appearing completely off to one side. The pore surface has **ridge-like veins running from the stem to the cap edge**.

NOTES: This species is named for the late bolete expert, Ernst Both. While seldom seen in large quantities, it is a common oak-associated species. Edibility is unknown and consumption is not recommended without further study.

Ash Bolete

Boletinellus merulioides

HABITAT: Found on the ground around ash trees. The Ash Bolete is not mycorrhizal with the tree but instead lives in a symbiotic relationship with the wooly ash aphid.

DESCRIPTION: This mushroom has a mottled brown cap that is **tacky** but not slimy when wet and looks almost polished or iridescent when dry and mature, much like the King Bolete (pgs. 44–47). Like many other boletes, it has a spongy yellow pore surface underneath the cap. Compared to other bolete varieties, however, it is easily recognized by its irregularities. The pore surface has a network of **ridge-like veins** running from the stem to the cap edges. The pores, which are large and somewhat angular, are arranged between the veins to form a **mesh-like surface**. The veins and pores run down the stem, which is **short, brown and not centered under the cap**; in many cases the stem grows completely off to one side. The caps, which are up to 8 inches wide, are **lobed and irregular**, growing very close to the ground on a stem that is generally 2 inches tall or shorter; the stem has no ring. If you come across a large group of these, it looks like a bag of russet potatoes has been dumped in the grass. The pore surface **bruises brown to bluish** after much handling.

SPORE PRINT: Olive-brown.

SEASON: Summer through fall.

OTHER NAMES: *Gyrodon merulioides*.

COMPARE: Several other mushrooms have similar overall appearances, but their pore surfaces lack the vein-like network. • Both's Bolete (pg. 172) has darker pores and a **central stem**. It occurs **under oak**. • Bay Bolete (pg. 186) has a **reddish-brown** cap that is more **regularly shaped**; the pore surface is creamy white to yellowish. It prefers pines.

NOTES: Ash Boletes are edible but not desirable, which is unfortunate because you are apt to find many at a time and they can be decent sized.

Veins on pore surface

FROM THE SOIL NEAR TREES

FALL

Slippery Jack

Suillus luteus

HABITAT: Slippery Jacks are mycorrhizal, growing in a symbiotic relationship with living trees. They are found in scattered clusters primarily under **conifers**. Occurs with two-needle pines, including red pine and Scots pines.

DESCRIPTION: *Suillus* species in general are called Slippery Boletes due to their frequently **slimy** cap surface. Like numerous other boletes, Slippery Jack has a **brown** cap and **pale yellow** pore surface underneath that darkens with age. The cap is up to 5 inches across and may become tan or yellowish with age. The stem is **white** and up to 3 inches tall; it is very sturdy and may be up to 1 inch thick. What makes the Slippery Jack distinctive is the **partial veil that breaks to form a prominent ring** on the stem. As the ring ages, it turns **dark purplish brown** and becomes sticky; with age it may disappear entirely. The flesh and pores **do not stain** when cut or bruised. The other notable feature is that there are **fine dots on the stem above the ring**, creating a texture similar to the pore surface. The dots are similar to the glandular dots on the stem of Dotted-Stalk Suillus (pg. 182), but on Slippery Jack the dots are only on the top portion of the stem, **above the ring**.

SPORE PRINT: Cinnamon-brown.

SEASON: Fall.

OTHER NAMES: Sometimes referred to as Sticky Bun.

COMPARE: The **Short-Stemmed Bolete** (*S. brevipes*) is very similar to Slippery Jack, but has **no ring** and it lacks the fine dots at the top of the stem. • **Slippery Jill** (*S. salmonicolor*; also known as *S. subluteus* or *S. pinorigidus*) is slightly smaller than Slippery Jack; it has an **orangish to brown** cap and pore surface. The stem is covered with **fine, dark dots overall** and has a **strong, white, skirt-like veil** that lacks the purplish coloration of Slippery Jack. • The **Larch Bolete** (pg. 190) has an **orange cap**, lacks the purplish ring color and **occurs under larch**.

NOTES: The *Suillus* species listed here are edible; opinions vary as to their desirability. The slippery caps remain slimy after cooking and may cause digestive problems, so some cooks prefer to peel the caps before cooking; however, some people get a skin rash from handling the sticky, uncooked caps.

green = key identification feature

Slippery Jack

Short-Stemmed Bolete

Pale Violet Bitter Bolete

Tylopilus violatinctus

HABITAT: The Pale Violet Bitter Bolete is found on the ground or in moss or humus in a mycorrhizal association with a variety of trees, including hemlock, red oak and beech. It can be found in forests and in urban parks, wherever its associated trees occur. It may be solitary but is usually found scattered or in small groups.

DESCRIPTION: This attractive mushroom has caps that are dry and somewhat velvety. With a cap that is 3 to 6 inches wide at maturity, it is a rather large mushroom. Caps are convex, becoming nearly flat in mature specimens. The margin is rolled under on young specimens. Cap coloration ranges from violet to grayish violet when young, becoming a pale pinkish-purple or brownish with almost no violet coloration at maturity. The **cap surface becomes dark violet to purple when rubbed**. The stem is usually equal but may be slightly club-shaped or bulbous. It is dry, solid and 3 to 6 inches in length. There is no veil or ring. **Coloration is similar to the cap but with whitish areas at the top and bottom**. When handled, yellowish stains may be noted. The stem may have an inconspicuous reticulation (mesh-like texture) at the very top. The pores are small, nearly round and randomly arranged. They are depressed around the stem but may rarely descend slightly onto the upper stem. The pore surface is white, becoming pinkish-brown to brown in age. Pores are unchanging when rubbed. The flesh is white, at time becoming pale grayish. Odor is mild and the taste is very bitter.

SPORE PRINT: Reddish-brown.

SEASON: Summer through early fall.

OTHER NAMES: None.

COMPARE: The **Violet-Gray Bolete**, *T. plumbeoviolaceus*, has a dark purple cap that becomes **brownish or grayish with age**. Its **stem is a persistently mottled purple**. • The **Reddish-Brown Bitter Bolete**, *T. rubrobrunneus*, has a **stem that develops olive stains**.

NOTES: This extremely bitter species and its look-alikes are considered inedible by most due to the unpleasant taste.

Pale Violet Bitter Bolete

Violet-Gray Bolete

Violet-Gray Bolete with brownish cap

FROM THE SOIL NEAR TREES

SUMMER THROUGH EARLY FALL

Bicolor Bolete

Baorangia bicolor

HABITAT: This mycorrhizal mushroom grows from the ground near oaks and other hardwoods. It may be scattered, in tight little clusters or alone.

DESCRIPTION: Fresh caps of this lovely mushroom are up to **6 inches wide** and **red**, ranging from rosy to purplish-red. The pore surface is **bright yellow**; stems are **red**. As it matures, the smooth cap surface becomes paler, more pinkish and at times, olive-brown. Older caps are sometimes cracked. Stems grow up to 4 inches tall and may be yellow toward the top; there is no ring. The **pore surface stains blue**, but this may be faint at times. The tubes are **very short in relation to the thick, pale-yellow flesh**. Bicolor Bolete can be distinguished from **toxic** blue-staining boletes (pgs. 67–69) by the way its yellow interior flesh stains blue **slowly and faintly**, if at all.

SPORE PRINT: Olive-brown.

SEASON: Summer through early fall.

OTHER NAMES: Two-Color Bolete, *Boletus bicolor*.

COMPARE: Many boletes have red caps and yellow pores; identification can be challenging. One to watch out for is **Brick-Cap Bolete** (pg. 68; **toxic**), which has a brick-red cap and **yellowish** stem that becomes reddish at the base; **pores and flesh stain blue instantly**. • Caps of **Ruby Bolete** (*Hortiboletus rubellus;* formerly *Boleteus rubellus* or *Xerocomellus rubellus*) and **Sulfur Bolete** (*H. campestris;* formerly *Boleteus campestris*) are less than 2 inches across and typically **deep rose to pinkish red**; with age, caps fade and often develop surface cracks. Pores are **deep and angular; pores and flesh stain blue quickly**. These two *Hortiboletus* are difficult to tell apart. Both were included with *Boleteus fraternus* as a species group, but recent DNA studies determined that *Boleteus fraternus* is identical to *H. rubellus*; all were moved to the *Hortiboletus* genus. While generally regarded as edible, they can be so similar to small Brick-Caps that even some experts do not collect them for the table. • Additionally, there are several varieties of **Bicolor Boletes**. Some mycologists believe there are other lookalikes that are undescribed, with the edibility untested.

NOTES: Some consider Bicolor Bolete almost as choice as the King Bolete (pgs. 44–47). However, this species should be consumed only after expert identification; it must be well cooked and should be eaten only in small quantities. Gastric problems have been reported with Bicolor Boletes and similar species.

Blue staining on pores

Split-open Bicolor Bolete

Ruby Bolete

Dotted-Stalk Suillus
Suillus granulatus (also listed as Suillus weaverae)

Dotted-Stalk Suillus is mycorrhizal, growing from the soil near pines. Caps are **pinkish-buff, brown or tan**, often spotted or streaked with cinnamon-brown. They are typically 2 to 4 inches wide and shiny when dry but sticky when damp. The pore surface is spongy and cream-colored, becoming coarse and yellow with age. When young and fresh, the spore-producing tubes may weep a milky fluid, giving this the alternate name of Weeping Bolete. Stems are up to 3 inches tall and **white** with **minute tan dots** that are **more concentrated at the top**; stems become yellow with age, particularly at the top. There is **no ring**. Flesh is white to yellow and **does not change color** when cut. Spores are cinnamon-brown. Found from spring through fall.

COMPARE: Chicken Fat Mushroom (pg. 185) is usually smaller, with **reddish streaks** on the **flat yellow caps**. Its pores are **large and angular**. • Slippery Jack (pg. 176) has a partial veil that breaks to form a **prominent ring** on the thick white stem. • The Short-Stemmed Bolete (pg. 176) has a **darker cap** and lacks the dots on the stem.

NOTES: Dotted-Stalk Suillus and the compares listed here are considered good edibles, but some people prefer to remove the slimy cap skin before cooking and eating, as it can cause digestive problems.

Red-Cracked Bolete

Xerocomellus chrysenteron (also known as *Boletus chrysenteron*)

This mycorrhizal species grows from the ground, scattered or in groups, near deciduous and coniferous trees. Caps are **olive-brown to brownish**, often with a reddish edge; the surface develops **pinkish to reddish-tinged cracks**. Smooth and velvety at first, caps grow to 3 inches wide, cracking as they expand. Pores are angular and moderately sized. The pore surface is **yellow** on young specimens, aging to brownish; when damaged, it slowly **bruises bluish**. The flesh inside is white to yellow and **slowly stains blue** when cut. The stem is up to 2½ inches tall and may appear subtly ridged; it is yellow at the top, turning reddish to purplish-red toward the bottom. The stem **bruises bluish-green**. There is no ring. Its spore print is olive-brown, and it grows from early summer through fall. This species is frequently infected and consumed with white mold.

COMPARE: *X. truncatus* is identical except for microscopic features. • The **Bicolor Bolete** (pg. 180) has a red cap up to **6 inches** wide, which can also be cracked when mature, especially in dry weather. However, the pore surface of older specimens bruises **blue** and the stem **does not bruise** when cut.

NOTES: Red-Cracked Bolete is edible, although the flesh is bland and mushy. Caution must be taken to avoid **toxic** Brick-Cap Bolete (pg. 68) and other look-alikes, which also may crack when old; these mushrooms **stain blue immediately** when cut. Expert Dr. Michael Beug warns that Red-Cracked Bolete can cause gastrointestinal distress when consumed with alcohol.

Ornate-Stalked Bolete

Retiboletus ornatipes (also known as *Boletus ornatipes*)

Ornate-Stalked Bolete is found in groups, scattered or singly under deciduous trees, particularly beech and oak. This mushroom gets its name from the **coarse mesh-like texture** covering the entire stem. The texture is created by ridges that are yellow at first, turning **brownish** when handled or with age. The stem is stocky and up to 6 inches tall; it is **bright yellow** and somewhat **powdery** and **bruises orangish-brown**. Yellow mycelium (thread-like fungal roots) may be present at the base of the stem; there is no ring. The cap is up to 8 inches wide; it is yellowish, brownish or olive-colored with a **dry or felt-like** surface. The pore surface is bright yellow, turning darker with age or handling. The flesh is bright yellow. Its spore print is olive-brown, and it grows from midsummer through early fall.

COMPARE: Butter Foot Bolete (pgs. 170–171) is the same size as Ornate-Stalked Bolete and has a tan cap with bright yellow stem and pores, but the stem has a **fine, yellow net-like pattern** on the top half and it **does not bruise**. · The Gray Bolete (*R. griseus*) has a gray cap, **whitish pore surface** and **white stem**. The **base of the stem bruises yellowish**; with age, the yellowish color moves upward on the stem. The stem is covered with a yellow netted pattern that, like that of the Ornate-Stalked Bolete, turns brownish to black when handled or with age.

NOTES: Ornate-Stalked Bolete is edible but is bitter; yellower specimens are the most bitter. Butter Foot Bolete and Gray Bolete are considered good edibles.

Chicken Fat Mushroom

Suillus americanus

This mushroom is also called the White Pine Bolete because it grows singly, scattered or prolifically from the soil **exclusively near white pine**. Of the many *Suillus* species, Chicken Fat is distinct because of its **small size**; it is typically less than 4 inches wide and tall. It has **yellow** caps that are **slimy** or slippery in moist weather; both the color and greasy feel account for its common name. Caps are fairly flat when mature, with only a slight peak in the center; they are often marked with reddish streaks. There may be veil remnants hanging on the cap edge; the stem may have a faint ring but it is usually absent. The stem is **slender** and often bent; it has small, raised **brown dots** and **stains brown** when handled. The flesh is yellow and **stains pinkish-brown** when cut or bruised. Pores are fairly large and angular; like the cap, the pore surface is yellow. Chicken Fat Mushroom has a cinnamon-brown spore print and is found from late summer through fall.

COMPARE: Dotted-Stalk Suillus (pg. 182) also occurs under white pine. Its caps are up to 6 inches wide; they are **brown to tan** and somewhat patchy. The pore surface is **spongy** rather than angular.

NOTES: Both of the mushrooms listed here are edible. The caps remain slimy when cooked and are often peeled before cooking; however, some people get a skin rash from handling the sticky, uncooked caps.

Bay Bolete or **Bay-Brown Bolete**

Imleria badia (also known as *Boletus badius, Xerocomus badius*)

This mushroom usually grows in pine forests but may be found in mixed woodlands with maple and birch. It grows from the soil near decayed wood, or directly on well-decayed wood. Caps of the Bay Bolete are reddish-brown to yellowish-brown. They are quite **rounded** at first, flattening as they grow; at maturity they may be up to 4 inches wide. They are usually tacky when young, becoming smooth and polished in old age. Both the pore surface and interior flesh are **creamy white to pale yellow**. The pores become greenish as they age and bruise **bluish-green**; the cut flesh may stain faintly blue. The pore surface may be sunken around the stem. The solid stem is the **same color as the cap** and has a **wrinkled** surface; it grows to 3½ inches tall. The stem has no ring. Bay Bolete has an **olive-brown** spore print and is found from late summer through fall.

COMPARE: The **Chestnut Bolete** (*Gyroporus castaneus*) is similar in size but grows near oaks, not conifers. It has a **light yellow** spore print. • The **Graceful Bolete** (*Austroboletus gracilis*) has a cap colored much like the Bay Bolete. It is a more slender species with pores that are **pinkish-gray to pinkish-brown**. Its spores are **pinkish-brown**.

NOTES: Many sources list this as a good edible and note that it is usually less bug-infested than other boletes. *Badius* means "brown" in Latin.

Shiny Cinnamon Polypore

Coltricia cinnamomea (also known as *Boletus cinnamomeus*)

This small, attractive mushroom grows singly or in small groups **from the ground** in mixed wooded areas; it is common in mossy areas and is often found along paths, even in hard soil. Its brown cap is **thin** and wavy, featuring **concentric brown rings** of varied color and texture, depending on age and weather conditions. Young ones are **shiny**, becoming velvety with age. Caps are mostly round and less than 2 inches wide. The short brown stem is up to 2 inches tall and has no ring. Sometimes funnel shaped, caps flatten out as they grow. Two or more individuals may fuse together, creating irregular shapes. Underneath the cap is a thin, **brown** pore surface. Its spore print is **cinnamon-brown**; it grows from late summer through fall but may be found year-round.

COMPARE: Tiger's Eye (*C. perennis*) is larger, with caps up to **4 inches wide**; its caps are **not shiny**. The pores under the cap **extend down the upper stem**. It is found in areas with **pines**. • Little Black Foot (pg. 166) is large like Tiger's Eye but lacks the distinct rings. The pore surface is **white**, and the bottom part of the stem is **black**. It grows **on wood**. • *Hydnellum concrescens* and other *Hydnellum* species resemble the Shiny Cinnamon Polypore but they are larger and have **spines**, not pores, on the underside. Their caps are **not shiny**.

NOTES: Even when fresh, this fungus is tough and leathery. It dries well and is used in decorative arrangements. It is being studied for medicinal uses.

Chrome-Footed Bolete

Harrya chromapes (also known as *Leccinum chromapes*, *Tylopilus chromapes*)

With its pinkish cap, this beautiful bolete is easy to spot in conifer woods. It is mycorrhizal and grows singly or scattered. The cap is **pinkish** and may be up to 6 inches across at maturity, although it is generally smaller; it turns tan with age. It is dry and often has a suede-like surface. Most of the stem is cream-colored to pale pink and **covered with fine scabers** (minute raised scales) that are generally **pinkish** but may be brownish; the bottom part of the stem is **bright yellow**. The stem is up to 6 inches tall on large specimens; the base may be pinched or narrowed. There is no ring. The pore surface is finely textured and somewhat sunken around the stem; it is white on young specimens, becoming yellowish, then pinkish and, finally, brownish with age. The flesh is white to pinkish; the flesh and the pore surface do not bruise. Its spore print is pinkish-brown; it is found from summer through fall.

COMPARE: Both the cap and stem of **Lilac Bolete** (pgs. 46–47) are **lilac-colored** when young; stems lack the scabers and the yellow base of Chrome-Footed Bolete. • **Violet-Gray Bolete** (pgs. 178–179) has a **dark purple** cap that becomes brownish or purplish-gray with age. Its stem is **mottled purple** with a whitish base; it has no scabers but may appear webbed at the top.

NOTES: Chrome-Footed Bolete and Lilac Bolete are edible, but Chrome-Footed Bolete is often infested with fly larvae. Violet-Gray Bolete is too bitter to eat.

Peppery Bolete

Chalciporus piperatus (also known as *Boletus piperatus*)

This small- to medium-sized mushroom grows from the soil in mixed woodlands. It has been found near birch and oak but seems to prefer conifers; the mycelium (thread-like fungal roots) has a symbiotic relationship with tree roots. Peppery Boletes grow alone, scattered or in large groups. This variety is smaller than other boletes. The cap is **1 to 3 inches wide**; it is rounded when young, becoming flatter with age. Young specimens are rust-red overall. With age, the pore surface becomes more reddish and the cap fades to a lighter tan. What distinguishes this species is the **bright yellow flesh** inside the cap and stem, which **bruises reddish-brown** when cut. The pores are **large and angular**, getting larger toward the stem; the pore surface **bruises dark brown** when damaged. The stem is up to 3 inches tall but is only ½ inch thick. Its base is **tapered,** rather than swollen like in many other boletes, and it has **no ring**. Distinctive **yellow roots** (mycelium) surround the stem base. Its spore print is **dark cinnamon brown**. It is found from late summer through fall.

COMPARE: *C. piperatoides* is nearly identical but its **pores stain blue when bruised**. Its spore print is **olive**.

NOTES: Peppery Bolete is edible when well cooked, however, many consider this species too peppery to be palatable.

Larch Bolete

Suillus grevillei (also known as *S. proximus*, Larch Suillus)

Also known as Tamarack Jack, Larch Bolete gets its common name from its mycorrhizal association with **larch (tamarack) trees**. Urban lawn areas with planted European larch produce this species as do boggy forests with native American larch. Caps are smooth and **slimy to sticky**; they are bald but may have patches of veil tissue at the margin. They are 2 to 6 inches wide and convex when young, flattening with age; there may be a raised area in the center. Caps vary from yellow to orangish-brown to dark reddish-brown. Stems are 1 to 4 inches tall, with an upward-flaring ring that is cottony, at times becoming gelatinous. Above the ring, the stem is pale yellow; below the ring it is orangish to reddish-brown and mottled with yellow. The surface is scurfy to granular. When cut, the stem may stain green at the bottom. Pores are small and rather angular. They are yellow, with ochre to olive tints at times; they **stain brown when bruised**. The spore print is olive-brown to cinnamon-brown. Larch Bolete are found in summer and fall.

COMPARE: Slippery Jack (pg. 176) has a brown cap and a **ring that turns dark purplish**; its pores **do not stain when bruised**, and the stem above the ring is covered with **fine dots**. Slippery Jack occurs with **pines**.

NOTES: Generally regarded as edible, although they are soft, with a mild to mediocre taste. As with all edible slimy-cap species, peeling the cap skin is recommended, as digestive issues have been experienced with unpeeled caps.

Old Man of the Woods

Strobilomyces 'floccopus,' S. confusus (S. 'floccopus' is also listed as S. 'strobilaceus')

These distinctive, medium-sized mushrooms grow singly or scattered from the ground near oaks and other deciduous trees; the mycelium (thread-like fungal roots) has a symbiotic relationship with tree roots. Caps are 1 to 6 inches wide; when young, they are white and covered with **shaggy black patches**. The patches tend to be slightly firmer and more upright on *S. confusus* than on *S. floccopus*, but a microscope is required to positively separate the two. Stems are 2 to 6 inches tall and proportionally thinner than stems of other boletes; they are **grayish to black** with a **shaggy** texture. The pore surfaces are white and sunken, darkening and bulging from under the cap with age. At the button stage, a partial veil covers the pore surface; as the cap expands, the veil leaves obvious flaps around the cap edges and may leave a faint ring on the stem. Both pore surface and flesh **bruise red** at first, then black. All parts of the mushroom become black with age. The spore print is dark brown to black. Found from summer through fall.

COMPARE: Black Velvet Bolete (*Tylopilus alboater*) is similar to mature Old Man in coloring and size. It has a **black** cap and stem that are both **smooth**, not shaggy like Old Man. The stem is **slightly thicker** and may bulge at the base. Like Old Man, it has a white pore surface that bruises red at first, then black.

NOTES: Old Man of the Woods is edible but not highly favored; older specimens are dark and unappealing. Black Velvet Bolete is edible, with a mild taste.

FROM THE SOIL

SUMMER THROUGH FALL

Stinkhorns (several)

Phallus and *Mutinus* spp.

HABITAT: Stinkhorns are saprobes, getting their nutrients from decaying organic matter. They are found in woods and fields and also appear in gardens, lawns and other cultivated areas; they often grow from wood chips.

DESCRIPTION: Stinkhorns start their lives encased in a universal veil, appearing like an egg (see pg. 62 for more details). Stinkhorns grow rapidly, rupturing the egg and attaining full stature of 6 to 9 inches in a day or less. A volva (a cup-like remnant of the universal veil) remains at the base of the stem, although it may be buried. Stems are hollow and slightly rough. Heads are covered with **dark, foul-smelling slime** that carries the spores; the tip is often free of slime. Flies strip away the slime, exposing the paler surface below. • **Common Stinkhorn** (*Phallus impudicus* and *P. hadriani*) have **ridged, pitted** heads and **whitish** stems. The volva of *P. impudicus* is whitish; that of *P. hadriani* is purplish. • **Ravenel's Stinkhorn** (*P. ravenelii*) is similar to Common Stinkhorn, but its head is **smooth to slightly granular**; the volva is **pinkish-tan**. • **Netted Stinkhorn** (*P. duplicatus*; also listed as *Dictyophora duplicata*) is similar to Common Stinkhorn but has a **white net-like skirt** hanging off the bottom edge of the head; the net encircles the stem loosely, hanging down to the ground. • **Devil's Stinkhorn** (*P. rubicundus*) has an **orangish to pinkish** stem with a **net-like** texture, a smooth, **cap-like head** and a tan volva. • **Dog Stinkhorn** (*Mutinus caninus, elegans and ravenelii*) closely resemble Devil's Stinkhorn, but there is **no distinct head**; it is merely a curved stem with brownish slime at the top that is eventually carried away by flies, leaving the bare stem.

SPORE PRINT: Impossible to make; likely brownish to olive-brown.

SEASON: Summer through fall.

OTHER NAMES: Common Stinkhorns are also called Morel Stinkhorns.

COMPARE: Common Stinkhorns may be mistaken for **Morels** (pgs. 24–27), but the caps of Morels are **not slimy** and there is **no volva** at the base of the stem. Morels grow in **spring**, while Stinkhorns grow in summer to fall.

NOTES: Mature Stinkhorns are considered inedible when gathered in the wild. They can be purchased dried in Asian markets. Cooked stinkhorn eggs are edible but opinions vary from not worth eating to revolting.

Common Stinkhorn

Ravenel's Stinkhorn with split egg

Netted Stinkhorn

Devil's Stinkhorn

Dog Stinkhorn

NEAR LIVE TREES   SUMMER THROUGH FALL

Elfin Saddles (several)

Helvella spp.

HABITAT: These unusual-looking mushrooms grow from the ground near living deciduous trees and conifers; they may also grow in grassy locations, along paths and in disturbed areas. Found singly or in small groups.

DESCRIPTION: Several Elfin Saddles are found in our area; they have thin-fleshed caps that appear **folded, lobed or saddle-like**. Stems of species discussed here are **chambered or hollow** and typically up to 4 inches tall; the flesh is brittle. • **Fluted White Helvella** (*H. crispa*) is the most common in our area. It has a **wide, heavily ribbed stem** that is whitish and may have a faint pink tinge. The cap is whitish to pale tan. It is saddle-shaped or irregularly folded and up to 2 inches across; the underside is **finely hairy**. • **Smooth-Stalked Helvella** (*H. elastica*) has a whitish to cream-colored stem that is **smooth** and **fairly slender**; it is **round** in cross-section. The cap is yellowish-brown, light brown or gray and usually less than 2 inches across. It typically has two lobes that appear to be folded together; edges are rolled slightly inward, giving a pillowy appearance. • **Fluted Black Helvella** (*H. lacunosa*) has a whitish to grayish stem that is wide and heavily ridged, with numerous pockets or cavities among the ridges; the stem may be up to **6 inches** tall. The cap is **dark gray, dark brown or black**; it is irregularly lobed and may seem **convoluted or brain-like**. It is usually about 2 inches across but some of the lobes may extend to nearly 4 inches across.

SPORE PRINT: White.

SEASON: Summer through fall.

OTHER NAMES: Elfin Saddle is a generic name for the species listed above.

COMPARE: **Saddle-Shaped False Morel** (*Gyromitra infula*) is similar; some sources list it as *H. infula*. Its caps are tan to brownish; they are up to 4 inches across and have two or three lobes. Stems are buff to whitish and up to 2 inches tall. It grows on **rotted wood** and woody debris that may be underground; the distinctions between this and the *Helvella* species are primarily microscopic. Saddle-Shaped False Morels are **toxic**.

NOTES: Elfin Saddles are sometimes listed as edible but are poor table fare; they may cause stomach upset and should be considered inedible.

Fluted White Helvella

Smooth-Stalked Helvella

Fluted Black Helvella

Saddle-Shaped False Morel

ON LIVE OR DEAD TREES AND LOGS

PRESENT YEAR-ROUND

Birch Polypore
Fomitopsis betulina

HABITAT: Found growing exclusively on birch trees, stumps and logs; more common on dead wood than on living trees. They grow as individual specimens, although there are typically multiple polypores on each tree. They cause brown rot, acting as both parasites and decomposers.

DESCRIPTION: Although this polypore takes several forms and appears in various colors, it is easy to recognize. It looks like a **pillowy growth** that may be shaped like a half-dome, a hoof, a projecting disk, a kidney or a half-bell that may be distorted. The top surface is dull white, gray or tan; it is **smooth** at first, often developing wide **cracks that expose the pale inner flesh**. The edge of the cap is rolled inward, creating a **thick, rounded overhang** that surrounds the pore surface. The cap may grow to 10 inches across but is usually smaller. There is no stem, although some specimens may have a thick neck at the point of attachment. The underside is whitish to buff, with small pores that may become tooth-like with age.

SPORE PRINT: White.

SEASON: Birch Polypore grows from spring through summer; they often persist over winter, appearing as darkened specimens the next year.

OTHER NAMES: Birch Bracket, Birch Conk, Ice Man Polypore, *Piptoporus betulinus*, *Polyporus betulinus*.

COMPARE: Tinder Polypore (pg. 198) grows in a similar fashion, but the surface is **banded** and it grows on a **wide variety of trees**. • Several other mushrooms that grow on trees may resemble Birch Polypore at a quick glance, but they have **gills** rather than pores. These include **Oyster Mushrooms** (pgs. 34–37), **Elm Caps** (pgs. 84–85) and **Bear Paw Lentinus** (pg. 223).

NOTES: Birch Polypore has long been used for medicinal purposes; indeed, it is one of the mushrooms found with the "Tyrolean Iceman," a mummified body from the mid-Neolithic era (the body was carbon-dated to between 3350 and 3100 BC) that was discovered in the Italian Alps in 1991, and is on display at the South Tyrol Museum of Archaeology in Bolzano, Italy. Birch Polypore are bitter and generally regarded as inedible.

ON LIVE OR DEAD TREES AND LOGS

PRESENT YEAR-ROUND

Tinder Polypore

Fomes excavatus (also listed as *F. fomentarius*)

HABITAT: Found growing on living or dead deciduous trees, stumps and logs. They grow as individual specimens, although there may be multiple poly-pores on each tree. Tinder Polypore causes white rot, acting as both a parasite and decomposer.

DESCRIPTION: This hard, tough-crusted gray to grayish-brown mushroom looks like a half-dome. It grows directly on the woody substrate and has no stem. The top side is **banded or ridged** both in texture and color; it is dull, dry and hard to the touch. The surface underneath is **brownish or gray** and is covered with fine, rounded pores. Caps are generally 2 to 8 inches across. Young specimens may be as tall as they are wide. With age, they become thicker and expand in width, particularly near the bottom; old specimens often look like a **hoof**. They may develop **slight cracks**.

SPORE PRINT: White.

SEASON: Growth takes place in spring and summer; present year-round.

OTHER NAMES: Firestarter Mushroom, Tinder Conk, Hoof Fungus, *Polyporus fomentarius;* called Amadou in Europe. *F. fomentarius* is listed in some sources as a synonym for *F. excavatus*; others describe these as two distinct species with very similar characteristics.

COMPARE: Willow Bracket (*Phellinus igniarius*; also known as *F. igniarius*) is similar in shape to Tinder Polypore, but its surface becomes blackened and develops **multiple, plate-like cracks**, giving it a **charred appearance**. It grows in the northern part of our area on willow, poplar, aspen, birch and other deciduous trees. • Birch Polypore (pg. 196) is similar to Tinder Polypore, but it **lacks the banding** and grows only on birch trees. • Artist's Conk (pg. 202) has **white** pores that instantly **bruise brown**.

NOTES: Tinder Polypore has long been used as a firestarter and an antibiotic; see the note on pg. 196 about the Tyrolean Iceman. Willow Bracket is used by the Inupiaq and Yup'ik peoples of Alaska to prepare a chewing mixture called Iqmik. The polypore is burned and its ashes are mixed with tobacco; the ashes amplify the effects of the nicotine, producing euphoria. Iqmik is used by young and old alike, even though it is addictive and causes tooth loss. There is a campaign by health officials to discourage this practice.

Tinder Polypore

Tinder Polypore

Pores of Tinder Polypore

Willow Bracket

ON DEAD AND DECAYING WOOD

PRESENT YEAR-ROUND

Turkey Tail
Trametes versicolor

HABITAT: Grows on dead wood such as fallen logs, stumps and standing dead trees; typically found on wood from deciduous trees but may occasionally grow on conifer wood. They are decomposers, causing white rot.

DESCRIPTION: These attractive, common shelf mushrooms grow as **thin, overlapping fan-shaped caps**. They may grow in a rosette, or may cover the wood like a scaly carpet. Individual caps have **concentric bands** of color. The outer band is **cream-colored or tan**, and the rest of the bands are shades of gray, blue, brown or reddish-brown. The surface is silky or velvety (a hand lens may be needed to see the hairs, but they can be felt with the fingers); the bands often alternate from smooth to hairy. Caps are **thin, leathery and flexible**; they range from 1 to 4 inches wide. Edges are **ruffled, scalloped or wavy**. The undersides are covered with **very fine, round pores** that are whitish, pale gray or yellowish. The caps have no stem, although they may narrow to a neck at the point of attachment.

SPORE PRINT: White to pale yellow.

SEASON: The Turkey Tail fruits from spring through fall; the caps are persistent and may be found for several years, continuing growth in successive seasons.

OTHER NAMES: *Coriolus versicolor, Polyporus versicolor.*

COMPARE: Several other shelf-type mushrooms that grow on wood appear similar but are distinguished by various features. • Caps of *T. pubescens* (also listed as *T. velutina*) are **velvety**; they are cream-colored to tan overall, **lacking the contrasting bands of color** found on Turkey Tail. • Caps of **Hairy Turkey Tail** (*T. hirsuta*) are **densely** hairy and gray to whitish overall; the outer band is typically **brownish** and the pores are larger than those of Turkey Tail. • **False Turkey Tail** (*Stereum ostrea*) looks just like Turkey Tail, but the underside is **smooth with no pores**. • The upper side of **Gilled Polypore** (pgs. 226–227) is similar to Turkey Tail, but the underside is covered with white **gill-like structures** rather than pores. • **Purple Tooth** (pg. 228) has **ragged purplish pores** underneath which become **tooth-like**.

NOTES: Turkey Tail and the look-alikes listed above are tough and inedible. They are used medicinally and are being studied for anti-cancer properties.

Turkey Tail rosette

T. pubescens

ON DEAD OR DECAYING WOOD (TYP.)

PRESENT YEAR-ROUND

Artist's Conk
Ganoderma applanatum

HABITAT: Found growing on living or dead trees, stumps and logs, primarily deciduous but also coniferous; more common on dead wood than on living trees. They grow as individual specimens, although there may be multiple polypores on each tree. Artist's Conk causes white rot, acting as both a parasite and decomposer.

DESCRIPTION: A tough, woody perennial that grows as a stemless, semicircular shelf, often with irregular, wavy or slightly scalloped edges; it may also appear hoof-like. Caps range from 2 to **25 inches** across; the body is thick on the side that attaches to the growing substrate, becoming thinner toward the edge. The top surface is **dull, dry and very hard**; it is tan, gray or brownish, often with concentric bands of color. It often develops ridge-like bands as it continues to grow each year; it may also become warty or bumpy and often develops furrows that run from the center toward the edge. The underside is covered with **fine white pores** that instantly turn **dark brown when scratched or bruised**; with age, the pore surface becomes buff-colored and less sensitive to scratches. If the mushroom is cut from top to bottom, **layers** of pores representing each year's growth will be visible. The mushrooms produce copious amounts of brown spores that are often seen on the growing substrate, or on plants and other nearby objects.

SPORE PRINT: Brown.

SEASON: Perennial; present year-round.

OTHER NAMES: Artist's Bracket. *G. megaloma* is sometimes listed as a synonym for *G. applanatum*, but there is evidence that there are differences between the two; some consider them a species complex.

COMPARE: Tinder Polypore (pg. 198) is a tough, dull polypore that is less than 8 inches across; its pore surface is **tan or gray** and does not bruise.

NOTES: Because it turns dark brown when scratched, Artist's Conk is often used as the medium for scratch art. The cap must be fresh, and the drawings should be done a few days after removing the cap from the tree. Once the cap dries out, it turns buff-colored; the brown engraved lines remain, creating an unusual piece of art. Tea made from the dried mushrooms is sometimes used medicinally.

Spores caught by spiderweb

Scratch art on Artist's Conk

Dyer's Polypore
Phaeolus schweinitzii

NEAR LIVE, DEAD OR DYING TREES

PRESENT YEAR-ROUND

HABITAT: A wood-rotting parasite, this mushroom is usually found at the base of conifers (rarely deciduous trees), growing from buried roots. It can sometimes be found growing directly from dead or dying wood.

DESCRIPTION: The color and shape of this fungus is quite variable, depending on the age and growing conditions. Single specimens can grow into large rosettes, up to a foot across, with overlapping shelves. Like the Tooth Mushrooms (pg. 254), this mushroom tends to envelop surrounding material as it expands and may simply look like a formless blob. When young, it is typically spongy and brown with a **yellow margin** and a velvety surface. With age, it becomes woody and dark brown to black, with intense yellow, orange or rust-brown bands of color. Underneath is a **greenish-yellow pore surface** that **bruises brown**. The pores are **large and rough**, becoming angular and almost tooth-like or maze-like with age. The entire mess grows from a stubby, brown stem.

SPORE PRINT: White to creamy yellow.

SEASON: Summer through late fall; grows annually but found year-round.

OTHER NAMES: Velvet Top Fungus, *Polyporus schweinitzii.*

COMPARE: Yellow-Red Gill Polypore (*Gloeophyllum sepiarium*, also known as Conifer Mazegill) is smaller, with rosettes less than 5 inches across. Underneath are distinct, **deep gill ridges** that are **golden brown**; they may be fused and maze-like. • **Orange Hydnellum** (pgs. 254–255) has fused or clustered caps up to 6 inches across. Caps are very bumpy and orange to brownish with a paler edge. Underneath are white **teeth** that turn brown with age except for the tips, which remain white. • Examples of *Ganoderma* **species** (pgs. 202, 206) growing from buried roots may look like the Dyer's Polypore, but they have a **fine, white** pore surface underneath.

NOTES: Though not edible, the Dyer's Polypore is a favorite of textile dyers because it contains an intense yellow pigment. This same mushroom used with a dye bath or wool treated with iron sulfate produces a beautiful green color. Yellow-Red Gill Polypore is regarded as inedible.

Bruised pore surface

Young specimen

Dyed wool yarn

ON LIVE OR DEAD TREES AND ROOTS

SPRING THROUGH LATE FALL

Lacquered Polypore
Ganoderma spp.

HABITAT: Our area has three species of Lacquered Polypore; they appear very similar, and are distinguished largely by habitat. All are saprobes that fruit on living or dead trees, as well as from buried roots; they are often found at the base of a tree. *G. sessile* and *G. curtisii* are found on **hardwoods**, while *G. tsugae* appears on **conifers**, primarily hemlock. They cause white rot.

DESCRIPTION: Lacquered Polypores are often strikingly beautiful, with a shiny surface banded with multiple colors. The classic form is a shelf-like bracket that may have a neck-like stalk or may be stalkless; *G. sessile* and *G. curtisii* frequently lack the stalk, but one is often present. Caps are **semicircular to fan-shaped**, with a **firm** texture and somewhat **lumpy** surface that appears **lacquered**; they are typically 3 to 6 inches across but may be up to 13 inches across. They often have concentric zones of color that may be dramatic or subtle. On many young specimens, the outer edge is **cream-colored, blending into yellow**; inner zones are **reddish to reddish-brown**. Other specimens are reddish, reddish-brown or brownish overall; older examples often have lumpy, ring-like bands. Undersides are covered with fine whitish pores that turn dull tan with age. The stalk, when present, is dark brown and twisted; it may be up to 5 inches long and is fairly thick. Lacquered Polypores fruit singly or in overlapping clusters. *G. sessile* also fruits on the ground, particularly in urban areas, on buried roots remaining where a tree was removed; it is generally circular when found in these locations. Mowing and foot traffic cause the mushroom to develop **multiple, overlapping lobes** that are bumpy and misshapen, often with grass and other vegetation growing between them.

SPORE PRINT: Brown.

SEASON: Spring through late fall; may persist into winter.

OTHER NAMES: Varnished Polypore, Reishi, Ling Chih. *G. sessile* is also listed as *G. lucidum*, which is an Asian species that does not occur in most of the U.S.

COMPARE: Beefsteak Fungus (pg. 217) is solid, deep red on top, with no banding; its pores are whitish to pinkish-yellow. It has a **very soft** texture.

NOTES: This fungus has been used for medicinal purposes for over 2,000 years in China. It is used to enhance longevity, boost the immune system, reduce blood pressure and treat cancer. Some people are allergic to it.

Terrestrial form of
G. sessile

ON DEAD TREES, STUMPS AND LOGS

FALL

Resinous Polypore

Ischnoderma resinosum

HABITAT: The Resinous Polypore is a saprobe that typically fruits on dead trees, both standing and fallen, as well as on stumps. It may occasionally appear on dying trees in areas where the wood has already succumbed to injury or disease. Although it is generally found on wood of deciduous trees, it occasionally appears on conifers. It may grow singly but is often seen in overlapping clusters.

DESCRIPTION: This mushroom's appearance changes considerably over time. Very young specimens are rounded or lumpy; they are thick, soft and **velvety**, with reddish-brown centers and a white margin. **Amber resin droplets** sometimes appear on cap edges. As the specimens age, they become wider and flatter; they are semicircular, often with wavy or scalloped edges. Mature specimens are up to 9 inches across and roughly ¾ inch thick. They are brownish to reddish-brown, often retaining the white margin; the color may be fairly consistent or it may be zoned into concentric rings. Old specimens become wrinkled and develop black, crusty-looking bands interspersed with brownish bands; the surface becomes dry and tough and may develop cracks that radiate from the center to the edges. The underside of young specimens is covered with white pores that **bruise brownish**; with age, the pore surface becomes tan.

SPORE PRINT: White.

SEASON: Fall.

OTHER NAMES: Late Fall Polypore.

COMPARE: Yellow-Red Gill Polypore (*Gloeophyllum sepiarium*; also known as Conifer Mazegill) looks similar to mature specimens of Resinous Polypore but is under 5 inches wide and has **slot-like pores and gills** underneath. The cap has concentric bands of color that may be subtle or distinct. Young specimens have bands of orange to rust-brown, while older specimens become dark brown or black in the center; edges are bright yellowish or whitish. It has a **corky** texture.

NOTES: Young, tender specimens of Resinous Polypore are edible when gently stewed; they have a moderately soft texture. Yellow-Red Gill Polypore is regarded as inedible.

Young specimens
with resin drops

Middle-aged specimens

Mature specimens

Marshmallow Polypore

Sarcodontia unicolor (formerly *Spongipellis unicolor*)

This unassuming white shelf mushroom grows singly or in sparse groups on dead or dying trunks and fallen branches of hardwood trees, especially oaks; it is also a parasite on living trees. It looks like many other polypores but is soft and **spongy**. The half-round domes are fuzzy or velvety on top and can grow up to **a foot across** and 8 inches out from the tree, although typical specimens are half that size. The pore surface is covered with large, angular pores that may be up to **1 inch deep**. With age the pores become coarser and sometimes more tooth-like or slot-like; the pore surface darkens to tan or yellowish. Its spore print is white; it is found in summer and fall.

COMPARE: *Irpiciporus pachyodon* (formerly *Spongipellis pachyodon*) is also called Marshmallow Polypore. Its caps are 2 inches wide or less; they grow in **large, fused clusters**, sometimes covering the side of a tree. The **tooth-like pore surface** is obvious, hanging out from the poorly formed caps, giving it the alternate name of Milk-White Toothed Polypore. Young specimens of *Irpiciporus pachyodon* can look more like a toothy crust growing on tree bark and could be confused with the even smaller, **hard-crusted** *Irpex lacteus* (pgs. 262–263), which is also called the Milk-White Toothed Polypore. • Birch Polypore (pg. 196) has **small pores** and occurs **only on birch logs and stumps**.

NOTES: The species listed are inedible. All cause white rot of the trees they infect.

Berkeley's Polypore

Bondarzewia berkeleyi (also known as *Polyporus berkeleyi*)

This polypore can grow to impressive sizes; clusters may be 3 feet across, with individual caps that are up to **10 inches** wide. They cause white rot, acting as both parasites and decomposers and are found near living, dying and dead deciduous trees, particularly oak; they typically grow at the base of a tree or from the ground over buried roots. Very young specimens look like a grouping of **knobby fingers**; these develop into caps that are fleshy and somewhat tough. Mature specimens grow as a **rosette** of overlapping caps that are roughly fan-shaped; the caps narrow down into a neck-like stalk. A tough, yellowish-brown stem may be found at the base of the rosette. Top surfaces are **cream-colored, tan or yellowish**, often with concentric bands of color that may be obvious or subtle; caps become dull orangish-brown with age. The surface is dry and may be smooth or lightly hairy. The lower surface is covered with medium-fine **whitish** pores that descend the stalk. Flesh of young specimens produces a milky sap when squeezed. Its spore print is white; it grows from midsummer through fall.

COMPARE: Hen of the Woods (pgs. 54–55) appears similar, but its caps are less than 3 inches across and are more delicate. • The **Chicken Mushroom** (pgs. 32–33) is **brightly colored**; pores of the most common variety are **yellow**. • The Black-Staining Polypore (*Meripilus sumstinei*) is similar, but it **stains black** when bruised.

NOTES: The finger-like stage is edible but developed caps are very bitter.

Smoky Polypore

Bjerkandera adusta (also known as *Polyporus adustus*)

From above, this polypore often looks like a cluster of generic-looking tan or grayish caps blanketing a dead deciduous tree; caps are semicircular or irregularly shaped and have no stem. Smoky Polypore is a saprobe that prefers the wood of deciduous trees but may be found on conifer wood. The caps are typically overlapping or fused together. They are 1 to 3 inches wide and **thin**, with a **velvety** surface and leathery texture; they are whitish, grayish or tan, frequently with concentric bands of color but sometimes fairly monotone. The surface underneath is covered with tiny pores that are **smoky gray**; they become darker when handled or with age. The edge is frequently whitish on both sides of younger specimens, turning black with age. The spore print is white. Smoky Polypore are found year-round.

COMPARE: Big Smoky Bracket (*B. fumosa*) is a related shelf mushroom that has a **buff to pale gray** pore surface. It may grow to nearly **6 inches** wide, and the caps are **thicker** and more fleshy than those of Smoky Polypore. Young specimens of Big Smoky Bracket smell like anise.

NOTES: When young, both of the *Bjerkandera* species discussed here may grow with only rudimentary caps or may appear nearly capless; they look like spreading patches of white or tan foam with blobs of velvety color. Both species are considered inedible.

Dryad's Saddle

Cerioporus squamosus (also known as Pheasant Back, *Polyporus squamosus*)

Both common names for this mushroom seem appropriate. The cap is elaborately patterned with flattened, dark brown scales that create a **feather-like pattern** on top of a tan to creamy yellowish background. It is semicircular or kidney-shaped, appearing like a **small saddle** suited to a woodland fairy. Some specimens have a short, thick stem that is attached off-center; it is cream-colored at first, turning black with age. Other specimens are attached directly to the wood. Dryad's Saddles act as parasites on living deciduous trees (particularly elms) and as decomposers of dead wood such as stumps and fallen logs. The cap may grow to over 12 inches across but is usually smaller; it often grows in small clusters but may also appear singly. The underside is covered with whitish to creamy yellow pores that are fairly large and angular; they do not bruise when handled. Flesh is soft when young, turning corky with age; it smells like **watermelon rind**. The spore print is white. Dryad's Saddle are most common in spring when they are often found by Morel hunters, but they may also be found in summer and fall.

COMPARE: Many other shelf mushrooms are similar in size, but they lack the distinctive, feathery pattern and large pores found on Dryad's Saddle.

NOTES: Young Dryad's Saddle are edible when cooked, although they have a rubbery texture.

Hexagonal-Pored Polypore

Neofavolus alveolaris

The small, bright caps of this mushroom can be a beautiful sight in the early spring woods. This polypore grows singly or in groups on branches and sticks of deciduous trees; it is usually seen on branches that have fallen to the ground. Caps are semicircular or kidney-shaped and may be up to 4 inches across but are typically much smaller. Young caps are tan to **bright orange** with a **feathered** surface (described as scaly in many field guides). Underneath the caps are white, **hexagonal-shaped** pores radiating from and running down the short to non-existent stem. Older caps may be white after exposure to the elements. Its spore print is white, and it is found from early spring through fall.

COMPARE: The Fringed Polypore (pg. 164) has a round cap that has a **hairy edge** and a **centrally attached brownish stem**. • Dryad's Saddle (pg. 213) has large angular pores, but its cap is much larger, growing up to a foot and a half across on trunks and stumps of dead or dying trees. Its surface is white with a feathery-looking pattern created by dark brown scales.

NOTES: This small mushroom has many names; it is also called Hickory-Stick Polypore, *Polyporus alveolaris, P. mori, Favolus alveolaris* and *F. canadensis*. Though tough, this mushroom is edible; young caps are a little more tender. It causes white rot of the wood on which it grows.

Cinnabar-Red Polypore

Trametes coccinea (also listed as Pycnoporus cinnabarinus, Polyporus cinnabarinus)

It's hard to miss this stunning mushroom in the woods; its bright **orangish-red** coloration draws the eye. It grows as a stemless semicircular or kidney-shaped cap that is attached to fallen or dead deciduous trees, particularly oak; it is occasionally reported on conifers. It typically is not found on very old, rotten wood. This species is most often found in open areas such as wood edges and power line cuts. Caps are up to 5 inches across; they are up to ½ inch thick with a thinner edge and are **tough and leathery**. They grow singly or in overlapping clusters. The surface is finely hairy on young specimens, becoming hairless but rough-textured, wrinkled or pockmarked with age; the color may fade to yellowish-orange. The underside is covered with **fine, bright reddish-orange pores** that are rounded or somewhat angular. Its spore print is white, and it grows from spring through fall in our area.

COMPARE: Tender Nesting Polypore (*Hapalopilus rutilans*; formerly *H. nidulans*) is a smaller polypore whose cap is **brownish-orange to cinnamon-colored**. Its pores are angular and **dirty orange to yellowish-brown**. • Beefsteak Fungus (pg. 217) is **deep red** and has a **very soft** texture. • *Pycnoporellus fulgens* (also listed as *Pycnoporellus fibrillosus* in older texts) has a **yellowish-orange cap** and **large pores** that are pale orangish to apricot-colored.

NOTES: Cinnabar-Red Polypore and Tender Nesting Polypore are inedible. Beefsteak Fungus is edible when young. Edibility of *Pycnoporellus fulgens* is unknown.

Red-Belted Polypore

Fomitopsis pinicola (also known as *Fomes pinicola*)

This mushroom grows on both living and dead trees and is frequently found on stumps and downed wood; it seems to prefer conifers but also grows on deciduous wood. Specimens may grow alone or there may be many on a single tree. It is perennial, persisting for several years. Each year it grows a new band of flesh on the outer edge of the older flesh, which is **hard and woody**. The new band is white to yellowish; there may be beads of moisture on its surface. As the mushroom grows, older portions darken, becoming reddish, then reddish-brown, gray and finally blackish; there is typically a **bright or deep red band** near the outer white edge. Younger bands typically have a glossy surface that looks lacquered; on some specimens the entire surface is glossy. The mushroom is typically hoof-shaped but may also be fairly flat, looking like a thick fan. Pores underneath are cream-colored, bruising yellow on young growth. The spore print is whitish.

COMPARE: Lacquered Polypore (pg. 206) is glossy and reddish to reddish-brown, but it is an annual and does not have the distinct, multiple layered bands of hard, woody flesh.

NOTES: Red-Belted Polypore has an important role in breaking down woody waste in forests, helping to create material for new soil. It also acts as a parasite on living trees, causing brown rot.

Beefsteak Fungus
Fistulina hepatica

This colorful mushroom is very noticeable. It grows singly or in small clusters on stumps and dead or dying trees; it is also found at the base of living trees. It prefers oak but also grows on chestnut and other deciduous trees. Caps are **deep to bright red or purplish-red** and generally fan-shaped or tongue-like, often with irregular or wavy edges; they are up to 10 inches across and typically **½ to 1½ inches thick**. The texture is **soft and fleshy**; it may be somewhat gelatinous, slimy or sticky. Caps may appear streaked or mottled; edges may be darker than the center. The pore surface underneath is whitish to pinkish-yellow on fresh specimens, turning reddish-brown when bruised. Unlike most other mushrooms with pores, the tubes are **separate** rather than fused together (a hand lens is needed to see this). Fresh specimens produce a **reddish liquid** when squeezed; the cut surface is red and really does resemble beefsteak. The spore print is pinkish or salmon-colored. Beefsteak Fungus grows from midsummer through fall.

COMPARE: Lacquered Polypore (pg. 206) may have a deep red cap, but its texture is **very firm** and it often has concentric bands of different hues. • Cinnabar-Red Polypore (pg. 215) is bright orangish-red and **thin** with a **tough** texture.

NOTES: Beefsteak Fungus is edible but has a bitter or tart taste; young specimens are preferred. Oak that has been parasitized by this fungus is prized by wood-workers because it develops dark, rich tones.

Blue Cheese Polypore

Cyanosporus caesius (also known as *Oligoporus caesius* and *Tyromyces caesius*)

This soft, watery polypore is a saprobe that prefers the wood of deciduous trees but may be found on conifer wood. It grows singly or in small groups that are often overlapping. The cap is roughly semicircular with wavy edges but may also be irregularly lumpy; it is up to 3 inches across and has no stem. The surface is **dirty white to grayish** and is covered with fine hairs that may be grayish-blue; it develops **bluish-gray or bluish patches** with age or handling. The bottom surface is whitish to gray, becoming grayish-blue or grayish-purple with age or handling; pores are moderately coarse and angular, developing a tooth-like appearance with age. The flesh is spongy and whitish, bruising grayish-blue; it has a pleasant fragrance. Its spore print is pale blue; it grows from midsummer through fall.

COMPARE: White Cheese Polypore (*T. chioneus* or *T. albellus*) is similar, but both surfaces are **white**, lacking the grayish or bluish tones; it grows on dead wood of deciduous trees, favoring birch.

NOTES: This mushroom has long been called *Postia caesia*, but that is a species that does not appear in North America; a handful of similar species, including *C. caesius*, may be listed as the *P. caesia* group. The polypores discussed on this page are inedible.

Chaga
Inonotus obliquus

Also called the Clinker Polypore or Birch Conk, this unusual, homely fungus would generate no notice at all if it were not used to make a highly regarded medicinal tea. It typically grows as a **bulging canker** on living trees, primarily birch; it may also grow as a snout-like or irregular projection rather than a bulge. Chaga may be a foot or more across. The surface is **black and heavily cracked**, often with brownish areas showing between the cracks; it looks **charred or burned**. The interior is yellowish-brown, with a **corky** texture. At this stage the fungus is sterile and does not produce spores. The fertile stage comes only after the host tree has died and a layer of tubes develops under the bark. These spore-producing tubes are quickly attacked and destroyed by beetles. Chaga grows in the fall but is present year-round. It is a parasite that will eventually kill the host tree in less than a decade.

COMPARE: The unusual burned appearance and birch tree habitat make this a distinct fungus. The yellowish-brown interior and corky texture will distinguish it from wood burls.

NOTES: Chaga is widely used in Slavic countries, Eastern Europe and some parts of Asia to make a tea that is believed to both prevent and cure cancer. It is rich in antioxidants and is also used to fight viruses, to cure disorders of the digestive system and as a general health tonic. A hatchet is generally needed to remove it from the host tree; the entire fungus is then pounded or ground and steeped to make tea.

Hairy Panus
Panus neostrigosus

ON DECAYING WOOD

EARLY SPRING THROUGH LATE FALL

HABITAT: Hairy Panus is a saprobe, getting its nutrients from decaying wood. It grows singly, in loose groups, or more often in tight clusters on dead **deciduous** wood, especially on cut or fallen logs and stumps.

DESCRIPTION: This mushroom, which is less than 4 inches across, presents itself in many different forms, from an almost stemless shelf to a short-stemmed funnel; it may be pink, purplish, tan or orangish. However, caps are **always furry**, a feature accentuated by the rolled-under cap edges. Gills are fine and closely spaced; they are colored like the cap when young, turning white with age. When a stem is present, it may be off-center with the **gills running down it** to meet the short, furry base.

SPORE PRINT: White.

SEASON: Early spring through late fall.

OTHER NAMES: Ruddy Panus, *Lentinus strigosus*, *Panus rudis*, *L. rudis*.

COMPARE: The **Smooth Panus** or **Conch Panus** (*Panus conchatus*; also listed as *L. torulosus*) is slightly larger than Hairy Panus, with a more obvious stem. It has a **smooth cap** and is more purplish, especially when young. • **Styptic Panus** (*Panellus stipticus*) is generally 1 inch across or less and grows in overlapping shelves. The semicircular cap fans outward from a short stem near the inside edge. Caps are tan, buff-colored or whitish; the top is velvety and edges are rounded or lobed. Gills are **abruptly attached** to the stem and do not run down it. They are light brown and forked, with numerous **cross-veins** (visible with a hand lens). Gills of young, fresh specimens glow in the dark (called bioluminescent), giving this species the alternate name of Luminescent Panus. • Orangish specimens of Hairy Panus may be mistaken for a pale **Orange Mock Oyster** (pg. 225), but Mock Oyster is **stemless** and more **brightly colored**; it has a **pink to tan** spore print. • Stalkless Paxillus (pg. 37) grows on dead **conifer** wood. Its gills have cross-veins and appear **wavy or corrugated**. The spore print is **yellowish to yellowish-brown**.

NOTES: Hairy Panus and Styptic Panus can be found in many seasons, shriveling up in dry weather and re-hydrating when wet. All the species noted above are inedible. Styptic Panus is used in traditional Chinese medicine as a blood thickener and purgative.

Hairy Panus

Smooth Panus

Styptic Panus

Split Gill
Schizophyllum commune

This small mushroom acts as both a parasite and decomposer, getting its nutrients from the wood of decaying or dead deciduous trees; it may also grow on processed lumber. Although small and easily overlooked, it has intriguing features when viewed closely; a hand lens is helpful. The cap is **fuzzy** and white to grayish above. It is up to 2 inches wide and fan-shaped or irregularly lobed; edges are minutely scalloped. It grows scattered, layered or in rosettes. The underside is pinkish-gray, with **doubled or split** gill-like structures that fan out from the center to the edge. These "gills" are really a folded pore surface; they pull together in dry weather to protect the spores within but open to release them when moisture is present. In fact, the entire mushroom will curl up and appear even smaller when dry but rehydrate and regain its shape when wet. This tough little shelf can last for many seasons. Its spore print is white; it is found year-round.

COMPARE: *Trametes pubescens* (pgs. 200–201; inedible) has a cap that is **velvety** but not fuzzy; it has a **white pore surface** below that yellows with age. • Styptic Panus (pgs. 220–221; inedible) has **sharp, single gills** attached to a **short stem**.

NOTES: Many experts call Split Gill the most common and widespread mushroom in the world. Although it is a traditional food in certain cultures, it is not recommended. It is small and tough, and has been known to infect humans with compromised immune systems. It is being studied for possible medicinal uses.

Bear Paw Lentinus
Lentinellus ursinus

This mushroom is a saprobe, getting its nutrients from decaying wood. It may grow singly but is usually found in overlapping clusters on dead deciduous trees, occasionally conifers. Bear Paw Lentinus gets its species name from *ursa*, the Latin word for bear, due to its brown color and **hairy surface**. Lacking a stem, fan-shaped caps grow to about 4 inches across with a lobed or wavy edge. They are usually lighter colored on the outer edges; some specimens may be tan all over and resemble an Oyster Mushroom (pgs. 34–37). However, unlike Oysters, the cap surface is **fuzzy**, especially near the base. Underneath, the **closely spaced**, white to pinkish gills have a distinct, **serrated** edge. Its spore print is white, and it is found from summer through late fall.

COMPARE: Fox Lentinus (*L. vulpinus*) is a similar size but caps grow from a **short stem** that may fuse with neighboring stems to form a thicker base. • The Shoehorn Oyster (*Hohenbuehelia petaloides*) has a **smooth, inrolled cap** and a wide neck, appearing funnel-like. • Oyster Mushrooms (pgs. 34–37) often appear similar but they **lack the cap hairs** and have a mild taste.

NOTES: *Lentinellus* species are said to have an extremely bitter or hot taste and are not collected for the table. This mushroom is also called Bear Lentinus, Bear Paw and Saw Tooth.

Creps (several)
Crepidotus spp.

These small, **flimsy** caps grow in loose groups on well-rotted deciduous wood, especially fallen logs and branches; when you first see them, you may think you've found a batch of baby Oyster Mushrooms (pgs. 34–37). Creps have white to tan caps with **crowded gills** underneath that fan out from where they are attached to the wood; there is no stem. When growing from the bottom of a log, they may be nearly circular. The gills are white at first, darkening to light brown; the spore print is brown. Creps are found from summer through late fall; they are common even in dry weather. • The **Flat Crep** (*C. applanatus*) is the most common, growing up to only 2 inches across; it is also called Little White Crep and Flat Oysterling. • The caps of the **Peeling Oysterling** (*C. mollis*) may grow slightly larger and have **minute brown scales** on top when dry. The flesh is **gelatinous**, giving it the alternate name of Jelly Crep.

COMPARE: The Orange Crep or Yellow Gilled Crep (*C. crocophyllus*) has buff to yellowish caps **overlaid with brownish fibers** that may be sparse or heavy. Gills of young specimens are **yellowish to orange**, turning brown with age.

NOTES: These fragile Oysterlings are not edible. Since Oysters have thicker flesh and often a short stem with gills running down it, you will know after inspecting only a couple whether you have an edible treat, or just a Crep.

Orange Mock Oyster
Phyllotopsis nidulans

Orange Mock Oysters grow singly or in loose groups but mostly in dense over-lapping clusters on dead and fallen wood of deciduous trees and conifers. They are saprobes, getting their nutrients from dead and decaying organic matter. Though small, these **fuzzy** little shelves are easy to spot because of their **bright yellow to orange** color. Caps are up to 3 inches across. Underneath the cap are closely spaced gills that are **the same bright orange color** and radiate out from the **stemless** connection point to the wood. Often the edge of the cap is rolled under, especially when young. The brightly colored cap surface fades to tan with age, but remains intensely furry at every stage. They often have a strong, unpleasant odor, but this may be absent. Despite their common name, they are not likely to be confused with a true Oyster Mushroom (pgs. 34–37) due to these characteristics. Their spore print is pink to tan; they grow from late summer through late fall.

COMPARE: Most Oyster Mushrooms (pgs. 34–37) are **cream-colored, tan or grayish-brown**, although caps of the **Golden Oyster** are bright yellow; however, true Oysters have **smooth** caps and **whitish** gills. *Panus* and *Lentinellus* species (pgs. 220 and 223) grow on wood and have densely **furry** caps, but they are not bright orange like the Orange Mock Oyster. • **Chicken Mushroom** (pgs. 32–33) is a prime edible shelf mushroom that is bright orange, but the underside is covered with **tiny pores** rather than gills and the top sides are **smooth** rather than fuzzy or hairy.

NOTES: Orange Mock Oysters are generally regarded as inedible.

ON DEAD WOOD

PRESENT YEAR-ROUND

Oak Maze Gill
Daedalea quercina

HABITAT: Grows on dead hardwood, especially oaks; *Quercus* is the Latin genus name for oak trees. It causes brown rot of the wood.

DESCRIPTION: This dull grayish to light brown shelf mushroom looks unremarkable until you turn it over. Underneath this woody bracket is a **deeply ridged** pore surface that looks like an intricate **maze** of thick gills. This spore-producing surface is white at first, turning tan with age. Individual caps have a bumpy but velvety surface and can grow to 8 inches wide, 3 inches out from the tree and **3 inches thick**. It lasts for many seasons on the same tree, getting darker over time. Although firm to the touch, it may surround sticks or other debris as it grows rather than pushing them away.

SPORE PRINT: White.

SEASON: Present year-round.

OTHER NAMES: Thick-Maze Oak Polypore, Oak Mazegill Bracket.

COMPARE: Caps of **Gilled Polypore** (*Trametes betulina*; also listed as *Lenzites betulina, L. betulinus*) grow only to about 4 inches wide and less than an inch thick. Underneath is a firm, elaborate pore surface composed of **thick, white gill-like structures**. *Betula* is the Latin genus name for birch and this is also called the Birch Mazegill, though it can be found on other deciduous trees and conifers. The cap surface has **distinct bands of color**, often including green from algae growth on old specimens. • **Thin-Maze Flat Polypore** (*Daedaleopsis confragosa*) grows mainly on birch and willow. Its bumpy to wavy cap surface varies in color from all-white, to gray or dark brown with **strong concentric zones**. It is also called Blushing Bracket, due to the tendency of its finer white to tan maze-like pore surface to **bruise pink to reddish** when young. • *Trametes gibbosa* and *T. elegans* are both referred to as Lumpy Bracket; DNA is required to positively separate the two. Lumpy Bracket is similar in appearance to Oak Maze Gill but is **up to 12 inches wide**; it is **white to gray** above and often discolored with green algae. Pores are often maze-like, but may also be round or angular. Lumpy Bracket is becoming more common in the Northeast. Current studies of species found in our area point to *T. gibbosa* rather than *T. elegans*, which is a subtropical species that is not found in the Northeast.

NOTES: All of the mushrooms listed above are inedible but quite decorative.

Oak Maze Gill

Gilled Polypore

Purple Tooth
Trichaptum biforme (also known as *T. biformis*)

These common, perennial mushrooms are saprobes that get their nutrients from dead and dying deciduous trees. They are fan-shaped, growing in overlapping shelf-like layers, often prolifically; on fallen logs, they may grow in a rosette. The Latin species name *biforme* ("two forms") was chosen because when young this mushroom has a **purple** pore surface that develops into minute **teeth** with age, fading to mauve or tan; outer edges with new growth are brighter and more pore-like. The top is hairy when young, with **bands** of **pink, purple, tan or brown** over the creamy white to grayish background. It becomes smoother and faded with age, sometimes becoming green from algae. Individual shelves are **paper-thin** and up to 3 inches across. The spore print is white. It grows from spring through early winter but is found all year.

COMPARE: *T. abietinum* is usually **smaller** and grows from dead or dying **conifers**. • **Turkey Tail** and its many look-alikes (pg. 200) grow in the same manner and have bands of colors but undersides are covered with **smooth whitish, pale gray or yellowish pores**. • From above, caps of **Gilled Polypore** (pgs. 226–227) look very similar to Purple Tooth, but they have **white gill-like structures** underneath.

NOTES: All of the mushrooms listed are decomposers, multiplying and persisting for years until the substrate is totally broken down. Some of these curl up in dry weather, and then rehydrate when moisture is present.

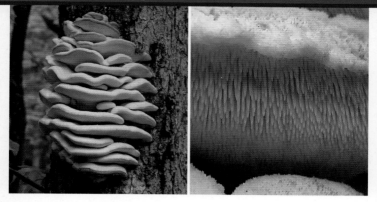

Northern Tooth
Climacodon septentrionale (also known as *C. septentrionalis*)

This large, creamy white shelf mushroom is a parasite, causing heart rot of deciduous trees, especially beech and maple; it fruits prolifically on the trees it has infected. The thick, tough caps can grow up to a foot across in densely overlapping clumps up the side or base of a tree. From a distance, it might look like a nice batch of Oyster Mushrooms (pgs. 34–37) or a pale version of the Chicken Mushroom (pgs. 32–33), but close viewing reveals quite different features. Growing from a thick, solid base, Northern Tooth caps are **fuzzy and bumpy** on top with clear zones of growth. Under the cap is a crowded surface of spore-bearing **teeth**. The entire fungus turns yellowish-brown when old and develops a rancid scent that some compare to rotting ham. Its spore print is white, and it grows from summer through late fall.

COMPARE: Hen of the Woods (pgs. 54–55) grows from the ground at the base of **oaks** and has a **fine white pore surface** under its caps, which are **smaller and thinner** than those of Northern Tooth. • All surfaces of *Hericium* species (pgs. 48–49) are **draped with white teeth**; several *Hericium* have branching forms.

NOTES: This large fungus is not edible, and worse than that, it likes to attack sugar maples! The name implies that it is a northern species (*septentrionale* means "northern" in Latin), but it is just as common in the southern parts of our area. It is also called Shelving Tooth.

Gem-Studded Puffball

Lycoperdon perlatum

HABITAT: This saprobic mushroom grows **from the ground**, usually in large groups or clusters. It is common in the woods but is also found in grassy urban areas.

DESCRIPTION: The Gem-Studded Puffball has a generally **spherical top** that may be up to 3 inches in diameter but is usually smaller. Rather than a true stem, it has an **elongated base** that varies from 1 to 3 inches tall, making the mushroom look like an upside-down pear; however, it often grows in tight clusters so only the spherical tops are visible. The outer skin is white, cream-colored or tan and is covered in **minute spines** that may disappear with age, leaving a slightly rough surface. As with other Puffballs (pgs. 41–43), the outer skin encases the interior spore-producing flesh. Initially smooth, white and edible, the flesh becomes yellowish-green and inedible, finally turning into a brown powder. Each sphere develops an opening at the top to release, or puff out, the spores.

SPORE PRINT: Brown.

SEASON: Early summer through fall; dried specimens can be found year-round.

OTHER NAMES: Common Puffball, Devil's Snuff-Box, *L. gemmatum*.

COMPARE: The slightly smaller **Pear-Shaped Puffball** (*Apioperdon pyriforme*; also listed as *L. pyriforme, Morganella pyriformis*) is similar to the Gem-Studded Puffball but grows in dense clusters from **decaying wood**. • The edible **Peeling Puffball** (*L. marginatum*) is up to 2 inches across; its skin is covered with **spines that have pyramidal bases**. It may be confused with species of **Spiny Puffball** (*L. curtisii, Vascellum curtisii, L. pulcherrimum, L. echinatum*), which are marble-sized and inedible. Peeling Puffball can be recognized at maturity when the skin **falls off in large sheaths**, revealing a smooth, brown surface.

NOTES: Most puffballs are edible when young but can be mistaken for various cap-and-stem species in the button stage, including **deadly** Amanitas (pgs. 62–66), **toxic** Agaricus (pg. 80) or the egg stage of Stinkhorns (pg. 192). Small puffballs growing from the ground should always be cut in half to make sure they are not overripe or young examples of another species such as an Amanita button (pg. 43); also see Earthballs, pg. 234. The ripe spores should not be inhaled, as they can cause respiratory distress.

Gem-Studded Puffball

Pear-Shaped Puffball

After releasing spores

Spiny Puffball

Earthstars (several)

Geastrum spp.

HABITAT: Earthstars grow from the ground singly or in groups near hardwoods and conifers. They are **saprobes**, getting their nutrients from leaf litter and dead wood; often found in large numbers near the stumps of dead trees.

DESCRIPTION: Earthstars begin their lives as small, smooth, tan spheres much like Puffballs (pgs. 41–43, 230), with a thick skin encasing a firm, spherical mass of spores. The skin splits and unfolds into a **star-shaped base** surrounding the sphere. The star is buff-colored to pinkish; it may be hidden by the dirt and debris it collects. With age, the sphere turns darker brown and develops a beak-like opening at the top for spore release. There are numerous species, each distinguished by slight variations. Most are less than 2 inches across, including the rays of the star. • **Rounded Earthstar** (*G. saccatum*) is the most common. It is attached to the ground at a **central point**; the sphere nestles tightly in its saucer-like star. The spore beak is surrounded by a **pale ring**. • Sessile Earthstar (*G. fimbriatum*) has a **wider connection** to the ground and **lacks the ring** around the spore beak. • **Collared Earthstar** (*G. triplex*) is up to **4 inches** across and has a much **thicker** base. The star has a **pinkish** surface that develops **dark brown cracks**. The arms may bend under so far that they break off.

SPORE PRINT: Brown.

SEASON: Fruiting summer through late fall, present year-round.

OTHER NAMES: Some American Indian tribes traditionally called them Fallen Stars and thought their appearance foretold of celestial events.

COMPARE: The **Hygroscopic Earthstar** (*Astraeus hygrometricus*) is also called the Barometer Earthstar because the rays **react to moisture**. In dry weather, they curl up to protect the interior but open when it rains to let the drops hit and disperse the spores. The rays can open wide enough to push the brown spore mass off the ground to give the spores a chance to be carried farther by wind. It grows in a symbiotic relationship with trees (called mycorrhizal) and is usually found in dry, sandy areas near pines.

NOTES: Earthstars listed here are inedible but are fascinating and beautiful.

Rounded Earthstar

Collared Earthstar

FROM THE SOIL NEAR TREES · SUMMER THROUGH FALL

Common Earthball

Scleroderma citrinum

HABITAT: Growing from the ground, singly or in groups, near living conifers and hardwoods; they are mycorrhizal and have a symbiotic relationship with the trees. They are fond of wet wooded areas and grassy lawns but are always near trees; they occasionally grow directly on rotted wood.

DESCRIPTION: This small sphere could almost be mistaken for a puffball, but it has a **yellowish to tan** exterior that is covered with a **dark brown, crackled texture**. This surface is actually a thick, tough skin surrounding the mass of spores. The sphere is 1 to 4 inches across; as it grows, it often flattens out slightly and may become oblong or slightly lobed. The interior is initially white like a puffball, but much **firmer**. As it matures, the interior darkens, turning **purplish-black** and, finally, **warmer brown to black**. Like a puffball, it develops a hole or expanding crack at the top through which the ripe, powdery spores are eventually released. Earthballs have **no stem** but are well-attached to the ground or wood by a cluster of rhizomorphs (root-like structures).

SPORE PRINT: Black to dark brown.

SEASON: Summer through fall.

OTHER NAMES: Pigskin Poison Puffball, Hard Puffball, *S. aurantium*, *S. vulgare*.

COMPARE: The **Potato Earthball** (*S. bovista*) is less than 2 inches across and has a **smooth** brownish surface, like a potato. It may narrow at the bottom where it is attached to the ground. With age it develops **fine cracks** on the surface; the spore mass inside becomes black to purplish-black. • The **Leopard Earthball** (*S. areolatum*) has thinner skin that is **cream to light brown** with fine, dark brown scales on the surface. • The **Earthstar Puffball** (*S. polyrhizum* or *S. geaster*) prefers **sandy soils**. It forms mostly underground so is typically **dirty brown**; it leaves quite a mark as it bursts through the soil. Its skin is **thick**; when it splits open to release its **purplish-brown** spores, it resembles a blackened Earthstar (pg. 232). • Small edible **Puffballs** (pg. 230) appear similar to some Earthballs, but their interiors are **soft and white**, becoming **yellowish**. When fully mature, Puffballs are filled with **brown powder**; they never have the firm, dark centers found in maturing Earthballs. • Also see the **Skull-Shaped Puffball** and the **Purple-Spored Puffball** on pgs. 42-43.

NOTES: Earthballs are **toxic**; take care not to confuse them with Puffballs.

Common Earthball

Darkened interior

Potato Earthball

Dyeball

Pisolithus arhizus (also known as *P. tinctorius*)

One of the least pleasant fungi to handle and arguably one of the ugliest, this fungus looks like a roundish puffball at first, but its interior has **pea-sized spore pockets that are embedded in a blackish liquid gel** that is sticky and stains the hands. As it elongates into an irregular club-like mass the spore pockets disintegrate from the top down into a mass of brown spores. It is 2 to 7 inches tall and 3 to 6 inches wide. The Dyeball's surface color ranges from various shades of brown to yellowish or purplish. Yellow strands (rhizomorphs) often are present at the base. With age, the fungus is covered in brown spore dust and the spore pockets disappear. It forms a symbiotic relationship with many plants but is most often found under conifers and oaks in the Northeast. The Dyeball can thrive in sandy and poor soils, making it an important fungus in reforestation projects. It is found from summer through fall.

COMPARE: Cutting the Dyeball in half will reveal the spore pockets and distinguish this from the **Potato Earthball** (pgs. 234–235) and other similar species.

NOTES: Also called Dyemaker's Puffball, this fungus is often used to dye wool yarn. It is inedible and possibly poisonous. Few would find it appetizing to look at, let alone eat!

Carbon Balls

Daldinia childiae (also known as *D. concentrica*)

These round to irregularly blob-shaped fungi are typically less than an inch across but can be up to 4 inches; they grow in **dense clusters** on fallen logs of deciduous trees, especially beech and ash. Light gray to pinkish-brown at first, they become black and shiny like coal when mature. Cutting them in half reveals the **concentric growth rings** that give them the Latin species name *concentrica*. The surface may appear **finely dotted** with spore-releasing openings before the ripe, **black** spores cover the surface of the balls and often become a sooty halo around them. They are found year-round.

COMPARE: Dead Man's Fingers (pg. 246) grow in a similar, clustered fashion but are grayish to greenish when young and are typically more **elongated**, like fingers. They have a black exterior, but the interior is firm and **white**.

NOTES: Though not edible, this common mushroom is also called King Alfred's Cakes or Cramp Balls in reference to old wives' tales. They are also called Coal Fungus and can be used in the woods for starting fires, like charcoal.

ON DECAYING WOOD   SPRING

Devil's Urn
Urnula craterium

HABITAT: Devil's Urns are saprobes, getting their nutrients from decaying deciduous wood. They are found on downed branches and logs and also on buried wood, appearing to grow from the ground; they frequently grow in moss. Found singly or in clusters that are often linear.

DESCRIPTION: Young Devil's Urn specimens look like an **inverted teardrop with a narrow opening** at the top; at the base they narrow down into slender, seamlessly connected **solid** stems that may be buried in ground litter and hard to spot. As specimens mature, the opening becomes wider, revealing a **hollow** interior; when the stems are visible, the mushrooms look like **black goblets**. Cups are generally 1½ to 2½ inches across and up to 4 inches tall; they are tough and leathery. Their insides are blackish-brown to jet-black and smooth; the outer surface is scruffy and grayish to brownish, turning black with age. The edge of the cup appears **torn** or toothy.

SPORE PRINT: Whitish to pale yellowish.

SEASON: **Spring**, typically early; often appears before Morels (pgs. 24–27).

OTHER NAMES: Black Tulip Fungus, Crater Cup.

COMPARE: Several other mushrooms with a similar appearance and growth habits are found in our area. **Hairy Rubber Cup** or **Peanut Butter Cup** (*Galiella rufa*; also listed as *Bulgaria rufa*) also look like goblets with torn edges, but the centers are **filled with a gelatinous substance** that is **tan to yellowish-brown** on top. The outside is blackish-brown and **downy**. Cups are less than 1½ inches across and feel **rubbery** when squeezed. They grow from **summer through fall**. • Black Trumpet (pgs. 50–51) is **trumpet-shaped**, with **rolled-over edges** turning outward; its stem is **completely hollow**. It grows from **summer through fall**. • Common Brown Cup (pg. 240) are **brownish, irregularly shaped** cups with **brittle** flesh; they have **no stems**. They grow from late spring to early summer.

NOTES: Devil's Urn and Hairy Rubber Cup are inedible. Common Brown Cup is edible but not particularly good. Black Trumpets are a prime edible.

green = key identification feature

Devil's Urn

Hairy Rubber Cup

Common Brown Cup

Phylloscypha phyllogena (formerly *Peziza phyllogena*)

HABITAT: These mushrooms are saprobes, getting their nutrients from decaying organic material that may be underground. They are typically found growing from the soil near white pines but are found near other conifers and also in deciduous forests; occasionally found on rotting wood such as downed logs. They grow singly or in clusters.

DESCRIPTION: Although large, these mushrooms often hide under leaves on the forest floor in spring. They are **cup-shaped** or bowl-shaped, narrowing down to the point of attachment; edges sometimes appear flared and trumpet-like but more commonly turn inward. Common Brown Cups have **no stems**, growing directly from the substrate. Individual cups are 1 to 4 inches across and typically as deep as they are wide. Insides are **matte brown**, sometimes with reddish or purplish areas; undersides are **yellowish-tan** and have a **finely granular** texture. Flesh is thin and **brittle**; the cups **crumble easily**. They appear somewhat translucent in the sunlight.

SPORE PRINT: White.

SEASON: Late spring to early summer.

OTHER NAMES: Pig's Ear, *Peziza badioconfusa*, *Peziza badio-confusa*.

COMPARE: Veined Cup (*Disciotis venosa*; also listed as *Peziza venosa*) grows from the soil and is up to **7 inches** across; it is found only in spring. Its upper surface is yellowish-brown to reddish-brown; the underside is **whitish to tan**. The center is pinched together and has **vein-like wrinkles**. • Spreading Cup (*Peziza repanda*) always grows **on wood**. Young specimens are **pale tan** and cup-like, with a **stem** that becomes less noticeable with age; the outer surface has a whitish bloom. Mature specimens are **flatter** and colored like Common Brown Cup. • *Gyromitra perlata* (also known as *Discina perlata* or *Discina ancilis*) is **reddish-brown**, with a **lumpy, irregular** surface. It is cup-like at first, becoming fairly flat with age. The underside is **pale** and grayish or yellowish-brown. It grows from the soil near conifers. • *Otidea* **species** are more irregularly shaped than Common Brown Cup and are **much paler brown to yellowish**.

NOTES: Common Brown Cup is edible but not very tasty; the others here are inedible. It's best to consider Common Brown Cup inedible due to difficulty in identification.

Common Brown Cup

Veined Cup

Spreading Cup (young)

ON DECAYING WOOD   SPRING THROUGH FALL

Wood Ear

Auricularia americana, Auricularia angiospermarum

HABITAT: These saprobes are found on dead and decaying wood including standing dead trees, stumps, downed logs and branches. *A. americana* fruits on **coniferous** wood, while *A. angiospermarum* is found on **hardwoods**.

DESCRIPTION: Fresh Wood Ears are irregularly shaped and look like flattened, wrinkled cups with shallow, irregular folds; they often appear ear-like, accounting for their common name. Individuals are 1 to **6 inches** wide. They usually appear slightly **puckered** at the point where they are attached to the substrate; the point of connection may be stub-like. Flesh is thin and **rubbery**. The spore-producing surface is smooth and grayish-tan to reddish-brown. The sterile (non-spore-producing) surface is tan to grayish-brown, occasionally with a slight violet hue; it is silky or downy and often has **vein-like** wrinkles. Either surface may be facing outward, although the spore-producing surface commonly faces the substrate.

SPORE PRINT: White to cream-colored.

SEASON: Spring through fall; they are least common in summer and most common in fall.

OTHER NAMES: Tree Ear, Jelly Ear. The two species above were originally considered a single species, listed as *A. auricula* and, in older texts, *A. auricula-judae*.

COMPARE: Copper Penny (*Pachyella clypeata*) has a somewhat similar appearance, but it is rarely wider than 3 inches across and usually closer to an inch. They are **disk-like** and stemless, usually with a **rounded cleft** on one side; they are much less wrinkled than Wood Ear. The **majority of the disk is attached** to the rotting wood on which these mushrooms grow; the edges are free. The upper surface is reddish-brown to copper-colored and generally shiny; the lower surface is tan. Very young specimens are pillow-like. • **Common Brown Cup** (pg. 240) grows as clusters of irregularly shaped brownish cups that may be found on rotting logs but typically grow from the soil; they have a **brittle** texture and **crumble easily**.

NOTES: Like the similarly named (and related) Tree Ears sold in Asian groceries, Wood Ears are edible. Both types of Wood Ears act as anticoagulants; caution is advised for persons taking blood-thinning medications.

Wood Ear

Copper Penny

Orange and **Red Cup Fungus** (several)
Aleuria and *Sarcoscypha* spp.

HABITAT: These two types of similar-appearing cup fungi grow in different habitats; each is described below. They are saprobes, getting their nutrients from dead and decaying organic matter that may be underground.

DESCRIPTION: Orange Peel Fungus (*A. aurantia*) grows in clusters on bare, **hard-packed soil**, such as along roads and trails; it also grows in disturbed areas including gardens and newly planted lawns. They are shallow cups that may be nearly 4 inches wide but are typically smaller; they have **no stem**. Edges are often irregular or wavy. The inner surface where spores are produced is **bright orange** and smooth, fading to orangish-yellow. The outside is whitish and is downy on young specimens. Their flesh is thin and brittle. • **False Orange Peel** (*A. rhenana*) is similar to the Orange Peel but slightly smaller; it has a **distinct stem** up to 1 inch long. It is found in **coniferous woodlands**, often in mossy areas. • **Scarlet Cup** (*S. austriaca*) grows on **fallen branches** from deciduous trees. Like Orange Peel, they look like shallow, wavy cups, but they seldom exceed 2 inches across. The inner spore-producing surface is **bright red** and glossy; outside is downy and pinkish, buff-colored or whitish. They may be stemless, or may have a short, thick stem at the base. Their flesh is thin and brittle. The related *S. dudleyi* and *S. coccinea* are indistinguishable from *S. austriaca* without a microscope. (*S. coccinea* is a western species that does not grow in our area, but it is often listed in field guides.) • **Stalked Scarlet Cup** (*S. occidentalis*) is a vermilion-red cup less than ⅜ inch across; like False Orange Peel, it has a **distinct stem** about 1 inch long. It grows on decaying wood.

SPORE PRINT: White.

SEASON: The *Aleuria* species above grow from summer through fall. *Sarcoscypha* species are one of the earliest mushrooms to appear in spring.

OTHER NAMES: Scarlet Cup is also referred to as Scarlet Elfcup.

COMPARE: Eyelash Cup (*Scutellinia scutellata*) is bright orange to red and only ¼ to ¾ inch wide; its edges have **dark hairs**. It grows on rotten wood.

NOTES: Orange Peel Fungus is edible when cooked; the others listed are inedible.

Orange Peel Fungus

Scarlet Cup

Eyelash Cup

ON DECAYING WOOD SPRING THROUGH FALL

Candlesnuff Fungus, Dead Man's Fingers

Xylaria hypoxylon, Xylaria polymorpha

HABITAT: These related species are saprobes, getting their nutrients from decaying deciduous wood that may be buried. Both grow in loose groups.

DESCRIPTION: Candlesnuff Fungus (*X. hypoxylon*) and Dead Man's Fingers (*X. polymorpha*) have two different forms: an immature stage during which they are pale and covered with powdery asexual spores and a mature stage when the surface is dark and covered with small bumps with pores (visible with a hand lens). The pores contain mature spores. Both species are **hard** and **somewhat woody**. • Candlesnuff Fungus is smaller and thinner, usually 1 to 3 inches tall and less than ⅜ inch thick. Immature specimens are often **branched**, with two to several thinner forks near the top; they are coated with **whitish** or grayish powder. They are often rounded but may be **somewhat flat**, especially toward the top. Mature specimens are carbon-like, black and pimply and are often unbranched; they appear **spindly or withered**. • Dead Man's Fingers are typically **unbranched** even when immature; they may be nearly **4 inches tall** and **1 inch thick**. Immature specimens are rounded, knobby or puffy-looking. They are coated with gray or **bluish** dust except at the very tip, which is white to cream-colored. Mature specimens are carbon-like, black and pimply and are much more **fleshy** than mature Candlesnuff.

SPORE PRINT: Black.

SEASON: The immature stage of both species is present in spring. Mature Candlesnuff is found throughout summer; mature Dead Man's Fingers are present from summer through fall.

OTHER NAMES: *X. hypoxylon* are sometimes called Carbon Antlers.

COMPARE: Several mushrooms are similar to Dead Man's Fingers in color and height; they are not hard and woody. **Stalked Xylaria** (*X. longipes*) is more slender and usually has a **thin stalk** at the base. • **Common Earth Tongue** (*Geoglossum difforme*) is more flattened and **tongue-like**; its surface is **glossy** and may be slimy. • **Velvety Earth Tongue** (*Trichoglossum hirsutum*) has a **flattened oval head** and a **rounded stalk**. Both the head and stalk are covered with stiff hairs.

NOTES: The species listed here are inedible.

Immature Candlesnuff

Mature Candlesnuff

Immature Dead Man's Fingers

Mature Dead Man's Fingers

ON DECAYING WOOD

EARLY SUMMER
THROUGH FALL

Crown-Tipped Coral

Artomyces pyxidatus

HABITAT: This lovely coral mushroom is a saprobe, growing **directly on decaying wood** of deciduous trees, particularly willow, aspen and maple.

DESCRIPTION: Although often found growing in large clusters, this coral may grow as a single specimen, making it easier to see its form. Individuals contain numerous branches that **curve away from the base**, similar to a **candelabra**. Specimens are 1½ to 4 inches wide and slightly higher; they are **white to pale yellowish-pink** when young, darkening to tan. Branches may divide into two or more stems at the top. Each stem is tipped with a **shallow, tiny cup** that has three to six points, appearing **crown-like**.

SPORE PRINT: White.

SEASON: Early summer through fall.

OTHER NAMES: *Clavicorona pyxidata, Clavaria pyxidata.*

COMPARE: Several *Ramaria* species have branches that split into two or more stems. However, *Ramaria* stem tips are **pointed or brush-like** rather than crown-like, and branches often grow from a thickened base. Their spore print is **yellow**; they grow from midsummer through fall. **Straight-Branched Coral** (*R. stricta*; also listed as *Clavaria stricta*) grows from decaying **conifer** wood that may be buried. Branches are **straight, upright and parallel** and often flattened. It is **buff-colored to yellowish-pink**, bruising purplish-brown; young stem tips are yellow. **Yellow-Tipped Coral** (*R. formosa*) grows **from the ground**. Branches are **pinkish**; stem tips are yellow. With age, the entire specimen turns orangish to tan. • **False Coral** (*Sebacina schweinitzii* or *Tremellodendron pallidium*) grows **from the ground**. It is composed of **very tough**, dry, whitish branching stems that are flattened and **partially fused** together. Found from **spring** through fall. • **Crested Coral** (*Clavulina coralloides* or *Clavulina cristata*) is whitish and grows **from the ground**. Branches are slightly flattened and have **tooth-like points**. A gray form is also found; some refer to it as *Clavulina cinerea*, while others regard it as a diseased specimen of *Clavulina cristata*.

NOTES: Crown-Tipped and Crested Coral are edible but easy to confuse with Yellow-Tipped Coral, which is **toxic**; the others listed are inedible.

Crown-Tipped Coral

Straight-Branched Coral

Yellow-Tipped Coral

False Coral

Crested Coral

FROM THE SOIL · SUMMER THROUGH FALL

Worm Corals (several)

Clavaria and *Clavulinopsis* spp.

HABITAT: These species grow **directly from the ground** in woodlands in clumps or bunches; they are often found in grassy or mossy woodland spots. Mycorrhizal associations are likely but have not been positively established.

DESCRIPTION: *Clavaria* species tend to be club-like; compared to the species discussed on pg. 248, they branch less frequently if at all. They have a **brittle** texture and **break easily.** · White Worm Coral (*Clavaria fragilis;* also listed as *Clavaria vermicularis*) looks like clumps of mung bean sprouts standing upright in the woods; it is generally unbranching, although some stalks may have small branches at the tips. Fresh stalks are **chalk-white**, becoming yellowish with age. They are cylindrical or slightly flattened, typically 2 to 6 inches tall and ⅛ to ¼ inch wide. Tips are **softly pointed** and may turn brownish. · Sometimes called **Smoky Spindles**, *Clavaria fumosa* are shaped like White Worm Coral but are **grayish, yellowish-tan or pinkish**; they are 1 to 5 inches tall. · Spindle-Shaped Yellow Coral (*Clavulinopsis fusiformis*) is similar in size and shape to White Worm but is **bright yellow**.

SPORE PRINT: White.

SEASON: Summer through fall.

OTHER NAMES: White Worm Coral is also called Fairy Fingers.

COMPARE: Violet Coral (*Clavaria zollingeri*) is **purple** and less than 4 inches high; unlike the other *Clavaria* species discussed above, its stalks **fork repeatedly**.

NOTES: The White Worm Coral is edible but insubstantial. The Spindle-Shaped Yellow Coral is considered edible by some authors, but it is extremely bitter. The others are generally regarded as inedible.

White Worm Coral

Smoky Spindles

Spindle-Shaped Yellow Coral

Violet Coral

Club-Shaped Coral

Flat-Topped Coral

Club-Shaped Coral

Clavariadelphus pistillaris (also known as Pestle-Shaped Coral)

Found growing from the soil in association with **deciduous** trees, particularly beech; they grow in loose clusters, looking like a collection of **tiny baseball bats**. Individuals are commonly 3 to **6 inches** high, although they may grow much **taller**. They are **club-shaped**, with a swollen, rounded top that narrows to a thick, rounded base; younger specimens are less club-like. Colors vary from yellowish to tan to orangish-brown, darkening with age; they turn brownish when bruised. The surface of young specimens is dry and smooth, becoming wrinkled or somewhat pockmarked. They grow from summer through fall and have a white to yellowish spore print.

COMPARE: *C. americanus* is virtually identical, but it grows under oaks and **conifers**. • Flat-Topped Coral (*C. truncatus*) has a **flattened** top; the edge is generally softly rounded but may also be somewhat abrupt, giving the impression of a small, solid trumpet. They are up to 6 inches tall; the top may be 3 inches across. Tops are **yellowish**; the stalks are **orangish** and often wrinkled. They are found near conifers. • Strap-Shaped Coral (*C. ligula*) are less than 4 inches tall, with a **slender** profile; they are usually less swollen at the top and may be somewhat flattened. They are salmon-colored to yellowish-brown and are found in mixed woods, often growing in conifer needles.

NOTES: Club-Shaped Coral and *C. americanus* are edible but often bitter. Flat-Topped Coral is a good edible; Strap-Shaped Coral is not eaten.

Velvet-Stalked Fairy Fan

Spathulariopsis velutipes (also known as *Spathularia velutipes*)

These pretty little mushrooms look like spatulas or fans that might be used by fairies. They grow on decaying wood that may be underground; they are typically found in loose clusters or groups, often under pine trees. Mature specimens are up to 2¼ inches tall; they are fairly soft and flexible. The stalk is brownish and has a **velvety** texture; orange mycelium (thread-like fungal roots) may be seen at the base. Topping the stalk is a **flattened head** that is fan-shaped to spoon-shaped. It is pale yellow to yellowish-brown and usually wavy; it is up to 1¾ inches wide. The bottom of the head runs alongside the stalk; the top of the head fans around the top of the stalk, forming a **flattened, partial ring** that encircles the top of the stalk. The heads are smoothly textured but may have wrinkles running from the stalk to the outer edges. Occasionally, stalks divide into two branches, each with its own head. Its spore print is white, and it is found from late summer to fall.

COMPARE: Yellow Fairy Fan (*Spathularia flavida*) is very similar, but its stalk is **smooth** rather than velvety and it is **yellowish overall**. It is found in the northern parts of our area. • Fan-Shaped Jelly Fungus (pgs. 256–257) has a similar shape, but it is smaller and has a jelly-like texture.

NOTES: Fairy Fans have not been reported as edible; they are best enjoyed for their unique, charming appearance.

Tooth Mushrooms (several)
Hydnellum spp.

HABITAT: This group of mushrooms grows from the ground under deciduous trees and conifers. They are mycorrhizal, growing in a symbiotic relationship with living trees. Due to their habit of enveloping surrounding debris, they may be attached to sticks or plants.

DESCRIPTION: It is hard to describe the shape of these mushrooms because they change drastically as they grow. Individual caps spread and may **fuse together**, engulfing anything in their path. The **velvety** cap surface may change color or texture as it grows. Undersides are covered with short spore-bearing **teeth**, which extend down the top of the stubby stem; the stem is often so short that specimens appear stemless. Many Hydnellum are pale and similar when young, but each species has at least one unique trait to distinguish it, especially at maturity. • **Orange Hydnellum** (*H. aurantiacum*) is the most common in our area, growing in large groups under conifers. Its **orange to brownish** caps have a **paler outer edge**; mature specimens are up to 6 inches across and extremely **bumpy**. Teeth are white, turning brown with age except on the **tips**, which remain **white**. • The tough caps of **Blue Tooth** (*H. caeruleum*) are up to 4 inches across. Margins of young specimens are **blue, pale blue or whitish**. The center is brownish; the entire cap becomes tan to brownish in older specimens. At times, the caps may ooze **drops of blue liquid that sit on top**, leaving a potholed surface when they evaporate. The teeth are blue, bluish gray to whitish, eventually turning tan. Stems are orange to brownish or tinted bluish. The **cut flesh has blue zones** and smells mealy or cucumber-like. Blue Tooth occurs most commonly under conifers. This is a variable mushroom which may eventually be determined to be several species, based on analysis of DNA examinations. • **Spongy Foot** (*H. spongiosipes*) has a flat, brown cap that is up to 4 inches across. They have a **spongy brown stem** and brown teeth that **bruise darker brown**. It is also called Velvet Tooth and grows with oaks.

SPORE PRINT: Brown.

SEASON: Summer through fall.

OTHER NAMES: Stiptate Hydnum (meaning, having a stem and teeth).

COMPARE: See **Hedgehogs** on pgs. 52–53.

NOTES: *Hydnellum* species are inedible but are used by dyers.

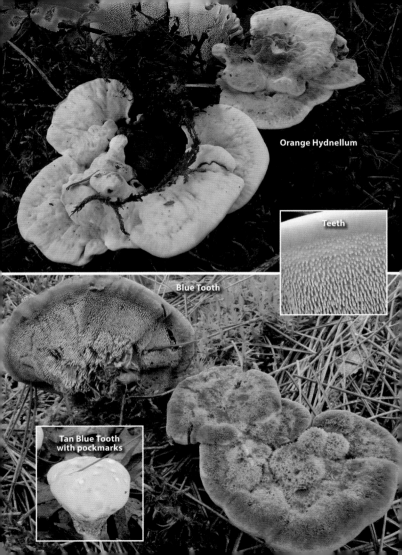

Orange Hydnellum

Teeth

Blue Tooth

Tan Blue Tooth
with pockmarks

Witches' Butter and Jelly Fungi
Various species

HABITAT: These jelly-like fungi grow on dead and decaying wood, including fallen logs, sticks and branches. They appear singly or in colonies.

DESCRIPTION: Several types of small, jelly-like fungi are often seen on wood; they grow in a variety of colors and are very different microscopically. They are gelatinous when fresh and moist; they shrivel in periods of dry weather but are revived by rain. • Two types are **yellow to orangish** and **irregularly lobed**; they become darker when dry. Lobes may be flattened or more swollen and brain-like; individuals are typically 1 to 3 inches wide and up to 1 inch high. **Orange Jelly** (*Dacrymyces chrysospermus*; also referred to as *Dacrymyces palmatus*) is **white** at the point of attachment; it grows on **coniferous** wood. **Witches' Butter** (*Tremella mesenterica*) tends to be yellow rather than orange and lacks the white at the point of attachment; it grows on **deciduous** wood. • Fan-Shaped Jelly Fungus (*Dacryopinax spathularia*) is orange. It consists of short, rounded stalks with **fan-shaped** tops; they are less than 1 inch tall. It grows from cracks in bare dead wood and may grow from construction lumber. • White Jelly Fungus (*Ductifera pululahuana*; also known as *Exidia alba*) is similar to Orange Jelly but is **white**, darkening with age; it has convoluted lobes that are often flattened. It grows on debarked deciduous wood. • Amber Jelly Roll (*E. crenata* or *E. recisa*) resembles a mass of **shiny, puckered brownish cups**. Individual lobes are up to 1½ inches across and attached to the wood by a stem-like point where the wrinkles come together.

SPORE PRINT: Not used for identification.

SEASON: Spring through fall.

OTHER NAMES: White Jelly Fungus is also listed as *Sebacina pululahuana*.

COMPARE: Black Witches' Butter (*E. glandulosa*; also called Black Jelly Roll) looks like **small, wrinkled black blobs**, each less than ½ inch across, fused together in a long, **linear cluster**. It grows on deciduous wood.

NOTES: Orange Jelly and Witches' Butter (yellow) are sometimes cooked in soup; Fan-Shaped Jelly Fungus is sometimes used in the Chinese dish called Buddha's Delight. Amber Jelly Roll is edible but has a gelatinous texture. The others listed above are generally considered inedible.

Orange Jelly

Fan-Shaped Jelly Fungus

White Jelly Fungus

Amber Jelly Roll

FROM THE SOIL NEAR TREES

LATE SUMMER THROUGH FALL

Lobster Mushroom

Hypomyces lactifluorum

HABITAT: Grows from the ground singly or in loose groups in mixed woods. It is a parasite of *Russula, Lactifluus* and *Lactarius* species, so it is found near fruiting bodies of those mushrooms.

DESCRIPTION: This unmistakable mushroom is colored like a cooked lobster shell; it also may smell somewhat fishy. The hard red shell is created when the *Hypomyces* parasite infects the fruitbody of the host mushroom, creating a new species; some mycologists believe that only white *Russula* and *Lactarius* species are parasitized by *H. lactifluorum*. The distinct cap and stem of the host species become a **misshapen** body with a hard, minutely **pimpled orangish-red surface**. Subtle gill-like folds are evident on some specimens; others appear like featureless, misshapen blobs. The spores are white and may cover the entire surface of the mushroom as well as the surrounding dirt or plants. Lobsters are notoriously dirty, but the white flesh is so **firm** that they can be scrubbed clean without damage. Older specimens turn darker red to bright magenta and become soft inside.

SPORE PRINT: White.

SEASON: Late summer through fall.

OTHER NAMES: None.

COMPARE: Other red- to orange-colored mushrooms include the red *Russula* **species** (pg. 138) and orange *Lactarius* **species** (pg. 128). These have well-defined gills and the classic cap-and-stem shape.

NOTES: Experts have determined that the main hosts of the Lobster fungus are *R. brevipes* and *Lactifluus piperatus*, but it is impossible to determine the host of any specific Lobster with certainty. Although concerns have been raised about eating Lobsters when the identity of the host is unknown, they have been safely consumed for a long time and are sold commercially in some areas. The host species probably affects the flavor of the Lobster. Some Lobsters taste like seafood, while others are bland; some may be peppery, and one of the authors has eaten Lobster Mushrooms that had a curry-like flavor. Lobster mushrooms should be fresh and firm; they should not be eaten if they are old and soft, or if they lack the bright orange, pimply surface.

Close-up

Misshapen specimens

GROWING ON OTHER MUSHROOMS

SPRING THROUGH FALL

Parasitic Fungi (several)

Various species

HABITAT: Numerous types of fungi grow on other mushrooms, parasitizing them and, in some cases, transforming them into another type of fungus. Each parasitic mushroom attacks a particular species (or genus), so they will be found where (and when) those mushrooms grow.

DESCRIPTION: Collybia Jelly (*Syzygospora mycetophila*; also listed as *Christiansenia mycetophila*) attacks **Oak Collybia** (pg. 98). It causes **gelatinous yellowish tumor-like growths** to develop on the host mushroom, frequently on the cap but also on the gills and stem. The tumors often fuse, appearing brain-like; they may also grow in large clusters around the base of the Oak Collybia. • The *Asterophora* **genus** contains two species, *A. lycoperdoides* and *A. parasitica*; these grow on the caps of old *Russula* and *Lactarius* mushrooms. *Asterophora* develop as small white cap-and-stem mushrooms; *A. parasitica* has **gills** under a **silky** cap, while *A. lycoperdoides* has **deformed gills or no gills** under its **rough-textured** cap. As the *Asterophora* mature, they produce powdery, buff-colored spores; the spores of *A. parasitica* develop **from the gills** under the cap, but spores of *A. lycoperdoides* appear **on top** of the cap. • Parasitic Bolete (*Pseudoboletus parasiticus*; also listed as *Boletus parasiticus*) **grows from Common Earthballs** (pg. 234). The bolete has a dry, tan to yellowish cap up to 3 inches wide. The stem is short and cream-colored and covered with fine brown fibers; it may curve as it grows around the Earthball. The pore surface under the cap may be dirty yellowish. • **Bolete Mold** (*Hypomyces chrysospermus*) attacks boletes (including Parasitic Bolete, above). The mold first appears on the pore surface as a white powder that soon covers the entire mushroom with a **cottony white blanket** that turns yellow before turning brown; even choice boletes become disgusting and toxic.

COMPARE: Lobster Mushrooms (pg. 258) are created when *Russula* or *Lactarius* species are attacked by another species of *Hypomyces*.

NOTES: None of these parasitic fungi except the Lobster Mushroom are recommended for consumption.

Collybia Jelly

A. parasitica

A. lycoperdoides

Parasitic Bolete

Bolete Mold

ON DEAD AND
DECAYING WOOD

PRESENT
YEAR-ROUND

Crust Fungi (several)
Various species

HABITAT: Crust fungi include both saprobic and symbiotic fungi. They are found on the wood of deciduous trees and, sometimes, conifers.

DESCRIPTION: These fungi have a texture and shape that is not what comes to mind when you think of mushrooms. Many are related to polypores but don't always grow into a shelf form. They have no stems and fuse to the material they are growing on. • Crowded Parchment (*Stereum complicatum*; also listed as *S. rameale*) covers logs, mainly oak, with sheets of flat to ruffled fungus that sometimes form **small fan-shaped brackets**. The top side is silky and colored with **orange to reddish-brown banding**; the spore-bearing surface below is **solid orange to cream** with a smooth texture. • Ceramic Parchment (*Xylobolus frustulatus*; also listed as *S. frustulosum*) looks like **white to buff-colored ceramic tiles** that may completely cover branches and logs, usually oak. Individual fruiting bodies are generally less than ½ inch across; they **turn black** with age. • Milk-White Toothed Polypore (*Irpex lacteus*) is a white to tan mass with hard spore-bearing **teeth** up to ¼ inch long. It sometimes develops a series of overlapping brackets, or can be a flat, toothy crust. It is found on deciduous trees, sometimes living trees.

SPORE PRINT: White (Crowded Parchment, Milk-White Toothed Polypore) or pinkish (Ceramic Parchment). Spore prints are difficult to obtain.

SEASON: Adds new growth annually but found year-round.

OTHER NAMES: Commonly called Crusts or Parchment Fungus.

COMPARE: False Turkey Tail (pgs. 200–201) is so closely related to Crowded Parchment that it has been found to occasionally cross (mate). Some experts regard them as varieties of the same species. • Young growth of **Purple Tooth** (pg. 228) is sometimes flat and crust-like. • *Irpiciporus pachyodon* (pg. 210) is also called Milk-White Toothed Polypore; it is a **polypore** with **tooth-like pores** on the underside.

NOTES: Most crusts are not edible due to their texture. The species listed here cause white rot of wood.

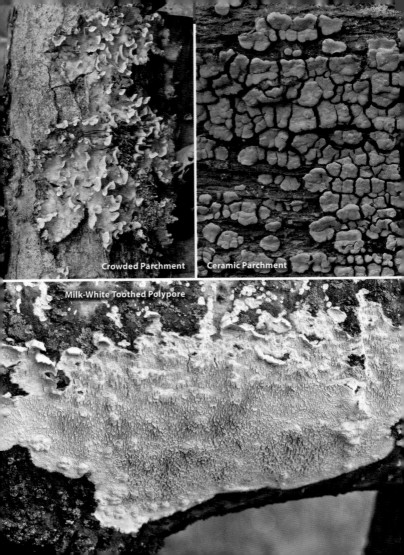

Crowded Parchment

Ceramic Parchment

Milk-White Toothed Polypore

Ochre Jelly Club
Leotia lubrica

These saprobes grow from the soil or from well-rotted wood, usually in profuse **clusters**, from early summer through fall. Also called Jelly Babies, these little fungi appear to have a long stem with a pillowy little cap. In actuality, they are a stemmed club with an **asymmetrical and often furrowed top** that may be rolled under to look like a cap. The colorless spores are produced on the surface of the cap-like top. Stems are up to 3 inches tall and may be minutely scaly on the outside; they are hollow or filled with jelly inside. The top is also **gelatinous** and is less than 2 inches across. The classic form has a cap that ranges from dull yellow, orange, tan to olive with a light yellow stem. With age, it darkens and becomes green. In the past, this green-headed form was considered a separate species, *L. viscosa*; however, recent DNA studies have suggested that this is simply a form of *L. lubrica* which has been attacked by a mold that turns the cap green. Another form is **green overall**; this is often listed as *L. atrovirens* but again, some experts believe that this is just another variation of *L. lubrica*. Some references list the all-green form as *Coryne atrovirens*.

COMPARE: *Cudonia* species look similar to Jelly Babies but they are **dry and not gelatinous**.

NOTES: The edibility of Jelly Babies and *Cudonia* species is unknown. They are related to Morels (pgs. 24-27) and other ascomycetes (see pg. 19).

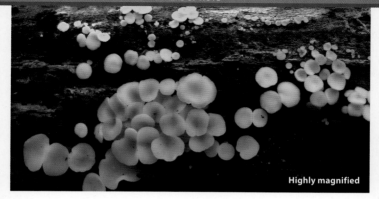

Highly magnified

Lemon Drops

Bisporella citrina (also known as Yellow Fairy Cups and Lemon Disco)

Lemon Drops are saprobes, getting nutrients from decaying or dead organic matter. They are found from summer through fall growing prolifically on the decaying wood of deciduous trees and conifers. These tiny fungi are usually not overlooked, even though individual cups are **⅛ inch** wide or less! Their **bright yellow** color and sheer numbers will make you take notice. With a hand lens, you can see the distinct **cup shape**, which may have a minute stem attaching it to the wood. Like other Cup Fungi (pg. 244) the spores are produced on the inner surface of the saucer. The discs become darker yellow to almost orange when old or dried out. The spores are colorless.

COMPARE: *Chlorencoelia versiformis* is larger, growing up to **1 inch** across; with age, the yellow cups develop a **green color inside**. • Witches' Butter (pg. 256) may be bright yellow and grows on decayed wood, but it is more **wavy and folded**, lacking the distinct cups. It is **gelatinous** in wet weather.

NOTES: The edibility of Lemon Drops is unknown; they are too small to eat.

Scaly Vase Chanterelle

Turbinellus floccosus (also known as *Gomphus floccosus*)

This sturdy, funnel-shaped mushroom is mycorrhizal, growing scattered or singly from the ground near conifers, especially hemlock; it is often found in mossy areas. It stands **3 to 7 inches tall**. When viewed from above mature specimens appear to have a cap, but there is no distinct separation between the underside and the stem. The top is **3 to 5 inches across**, with a central depression that becomes more funnel-like with age. Its surface is **orange to reddish**, with numerous **darker scales** that become downturned in the center. The margin is even to slightly wavy and may appear yellow on young specimens. The underside is **cream-colored** and shallowly wrinkled or ribbed; it may bruise purplish. The stem is **hollow** and tapers toward the base. It is white to cream-colored and wrinkled at the top, becoming smooth toward the base. Flesh is thick and whitish, sometimes bruising brownish. The spore print is light brownish-orange to yellowish-brown. Scaly Vase Chanterelle grows throughout summer and early fall.

COMPARE: Chanterelles (pgs. 38–40) are generally smaller and their caps are **smooth**, not scaly. When cut open, their stems are **solid**. • The top of Pig's Ear Gomphus (*G. clavatus*; edible) is **pale brown to lilac** and has **few or no scales**.

NOTES: Scaly Vase Chanterelles are **toxic**, although a few people can tolerate them without incident. Most suffer nausea, vomiting and diarrhea. Other common names include Wooly Chanterelle, Wooly Gomphus and Shaggy Chanterelle.

White-Egg Bird's Nest   Highly magnified

Bird's Nest Fungi (several)
Crucibulum and *Cyathus* spp.

Although they are tiny, these unusual fungi are fascinating and lovely. They are easiest to identify in the mature stage, when they look like **tiny, cone-shaped nests** ½ inch or less across, with even tinier **flattened spheres inside**. On young specimens, a dome-like lid covers the top, appearing cushion-like. The lid eventually falls away, revealing the interior with two to numerous "eggs" that are less than ⅟₁₆ inch wide and contain the spore-producing structures. Bird's Nest Fungus grows singly, scattered or in dense clusters on downed branches, woodland debris and even on old planks. They are found from spring through fall. Several varieties appear in our area. • White-Egg Bird's Nest (*Crucibulum laeve*) are **yellowish to tan** and often **velvety** on the outside; the inside is smooth and tan to grayish. Eggs are **white**. • Dung-Loving Bird's Nest (*Cyathus stercoreus*) is **brownish** and **shaggy** outside, with smooth **grayish interiors and eggs**; it is often found on manure but also grows on woody debris. • Striate Bird's Nest (*Cyathus striatus*) is more vase-shaped. The outside is dark grayish-brown to brownish and covered with **shaggy hairs**; the interior is distinctly **ribbed** and shiny and ranges from tan to gray. Eggs are grayish to whitish.

COMPARE: Other than additional Bird's Nest species (including those in the *Nidula*, *Nidularia* and *Mycocalia* genera), nothing resembles these fungi.

NOTES: Bird's Nest are best appreciated when viewed with a hand lens, and make splendid subjects for macro photography. They are inedible.

green = key identification feature   267

Helpful Resources and Bibliography

Information on mushrooms is readily available in books, magazines and on the Internet; note, however, that some websites are less reliable than others. Here is a list of some websites and books that provide reliable information that may be of interest to readers.

WEBSITES

Mycological societies

North American Mycological Association (namyco.org)

For a listing of NAMA-affiliated mycological societies in each state, consult the state-by-state list at www.namyco.org/clubs.php

University or independent websites

American Mushrooms, David Fischer
(americanmushrooms.com)

Fungi magazine (fungimag.com)

Indiana Mushrooms (indianamushrooms.com)

Messiah College, Gary Emberger, fungi on wood
(messiah.edu/Oakes/fungi_on_wood/index.htm)

Mushroom Expert, Dr. Michael Kuo (mushroomexpert.com)

Mushroom Observer (mushroomobserver.org)

MykoWeb: Mushrooms and Other Fungi on the Web (mykoweb.com)

University of Wisconsin/LaCrosse, Tom Volk's page
(botit.botany.wisc.edu/toms_fungi)

Urban Mushrooms (urbanmushrooms.com)

BOOKS

Arora, David. *Mushrooms Demystified*. Berkeley: Ten Speed Press, 1986.

Barron, George. *Mushrooms of Northeast North America: Midwest to New England*. Auburn, WA: Lone Pine Publishing, 1999.

Bessette, Alan E. and Arleen R.
   —and David W. Fischer. *Mushrooms of Northeastern North America*. Syracuse, NY: Syracuse University Press, 1997.

   —and William C. Roody and Walter E. Sturgeon. *Waxcap Mushrooms of Eastern North America*. Syracuse, NY: Syracuse University Press, 2012.

Kuo, Michael. *Morels*. Ann Arbor: The University of Michigan Press, 2005.

   —*100 Edible Mushrooms*. Ann Arbor: The University of Michigan Press, 2007.

Lincoff, Gary H. *National Audubon Society® Field Guide to North American Mushrooms*. New York: Alfred A. Knopf, 2011 (24th printing).

   —*The Complete Mushroom Hunter*. Beverly, MA: Quarry Books (Quayside Publishing Group), 2010.

Marrone, Teresa and Kathy Yerich. *Mushrooms of the Upper Midwest;* second edition 2020. Cambridge, MN: Adventure Publications, 2014.

McFarland, Joe and Dr. Gregory M. Mueller. *Edible Wild Mushrooms of Illinois & Surrounding States: A Field-to-Kitchen Guide*. Urbana and Chicago: University of Illinois Press, 2009.

McKnight, Kent H. and Vera B. *A Field Guide to Mushrooms: North America* (A Peterson Field Guide). New York: Houghton Mifflin Company, 1987.

Pacioni, Giovanni; Gary Lincoff, U.S. editor. *Simon & Schuster's Guide to Mushrooms*. New York: A Fireside Book, published by Simon & Schuster Inc., 1981.

Rhodes, Landon H., Britt A. Bunyard, Walter E. Sturgeon and Sarah D. Ellis. *Mushrooms and Macrofungi of Ohio and the Midwestern States*. Columbus, OH: The Ohio State University, 2013.

Roody, William C. *Mushrooms of West Virginia and the Central Appalachians*. Lexington, KY: The University Press of Kentucky, 2003.

Spahr, David L. *Edible and Medicinal Mushrooms of New England and Eastern Canada*. Berkeley: North Atlantic Books, 2009.

Glossary

Aborted: A mushroom whose growth is stunted, deformed or mutated. This often occurs after contact with another organism, possibly even another mushroom.

Agarics: A large family of mushrooms (both edible and poisonous) with a stem and a distinct cap with gills. Sometimes used as a general term for multiple species of mushrooms growing in this form.

Amatoxins: Lethal toxins present in some species of mushrooms, including some *Amanita*, *Galerina*, *Lepiota* and *Conocybe* species. Ingestion causes extreme sickness and may cause death.

Annual: A mushroom whose fruitbody appears once a year in a particular season. (*Compare:* Perennial)

Ascomycete: Scientific name for a group of mushrooms whose spores develop in a sac-like container called an ascus. When the spores are ripe, the end of the sac opens to eject them. (*Compare:* Basidiomycete)

Ascus: The sac-like container that produces spores on the group of mushrooms called ascomycetes. (*Plural:* asci)

Attached gills: Gills that are attached to both the underside of the cap and to the stem. (*Compare:* Free gills)

Basidiomycete: Scientific name for a group of mushrooms whose spores develop on microscopic club-shaped appendages called basidia. This includes most mushrooms with gills and pores, as well as puffballs. (*Compare:* Ascomycete)

Basidium: Microscopic club-shaped appendage with tiny prongs that carry spores. (*Plural*: basidia) *See also* Basidiomycete.

Bolete: General name used for mushrooms that have a cap and stem with a pore surface under the cap rather than gills or teeth. Many are in the *Boletus* genera; others are not but are still commonly referred to as "boletes."

Bracket: Term used to describe mushrooms that grow laterally (sideways) from a tree or another object, usually without an obvious stem. (*Synonym:* Shelf)

Branching: The growth habit of a mushroom or part of a mushroom that has multiple stems or limbs, resembling the branches of a tree. (*Compare:* Unbranching)

Brown rot: A condition where a fungal organism breaks down and consumes the cellulose of a tree, leaving behind the lignin as a brown, corky material. (*Compare:* White rot)

Bruise/bruising: A color transformation, usually in the cut or damaged flesh, gills or pore surface of a mushroom.

Bulbous: Abruptly swollen or rounded; generally refers to the base of a mushroom stem. (*Compare:* Club-shaped)

Button: An immature or newly emerging mushroom on which the gills or pores underneath the cap are not visible yet. Usually spherical or egg-shaped.

Canker: A sore or tumor-like growth, derived from the Latin word *cancer*.

Cap: The top or head of the mushroom, usually used in reference to mushrooms with a stem. In forms with lateral (sideways) or less prominent stem growth, the cap may be more shelf-like. Called the pileus in some sources.

Chambered: A cavity that is broken into multiple enclosed spaces. In mushrooms, it may occur in the stem or inside the entire fungus.

Close gills: Numerous gills that are closely spaced but still have slight separation from one another.

Club-shaped: Gradually swollen; refers to the base of a mushroom stem. (*Compare:* Bulbous)

Concentric: Usually refers to ridges, lines or other bands of texture or color that are circular and parallel, surrounding a central point. (*Compare:* Radiate)

Coniferous: A tree or shrub with needle-like or scale-like leaves (usually evergreen) whose seeds are contained in cones. (*Compare:* Deciduous, Hardwood)

Cortina: A partial veil over the gills that resembles cotton fibers or a spiderweb.

Cross-veins: Connecting ridges between the gills or gill-like folds of some mushrooms; appears as a net-like pattern.

Crowded gills: Numerous gills that are so tightly packed that the spaces between them are not visible.

Crust: Mushrooms growing as a thin layer covering a surface, usually on dead or decaying tree branches or logs.

Cup: Multiple meanings. Usually refers to the shape of a mushroom whose cap or entire body is concave, like a bowl. Also used to describe the sac-like structure found at the base of the stem on some species (especially Amanita). Cup Fungi is additionally used as a general term for members of the Ascomycete group, which have sac-like structures that produce spores. *See also* Ascus, Volva.

Deciduous: Trees and shrubs that lose their leaves each year, rather than being evergreen; also referred to as hardwoods. (*Compare:* Coniferous)

Decomposer: Something that hastens or facilitates decay or decomposition.

Decurrent gills: Gills that are attached to the stem and run down it. (*Compare:* Free gills) *See also* Attached gills.

Deliquesce: To dissolve, turning to liquid.

Eccentric: Off-center; for mushrooms it is usually used in reference to the placement or the growth of the stem in relation to the cap.

Egg: The immature stage of growth where a mushroom is entirely covered by a thin membrane called a universal veil.

Fairy ring: A group of mushrooms growing in a circle or an arc.

Fertile: Capable of reproduction; for mushrooms, "fertile surface" refers to the surface that holds and releases spores. (*Compare:* Sterile)

Filament: A thin, string-like piece of material.

Flesh: For mushrooms, a term describing the interior that is revealed when the mushroom is cut.

Folds: Gill-like ridges found under the cap of some mushrooms (notably Chanterelles); like gills, the folds contain the microscopic spore-bearing structures.

Forked gills: Gills that branch into two (or more) sections, often near the cap edge.

Free gills: Gills that are attached to the underside of the cap but are not attached to the stem. (*Compare:* Attached gills)

Fruit/fruiting body: The part of a fungal organism that is visible above the ground or other growing medium; another word for what we generally call a mushroom.

Fungus: The scientific Kingdom that is neither plant nor animal; includes yeasts and molds as well as the fleshy fruit bodies we commonly call mushrooms. (*Plural:* fungi) *See also* Kingdom.

Gastrointestinal: The lower digestive tract of the body. "Gastrointestinal problems" refers to a stomachache, cramps and/or diarrhea.

Genus: Scientific classification in biology; the second-to-last level of Latin naming for a living organism. Could be considered the Latin "last name" for a living organism but is listed before the species name. (*Plural:* genera. *Compare:* Phylum, Species) *See also* Kingdom.

Gills: Blade-like or plate-like structures attached to the cap underside of some mushrooms; the gills contain the microscopic spore-bearing structures. Some sources refer to gills as lamellae. (*Singular:* lamella)

Glandular dots: Textural markings that are minutely raised and usually of a different color than the background; found on the stem of some mushrooms. Glandular dots are smaller than scabers. *See also* Scabers.

Habitat: A term used to describe the area where a mushroom grows, including geography, type of soil or other substrate, and other species of plants (usually trees) nearby.

Hand lens: A small, hand-held magnifying glass, used to see minute but not microscopic features. (*Synonym:* Loupe)

Hardwood: A broad-leaved tree whose seeds are contained in fruits or nuts; also referred to as deciduous trees. (*Compare:* Coniferous)

Host: A term used to describe an organism on which a mushroom (or other organism) is growing; the host may be a tree, plant or another mushroom. *See also* Parasite.

Humus: Decayed leaves and organic matter.

Hygrophanous: An adjective that describes a type of mushroom whose tissue changes appearance (color or texture) based on the amount of moisture present.

Kingdom: Scientific classification in biology; the first level of Latin naming for a living organism. Fungi are called the third kingdom, after plants and animals. The 7 levels of this classification are: Kingdom, Phylum, Class, Order, Family, Genus, Species.

Latex: Thickened fluid that comes from slicing the flesh or gills of *Lactarius* and some other species of mushrooms.

Loupe: A small, hand-held magnifying glass, used to see minute but not microscopic features. (*Synonym:* Hand lens)

Macro fungi: The fruiting body or reproductive structure of a fungus that is visible to the naked eye.

Margin: The edge, usually referring to the outer portion of a mushroom's cap.

Marginate: To have a well-defined border; with mushrooms, usually in reference to the edge of the cap or the bottom edge of the gills.

Membrane: Skin-like tissue; with mushrooms, usually used in reference to a partial or universal veil.

Milky: A term used to refer to some species of mushrooms that ooze a fluid when cut or scored across the gills or flesh. *See also* Latex.

Mixed woods: An area that has both deciduous and coniferous trees.

Morphology: The study or categorization of an organism based on its physical structure or appearance. (*Compare:* Taxonomy)

Mushroom: The general term for the fleshy fruitbody of a fungal organism.

Mycelium: The collective name for the root-like filaments of a fungal organism.

Mycology: The study of mushrooms.

Mycorrhizal: An adjective that describes a mushroom that grows from the ground but has a symbiotic relationship with the roots of trees. (*Compare:* Saprobe)

Notched Gills: Having a notch or cutout where the gills attach to the stem. (*Compare:* Attached gills, Decurrent gills) *See also* Free gills.

Parasite: An organism that grows on another living organism in a relationship that benefits one organism to the detriment of the other; feeding off something while it is still alive with no benefit to the host. *See also* Host.

Partial veil: A membrane on the underside of the cap of some immature mushrooms; it stretches from the stem to the cap edge, covering the gills or pores. When the cap expands as the mushroom matures it breaks the partial veil, sometimes leaving fragments on the cap edge and a ring on the stem. (*Compare:* Universal veil) *See also* Ring, Ring zone.

Patches: Small to medium-sized, irregularly shaped pieces of tissue attached to the surface of a mushroom cap; they are remnants of a universal veil. *See also* Warts.

Perennial: A mushroom whose fruitbody persists over several years; new growth layers are added to the existing fruitbody each year. (*Compare:* Annual)

Phylum: Scientific classification in biology; the second level of Latin naming for a living organism. (*Plural:* phyla. *Compare:* Genus, Species) *See also* Kingdom.

Polypore: Literally means "having many pores"; refers to a group of mushroom species that release their spores from a surface covered with minute holes.

Pores: Minute holes or openings. In mushrooms, usually part of the fertile, or spore-producing, surface. *See also* Polypore.

Pubescent: Having minute hairs.

Radiate: With mushrooms, refers to lines, ridges or grooves that emanate from a central point, like the spokes of a wheel. The lines, ridges or grooves are often faint and only the outer portions may be visible. (*Compare:* Concentric)

Resupinate: A stemless fruitbody that appears to grow upside-down, with its back fused onto the substrate and its fertile surface facing upward. Usually found growing on fallen logs or other horizontal surfaces. *See also* Crust.

Reticulation: A net-like pattern of raised ridges.

Ring: A band of tissue encircling the stem of mushrooms that have a partial veil. It may be large and skirt-like, or small and fragile; it may be firmly attached to the stem or free. Also called an annulus. (*Compare:* Ring zone) *See also* Partial veil.

Ring zone: The place on a mushroom stem where a partial veil was once attached. The ring (see pg. 273) may move or deteriorate with age, leaving a zone where the stem texture or color may be different. It may also collect the spores that have been released from above. *See also* Partial veil.

Rosette: Growing in a circular and layered pattern, like a flower; rose-like.

Saprobe: Mushrooms that get their nutrients from dead or decaying organic matter are called saprobic. (*Compare:* Mycorrhizal)

Scabers: Minute raised scales on the stems of some mushrooms; often a different color than the stem. Scabers are larger than glandular dots. They are a key ID feature for some mushrooms, especially the *Leccinum* species, which are called scaber stalks. *See also* Glandular dots.

Scales: Raised growths that are generally minute to small. There are various textures possible, from fibrous and tufted, to pointy and sharp. The nature of the scales is usually a key ID feature. May be called scabrous in some sources.

Serrate: Jagged in appearance, like the edge of a saw blade. Usually in reference to the edges of gills.

Shelf: Term used to describe mushrooms that grow laterally (sideways) from a tree or another object, usually without an obvious stem. (*Synonym:* Bracket)

Species: Scientific classification in biology; the final or last level of Latin naming for a living organism. Could be considered the Latin "first name" for a living organism but is listed after the genus name. (*Compare:* Genus, Phylum) *See also* Kingdom.

Spore deposit: Visible ripe spores that have been released by a mushroom; may be seen on nearby plants, objects or other mushrooms. *See also* Spore print.

Spore print: A spore deposit deliberately caught on a piece of paper; spore prints are made by mushroom enthusiasts for purposes of identification.

Spores: Microscopic reproductive structures, like the "seeds" of mushrooms. Spores are part of sexual reproduction in fungi, as opposed to the same organism growing and spreading to produce additional fruit bodies.

Stem: The part of the mushroom on some species that grows to support a cap. Referred to as the stipe in some sources.

Sterile: Incapable of reproduction; for mushrooms, "sterile surface" refers to the non-spore-producing surface. (*Compare:* Fertile)

Striate: Lines or ridges on a mushroom, usually visible on the cap surface or on the stem.

Substrate: The material or medium on which a mushroom is growing: wood, soil, leaves, straw, compost, wood chips, etc.

Symbiotic: A mutually beneficial relationship, where one organism provides benefits to another in exchange for something it needs. (*Compare:* Parasite) *See also* Mycorrhizal.

Tawny: A color that ranges from tan to light brown, sometimes having a yellowish or reddish hue.

Taxonomy: The science of classifying and naming living organisms based on biological characteristics and relationships. Groups such as genus and species are called taxa. (*Singular:* taxon. *Compare:* Morphology)

Terrestrial: Growing from the ground. *See also* Substrate, Habitat.

Toadstool: Synonym for mushroom; often used to refer to poisonous species.

Tomentose: Having a dense covering of fine, short hair.

Tubes: Hollow cylindrical structures on some mushrooms, especially boletes, that contain the spore-producing structures. The pores are packed tightly together under the cap; openings in the bottoms of the tubes create a spongy texture known as a pore surface.

Umbo: A bump, knob or nipple-like protrusion at the top of a mushroom cap; a cap with this feature is called umbonate.

Unbranching: The growth habit of a mushroom or part of a mushroom that has a single stem or member. (*Compare:* Branching)

Uniform: Even all over. Usually in reference to a color, texture, size or other growth pattern.

Universal veil: A thin membrane that completely surrounds an immature or developing mushroom. As the mushroom grows, it breaks the partial veil, sometimes leaving fragments on the cap surface and around the base of the stem. (*Compare:* Partial veil) *See also* Button, Egg, Patches, Volva, Warts.

Veil remnants: The remains of a partial or universal veil on a mature mushroom. Partial veil remnants are typically shaggy, tissue-like pieces hanging from the cap edges. Universal veil remnants may appear as warts or patches on the top of a cap.

Viscid: Having a sticky, but not slimy, surface. The caps of some mushroom species react to moisture in the air and are tacky when wet.

Volva: The fragile, sac-like structure that remains at the base of the stem on species that have a universal veil. As the mushroom grows, it breaks through the membrane, leaving this sac at the base of the stem. It is a common feature of *Amanita* and *Volvariella* species and is sometimes called a cup.

Warts: Small, irregularly shaped pieces of tissue attached to the surface of a mushroom cap; they are remnants of a universal veil. *See also* Patches.

White rot: A condition where a fungal organism uses the lignin of a tree and replaces it with cellulose, leaving a soft, white rotted material behind. (*Compare:* Brown rot)

Zonate: Having distinct stripes, bands or zones of color or texture.

Index

Note: **Bold text** indicates complete species description